The Globalization
of Higher Education

Published by Economica Ltd,
9 Wimpole Street
London W1M 8LB

© *Economica Ltd, 2008*

First published 2008

Printed in France

Luc E. Weber and James J. Duderstadt
The Globalization of Higher Education
ISBN 978-2-7178-5507-4

The Globalization
of Higher Education

Edited by

Luc E. Weber

James J. Duderstadt

ECONOMICA

Glion Colloquium Series N°5

London • Paris • Genève

Titles in the Series

Governance in Higher Education: The University in a State of Flux
Werner Z. Hirsch and Luc E. Weber, eds, (2001)

As the Walls of Academia are Tumbling Down
Werner Z. Hirsch and Luc E. Weber, eds, (2002)

Reinventing the Research University
Luc E. Weber and James J. Duderstadt, eds, (2004)

Universities and Business: Partnering for the Knowledge Economy
Luc E. Weber and James J. Duderstadt, eds, (2006)

The Globalization of Higher Education
Luc E. Weber and James J. Duderstadt, eds, (2008)

Other publications of the Glion Colloquium

The Glion Declaration: The University at the Millennium
The Glion Colloquium, (1998)

Challenges Facing Higher Education at the Millennium
Werner Z. Hirsch and Luc E. Weber, eds, American Council on Education/Oryx Press, Phoenix and IAU Press/Pergamon, Paris and Oxford, (1999)

To Jean Pavlevski,
Founder and President of ECONOMICA.

Thanks to this respected scholar and unique,
entreprising and independent publisher,
thousands of young men and women, as well
as established authors and books editors,
have been able to fulfil their dreams of sharing
with the public the results of their individual
or collective work.

His colleagues and friends dedicate this book
to him with admiration and gratitude for his
enthusiastic early interest and continued com-
mitment to publishing the analysis and thoughts
developed at five Glion Colloquia.

CONTENTS

PREFACE

The Sixth Glion Colloquium brought together university leaders from around the world in Glion above Montreux, Switzerland, to consider the challenges, opportunities and responsibilities presented to higher education by the emerging global, knowledge-driven economy. Launched in 1998 by Professors Luc Weber (University of Geneva) and Werner Hirsch (University of California), the Glion Colloquium has brought together university leaders from Europe and North America to discuss the future of higher education, frequently joined by leaders from business, foundations and government. Topics have included the rapidly changing nature of research universities, university governance, the interaction between universities and society, the future of the university and the responsibilities of higher education, as articulated in the important document, *The Glion Declaration: The University at the Millennium*, prepared for the UNESCO World Conference on Higher Education in 1998. The papers presented and associated discussion at each colloquium have subsequently been published in a series of books that can be found on the Glion Colloquium website at http://www.glion.org.

The Glion VI Colloquium departed from its customary transatlantic dialogue by broadening participation to embrace global representation, including university leaders from around the world representing 18 nations and five continents, to consider the globalization of higher education. The emergence of a global, knowledge-driven economy is driven by a radically new system for creating wealth that depends upon the creation and application of new knowledge and hence upon advanced education, research, innovation and entrepreneurial activities. Both mature and developing nations are making major investments in building the knowledge infrastructure — schools, universities, research institutes, high-tech industry, cyberinfrastructure, public policies and programmes — necessary to achieve prosperity and security in the knowledge economy.

In parallel with these trends, there is a strong sense that higher education is also in the early stages of globalization, both through the increasing mobility of students and faculty and the rapid growth in international partnerships among universities. Some even conjecture that soon we will see the emergence of truly global universities, which not only intend to compete in the global marketplace for students, faculty and resources, but also are increasingly willing to define their public purpose in terms of global needs such as public health, environmental sustainability, and international development. The aim of this meeting was to provoke a stimulating discussion among leaders of research universities from around the world — both from mature nations in Europe, North America and Asia and from developing nations throughout the world — to explore both the challenges and opportunities inherent in the globalization of higher education. Using the highly interactive framework of the Glion meetings, the aim was to identify the key issues and build the relationships necessary for higher education to play a key role in the global economy. The colloquium was organized into six sessions, each structured around the presentation of several papers accompanied by extensive discussion. These papers and a summary of the associated discussions have been included in this book.

The first session aimed at providing a context for the subsequent discussion of the impact of globalization on the university from the perspective of a university leader (Deepak Nayyar), an industry executive (Wayne Johnson) and a foundation president (Carl Schramm). It was noted that despite the common image of isolated ivory towers, universities have long embraced the world beyond their national horizon. Initially scholars travelled from country to country in search of a student audience. Now students in millions are internationally mobile in search of university degrees and cross-cultural experiences. Yet globalization is a deeper and more profound phenomenon, implying integration into the world economy and extending far beyond economics to include culture and politics. Market forces driven by global competition have reshaped many aspects of higher education as businesses, while rapidly evolving information and communications technologies are obliterating the constraints of space, time and monopoly to enable the emergence of entirely new paradigms for learning. It was noted that nothing provides clearer evidence of global competition in higher education than the recent popularity of worldwide rankings of universities.

Yet, while some economic sectors such as industry have been restructuring their processes and work flows to forms better suited to a globalized world, universities are only at the beginning of their comparable journey. Concerns were raised not only about the ability of universities to adapt to the rapidly changing, highly entrepreneurial, and aggressively competitive nature of the global economy, constrained as they are by tradition, culture and campuses, but also about whether in their efforts to adapt — to globalize — universities would leave behind some of their most important roles such as serving as critics of society or sustaining their regional cultures.

The second session turned to the global strategies of established universities from several nations: the United States (Robert Berdahl), the United Kingdom (Howard Newby), Austria (Georg Winckler), Australia (John Niland), Japan (Yuko Harayama & René Carraz) and Russia (Vladimir Troyan). There were several common themes of this discussion. The workforce competitiveness requirements of the global economy has stimulated massification, the effort to expand the proportion of the population receiving higher education qualifications. International competitiveness also demands that nations sustain and enhance the quality of their higher education systems, even as they expand them. Yet governments around the world seek to expand the sector and enhance quality while simultaneously reducing the burden of resources this requires from public finances, if not in absolute, then certainly in proportional terms. To enable universities to respond to these conflicting challenges, many governments are beginning to grant greater autonomy to institutions, e.g. "incorporating" them separate from government, to enable more agility, flexibility and freedom from bureaucratic controls — and perhaps as well less public support.

A quite different perspective was provided by the participants in the third session, discussing strategies for emerging universities and university systems and representing China (Jie Zhang), Singapore (Tony Tan), Korea (Nam Suh), and Brazil (Carlos de Brito Cruz). All of these nations were experiencing very rapid economic growth, both stimulated by and requiring increasingly sophisticated workforces, technological capability and global reach. While Singapore and Korea had rapidly developed higher education resources to achieve high levels of participation, others such as China and India faced considerable challenges in meeting the higher education needs of vast populations. Just as for established universities, all were sensitive to the importance of building universities capable of competing at world-class quality, both through substantial investments and partnerships with other leading universities.

The next two sessions turned to a broader discussion of global competition and cooperation within the context of changing paradigms in higher education, with participants from an unusually broad range of institutions including business schools (Peter Lorange), industry (Dennis Tsichritzis), scientific academies (James Duderstadt), open universities (Brenda Gourley) and technology institutes (Charles Vest and Patrick Aebischer & Jean-François Ricci). Here the focus was very much on changing paradigms in education and research, driven and enabled by rapidly evolving technologies such as the Internet, and whether these would lead to truly global universities. It was noted that the open university paradigm, best exemplified by the United Kingdom's Open University, had already achieved global span through the use of many technologies and practices such as lifelong learning, distance education, open source and content educational resources, and peer production. Yet there were also concerns raised that many of the characteristics of global business such as standardization, networked resources and virtual organizations seemed incompatible with the fundamental characteristics of contemporary universities, currently based upon highly customized, campus-based, and face-to-face educational experiences.

The final session turned to a discussion of the broader global responsibilities of higher education from the perspective of Europe (Luc Weber), the Middle East (John Waterbury) and America (Robert Zemsky and David Ward). It was stressed that in their efforts to globalize, universities should resist the tendency to adopt colonial strategies, in which their outreach activities were primarily designed to attract new resources — students, faculty, fee income — for their home campuses. Instead they should attempt to be not only responsive but also responsible in their globalization efforts by accepting responsibility for enhancing the development of higher education systems elsewhere along with a broad commitment to enabling sustainable societies in all their facets: environmental, economic, and political. Here there was also the caution raised that universities were most effective and constructive when they focused on their traditional roles of education and scholarship within academic communities based upon academic freedom and democratic processes.

The Glion VI Colloquium was arranged under the auspices of the University of Geneva and made possible by the generous support of the Hewlett Packard Corporation in both the United States and Europe, the Ewing Marion Kauffman Foundation in the United States and, in Switzerland, the State Secretariat for Education and Research. We are particularly grateful for the efforts of those who contributed to the production of this book, including Gerry Taggart from the Higher Education Funding Council of England who took extensive notes from the sessions, Edmund Doogue in Geneva, who provided rigorous editorial assistance, and Martina Trucco, HP University Relations, and Natacha Durand, University of Geneva, for their energetic and efficient help in making certain the colloquium ran smoothly.

Luc E. Weber   James J. Duderstadt
University of Geneva   *University of Michigan*

CONTRIBUTORS
AND
PARTICIPANTS

CONTRIBUTORS

Patrick AEBISCHER

Patrick Aebischer trained as an MD (1980) and a Neuroscientist (1983) at the Universities of Geneva and Fribourg in Switzerland. From 1984 to 1992, he worked at Brown University in Providence (Rhode Island, US) as an Assistant and then Associate Professor of Medical Sciences. In 1991, he became chairman of the Section of Artificial Organs, Biomaterials and Cellular Technology of the Division of Biology and Medicine of Brown University. In 1992, he returned to Switzerland as a Professor and Director of the Surgical Research Division and Gene Therapy Center at the Centre Hospitalier Universitaire Vaudois (CHUV) in Lausanne. In 1999, Prof. Aebischer was appointed President of the Ecole Polytechnique Fédérale de Lausanne (EPFL) by the Swiss Federal Council, taking office in March 2000. He is a member of numerous professional societies, both in Europe and America, and a fellow of the American Institute for Medical and Biological Engineering and of the Swiss Academy of Medicine. He is also the founder of two biotechnology companies: CytoTherapeutics (today Stem Cell In) and Modex Therapeutics (today IsoTis). His current research focuses on the development of cell and gene transfer approaches for the treatment of neurodegenerative diseases.

Robert BERDAHL

Robert M. Berdahl is president of the Association of American Universities. From 1997 to 2004, he was chancellor of the University of California, Berkeley. Before his move to Berkeley, he served as president of the University of Texas at Austin, Vice Chancellor for Academic Affairs at the University of Illinois in Urbana-Champaign, and dean of the College of Arts and Sciences at the University of Oregon. His research specialty has been German history, and he is author or co-author of two books and numerous articles; he has taught courses in European history and, more recently at Berkeley, public policy. He has received a number of awards and was elected to the American Academy of Arts and Sciences.

Carlos Henrique de BRITO CRUZ

Carlos Henrique de Brito Cruz was born in Rio de Janeiro, Brazil. He graduated in Electrical Engineering from Instituto Tecnológico da Aeronáutica (ITA), received an MSc and a DSc degree in Physics, both from the Physics Institute "Gleb Wataghin" at the State University at Campinas (Unicamp). He has been a researcher at the Quantum Optics Laboratory, at the University of Rome, and a resident visitor at AT&T Bell Laboratories in Holmdel, NJ, and in Murray Hill, NJ, in the US. Dr Brito Cruz works in the field of ultrafast phenomena in physics, using femtosecond pulse lasers to study fast processes in condensed matter. He has been Vice-President of the Brazilian Physics Society and served as a member of the International Advisory Committee of the Optical Society of America (OSA). He was the Director of the Physics Institute at Unicamp for two terms. He has been the Dean of Research at the State University at Campinas (Unicamp) and, from 1996 till 2002, he served as President of the Foundation for the Support of Research in the State of São Paulo (Fapesp). From April 2002 to April 2005, he was Rector of the State University of Campinas, Unicamp. Since April 2005 Prof. Brito Cruz has been the Scientific Director of Fapesp. He is also is a member of the Brazilian Academy of Sciences.

René CARRAZ

René Carraz is a Ph.D. candidate from the French-Japanese Doctoral School. He was awarded a scholarship from the French Ministry of Foreign Affairs to conduct research about the Japanese university-industry relationship. After training in economics and mathematics, he became interested in the economics and management of innovation. He is currently a teaching assistant at Université Louis Pasteur where he teaches Industrial Economics.

James J. DUDERSTADT

James J. Duderstadt is President Emeritus and University Professor of Science and Engineering at the University of Michigan. A graduate of Yale and

Caltech, Dr Duderstadt's teaching and research areas include nuclear science and engineering, applied physics, computer simulation and science policy. He has served as chair of numerous national Academy and federal commissions, including the National Science Board. In 2005-2006 he served as a member of the Secretary's Commission on the Future of Higher Education (best known as the Spellings Commission).

Brenda M. GOURLEY

Brenda Gourley has been Vice-Chancellor of The Open University since 2002. She is a member of the Board of the International Association of Universities and chairs the Association of Commonwealth Universities Board, as well as the Talloires Network's Global Project on literacy. A frequent speaker on a broad range of platforms and issues, as well as a contributor to publications around the world, Prof. Gourley has received several honorary degrees for her contributions to Higher Education. She has been named as one of the Global Business Network's "remarkable people". Previously Vice-Chancellor at the University of Natal in South Africa, Prof. Gourley is a qualified Chartered Accountant by profession and began her career in the private sector before moving into academia.

Yuko HARAYAMA

Yuko Harayama received her Ph.D. in Education Science in 1996 and a Ph.D. in Economics in 1997, both from the University of Geneva, Switzerland. Dr Harayama has a broad range of experience that encompasses work as an Assistant Professor in the Department of Political Economy at the University of Geneva and as a Fellow at the Research Institute of Economy, Trade and Industry in Japan. She currently serves as a Professor in the Management Department of Science and Technology at the Graduate School of Engineering of Tohoku University, Japan, and as an executive member at the Council for Science and Technology Policy in Japan.

Wayne C. JOHNSON

Wayne Johnson is Vice-President for University Relations Worldwide at Hewlett Packard in Palo Alto. He is responsible for higher education programmes in research, marketing and sales, recruitment, continuing education, public affairs and philanthropy. During his career, he has gathered significant management experience across a diversified set of business operations, including university relations management, engineering management, programme management, international training and logistics, research, international business development and commercial business development, mainly with Raytheon in different locations, as well as with Microsoft Research. Wayne Johnson received his B.A. from Colgate University, Hamilton, NY, and his M.B.A. from Boston

College's Carroll School, Boston, MA. He was an Adjunct Professor of Management at Boston University from 1977 to 1999.

Peter LORANGE

Peter Lorange was President of IMD from July 1993 until April 2008. He was formerly president of the Norwegian School of Management in Oslo. Before this, Dr Lorange was affiliated with the Wharton School, University of Pennsylvania, for more than a decade, in various assignments, including director of the Joseph H. Lauder Institute of Management and International Studies, and the William H. Wurster Center for International Management Studies, as well as the William H. Wurster Professor of Multinational Management. He also taught for eight years at the Sloan School of Management (MIT). Dr Lorange received his undergraduate education from the Norwegian School of Economics and Business, was awarded an M.A. in operations management from Yale University, and his Doctor of Business Administration degree from Harvard University. Dr Lorange has written or edited 15 books and some 110 articles.

Deepak NAYYAR

Deepak Nayyar is Professor of Economics at Jawaharlal Nehru University, New Delhi. He has previously taught at the University of Oxford, the University of Sussex and the Indian Institute of Management, Calcutta. He was Vice Chancellor of the University of Delhi from 2000 to 2005. He served as Chief Economic Advisor to the Government of India and Secretary in the Ministry of Finance from 1989 to 1991. He was educated at St Stephen's College, University of Delhi. As a Rhodes Scholar, he went on to study at Balliol College, Oxford, where he obtained a B. Phil. and a D. Phil. in Economics. He has published several books and articles in professional journals. He has been a Member of the World Commission on the Social Dimension of Globalization, a Member of the Board of Directors of the Social Science Research Council in the United States, and Chairman of the Advisory Council for the Department of International Development, Queen Elizabeth House, University of Oxford. He is an Honorary Fellow of Balliol College, Oxford. Professor Nayyar is Chairman of the Board of Governors of the UNU-WIDER Helsinki, a member of the National Knowledge Commission in India, and Vice President of the International Association of Universities, Paris.

Howard NEWBY

Sir Howard Newby will take up his post as Vice-Chancellor of Liverpool University in May 2008. He was Vice-Chancellor at the University of the West of England and Chief Executive of the Higher Education Funding Council for England between 2001 and 2005. Previous to that, he was Vice-Chancellor of the University of Southampton. In 2001-2002 he was President of Universities UK, and President of the British Association. Sir Howard has published many books and articles on social change in rural England and was for eight years a Rural Development Commissioner. Sir Howard was awarded a CBE in 1995 for his services to social sciences and a knighthood in 2000 for his services to higher education.

John NILAND

John Niland is Professor Emeritus (in Economics) at the University of New South Wales, where he was Vice Chancellor and President from 1992 to 2002. He served a term as President of the Australian Vice Chancellors' Committee and was a founding director of Universitas 21. He now serves on a number of Boards. In the university sector, he is on the Board of Trustees of Singapore Management University and is a member of the University Grants Committee of Hong Kong. In the corporate world he is an Independent Director of Macquarie Bank Limited, and is Chairman of Campus Living Villages Limited, a significant private provider of student accommodation in the US, New Zealand and Australia.

Jean-François RICCI

Jean-François Ricci was born in Geneva and trained as a civil engineer at EPFL where he took his diploma in 1989. From 1989 to 1991 he worked as a teaching and research assistant in the civil engineering department of EPFL. He then spent a year in Japan as a visiting scientist with the support of the Swiss Academy of Engineering Science. He returned to Switzerland in 1992 to work for WGG Schnetzer Puskas Ingenieure AG as a structural engineer on various large construction projects (bridges, stadium, buildings, etc). He joined EPFL in 1997 as head of strategic planning. He has a member of the senior management team of EPFL since 2000, and as a Senior Advisor to the President, he is involved in the strategic and operational conduct of EPFL.

Carl J. SCHRAMM

President and CEO, Kauffman Foundation. Carl Schramm is recognized as one of the world's foremost thinkers on the importance of entrepreneurship to a nation's economic growth. His recent books, *Good Capitalism, Bad Capitalism* and *The Entrepreneurial Imperative*, are regarded as emerging classics, providing new insight into the American and international economies. In 2007, US Secretary of Commerce Carlos Gutierrez tapped Schramm to chair the Department of Commerce's Measuring Innovation in the 21st century committee. Trained as an economist and lawyer, with experience in business, public policy and academia, Schramm has founded and co-founded several health care, finance and information technology companies. He is a Batten Fellow at the University of Virginia's Darden School of Business and a member of the Council on Foreign Relations.

Nam Pyo SUH

Nam Pyo Suh is the President of Korea Advanced Institute of Science and Technology (KAIST). Before taking up this position in 2006, he was at MIT, where he was the Cross Professor, Director of the Park Center for Complex Systems, Director and Founder of the Laboratory for Manufacturing and Productivity, and the Head of the Department of Mechanical Engineering. In 1984-1988, he took leave from MIT to accept a Presidential Appointment at the National Science Foundation. He holds five honorary doctorates from four continents and numerous awards for his contributions in tribology, design and complexity theory, and materials processing.

Gerry TAGGART

Dr Gerry Taggart is Executive Assistant to the Chief Executive of the Higher Education Funding Council for England (Hefce). Having joined Hefce in 1978, Taggart has worked on various task teams and international policy initiatives, and a major focus of Taggart's current role is as researcher and speech-writer for the Chief Executive. A member of the Hefce senior management team, Taggart also has varied stakeholder responsibilities within the organization, including Hefce's relationship with HM Treasury and the House of Commons Education Select Committee. His doctorate (on the role of the funding council and its relationship with universities and the state) was awarded by the University of Bristol in 2004. Taggart has two adult sons and lives in Bristol.

Tony TAN KENG YAM

Tony Tan Keng Yam graduated from the University of Singapore in 1962 with First Class Honours in Physics. He continued his studies at the Massachusetts Institute of Technology (1962-1964) and at the University of Adelaide where he received a Ph.D. in Applied Mathematics. He was appointed a Lecturer in Mathematics in the University of Singapore. In 1979, he was elected to Parliament and was appointed Minister for Education in June 1980 and, concurrently, the Vice-Chancellor of the National University of Singapore. In the years that followed, he held major government posts — Minister for Trade and Industry and Minister-in-charge of the National University of Singapore and the Nanyang Technological Institute, Minister for Finance, Minister for Education and Minister for Health. In 1991, Dr Tan stepped down from the Cabinet to return to the private sector as Oversea-Chinese Banking Corporation's Chairman and Chief Executive Officer. He rejoined the Cabinet in August 1995 and was appointed Deputy Prime Minister and Minister for Defence. In September 2005, he retired from the Cabinet and took up the posts of Deputy Chairman and Executive Director of the Government of Singapore Investment Corporation Private Limited, Chairman of the National Research Foundation and Deputy Chairman of the Research, Innovation and Enterprise Council, and Chairman of Singapore Press Holdings Limited.

Vladimir TROYAN

Vice-rector for research at the University of St Petersburg since 1993 and head of the Physics of the Earth Department at the same university since 1988, Vladimir Troyan is a specialist on a wide range of subjects, from inverse geophysical problems, application of geophysical methods to the solution of the environmental problems, geophysical tomography methods, statistical methods for processing of geophysical data, prediction of earthquakes and natural disasters to the application of statistical methods in climatology. He began his tertiary studies at the University of St Petersburg, obtaining a Diploma in Geophysics in 1963, a Ph.D. in Geophysics (1967) and a Dr Sci. (1980) at the same university. From 1967-1972, he was also Assistant professor in the Physics of the Earth Department at the University of St Petersburg, and went on to hold senior departmental posts in the 1970s and 1980s, as well as being a consultant to VEB Geophysics, Leipzig, Germany, from 1972 to 1977.

Dennis TSICHRITZIS

Dennis Tsichritzis obtained his Ph.D. in 1968 at Princeton University in Computer Science. He taught for several years at the University of Toronto, University of Crete and University of Geneva. He was President of GMD, the German National Research Centre on Information Technology, and then Senior Vice President of Fraunhofer Gesellschaft in Germany. He currently serves on different boards internationally.

Charles M. VEST

Charles M. Vest is president of the National Academy of Engineering and served as president emeritus of the Massachusetts Institute of Technology. A professor of mechanical engineering at MIT and formerly at the University of Michigan, he has served on the US President's Council of Advisors on Science and Technology since 1994, and has chaired the President's Committee on the Redesign of the Space Station and the Secretary of Energy's Taskforce on the Future of Science at DOE. He has also served as a member of the Commission on the Intelligence Capabilities of the United States Regarding Weapons of Mass Destruction and on the Secretary of Education's Commission on the Future of Higher Education. He was vice chair of the US Council on Competitiveness for seven years. He holds ten honorary doctorates and received the 2006 National Medal of Technology.

David WARD

A leading spokesperson for American higher education, David Ward became the 11th president of the American Council on Education in September 2001, after serving as Chancellor of the University of Wisconsin-Madison where he also received his doctorate in Geography in 1963. He received his B.A. and M.A. in geography from the University of Leeds, UK, before emigrating to the US. At the University of Wisconsin-Madison, he was Andrew Hill Clark Professor of Geography. In 1989 he was elected President of the Association of American Geographers. His services to higher education include the chairmanship of the Board of Trustees of the University Corporation for Advanced Internet Development, a non-profit group that spearheaded the development of Internet 2 and as a member of the Kellogg Commission on the Future of State and Land-Grant Universities.

John WATERBURY

John Waterbury became the 14th President of the American University of Beirut in January 1998 and the first President to reside in Beirut since 1984. In his tenure at AUB, he has sought to restore the university to its long-standing place and reputation as an institution of higher learning, meeting the highest international standards. Before joining AUB, Dr Waterbury was, for nearly 20 years, Professor of Politics and International Affairs at Princeton University's Woodrow Wilson School of Public and International Affairs. He took his Ph.D. in Public Law and Government at Columbia University in 1968, and went on to the University of Michigan as Assistant Professor of Political Science. In 1971 he joined the American Universities Field Staff, a consortium of US Universities, which he represented in Cairo from 1971 to 1977. Dr Waterbury has published widely on the politics of the Middle East, the political economy of public enterprise, and on the development of international river basins. His latest book, *The Nile Basin: National Determinants of Collective Action*, was published by Yale University Press in 2002.

Luc E. WEBER

Educated in the fields of economics and political science, Luc Weber has been Professor of Public Economics at the University of Geneva since 1975. As an economist, he serves as an advisor to Switzerland's federal government, as well as to cantonal governments, and has been a member of the Swiss Council of Economic Advisers for three years. Since 1982, Prof. Weber has been deeply involved in university management and higher education policy, first as vice-rector, then as rector of the University of Geneva, as well as Chairman and, subsequently, Consul for international affairs of the Swiss Rectors' Conference. He is the co-founder, with Werner Hirsch, of the Glion Colloquium and vice-president of the International Association of Universities (IAU). He is also a founding Board Member of the European University Association (EUA). He served for eight years on the Bureau of the Steering Committee for Higher Education and Research of the Council of Europe and was its chair over the last two years. Prof. Weber was recently awarded an honorary degree by the Catholic University of Louvain-la-Neuve for his contribution to Higher Education.

Georg WINCKLER

Georg Winckler studied at Princeton University and also at the University of Vienna, where he was appointed Full Professor of Economics in 1978. He has been Visiting Scholar at the International Monetary Fund (1990-1991), Visiting Professor at Georgetown University (Fall 1995) and at other universities, and Rector of the University of Vienna since 1999. He was President of the Austrian Rectors' Conference (2000-2005), Vice-President of the European University Association (2001-2005) and President since March 2005. He has been a member of the European Research Advisory Board since 2004.

Robert ZEMSKY

Robert Zemsky is the Chair and CEO of The Learning Alliance at the University of Pennsylvania. From 1980 to 2000, Professor Zemsky served as the founding director of Penn's Institute for Research on Higher Education. In 2005-2006 he served as a member of the Secretary's Commission on the Future of Higher Education (best known as the Spellings Commission).

Jie ZHANG

Zhang Jie took his Ph.D. in Optical and Atomic and Molecular Physics from the Institute of Physics, Chinese Academy of Sciences, Beijing, in 1988. He then started his career as a research scientist in the Institute of Physics, Chinese Academy of Sciences, where he received numerous academic honours in areas such as x-ray lasers, high field physics and laser-plasma physics. In 2003 Professor Zhang was elected Academician of the Chinese Academy of Sciences, the highest academic title in China. Before his appointment in November 2006 as President of Shanghai Jiao Tong University, he held positions as Director General, Bureau of Basic Sciences, Chinese Academy of Sciences (2003-2006), Director, Chinese Spallation Neutron Source (2002-2006), and Deputy Director, Institute of Physics, Chinese Academy of Sciences (1998-2003).

PARTICIPANTS

The following personalities participated in the Sixth Glion Colloquium and contributed comments and statements to the discussion:

Michel BENARD, Director, HP University Relations Technology Programs.

Daniel STANGLER, Office of the President of the Kauffman Foundation.

PART I

•••••••••••••

The Context

CHAPTER 1

Globalization: What does it Mean for Higher Education?

Deepak Nayyar

lobalization is centre-stage in the contemporary world. It interests almost everyone. Education, alas, is back-stage somewhere in the midst of the props. It interests some of us. Globalization and education, together, is a relatively unexplored subject, particularly among economists. The object of this essay is to reflect upon the intersection of, and explore the interconnections between, globalization and higher education in the wider context of development.

The structure of the paper is as follows. Section I outlines the essential characteristics of globalization, to set the stage before the play begins. Section II develops an analytical framework to consider how globalization relates to, or influences, the world of higher education. Section III examines what globalization means for higher education in different spheres. Section IV analyses the implications of markets and commercialization for universities which are, perhaps, the most important dimension of higher education. Section V seeks to focus on the globalization of higher education, to discuss its consequences for people and for education in the process of development. In conclusion, Section VI attempts to address a question that is simple enough to pose but difficult to answer: what is to be done?

GLOBALIZATION: MEANING AND DIMENSIONS

Globalization means different things to different people. What is more, the word globalization is used in two ways, which is a source of some confusion. It is used in a *positive* sense to *describe* a process of integration into the world economy. It is used in a *normative* sense to *prescribe* a strategy of development based on a rapid integration with the world economy.

Even its characterization, however, is by no means uniform. It can be described, simply, as an expansion of economic activities across national boundaries. There are three economic manifestations of this phenomenon – international trade, international investment and international finance – which also constitute its cutting edge. But there is much more to globalization. It is about the expansion of economic transactions and the organization of economic activities across political boundaries of nation states. More precisely, it can be defined as a process associated with increasing economic openness, growing economic interdependence and deepening economic integration in the world economy (Nayyar, 2006).

Economic *openness* is not simply confined to trade flows, investment flows and financial flows. It also extends to flows of services, technology, information and ideas across national boundaries. But the cross-border movement of people is closely regulated and highly restricted. Economic *interdependence* is asymmetrical. There is a high degree of interdependence among countries in the industrialized world. There is considerable dependence of developing countries on the industrialized countries. There is much less interdependence among countries in the developing world. Economic *integration* straddles national boundaries as liberalization has diluted the significance of borders in economic transactions. It is, in part, an integration of markets (for goods, services, technology, financial assets and even money) on the demand side, and, in part, an integration of production (horizontal and vertical) on the supply side.

It is essential to recognize that economics provides a critical but limited perspective on globalization which is a multi-dimensional phenomenon. It extends much beyond the economy to polity and society (World Commission on the Social Dimension of Globalization, 2004). And it would be no exaggeration that the whole is different from, possibly greater than, the sum total of its parts. The multiple dimensions — political, social and cultural — deserve mention, even if briefly.

In the political dimension, the momentum of globalization is such that the power of national governments is being reduced, through incursions into hitherto sovereign economic or political space, without a corresponding increase in effective international cooperation or supra-national government, which would regulate or govern this market-driven process. Simply put, there is a mismatch between economies that are global and polities that are national or local (World Commission on the Social Dimension of Globalization, 2004).

In the social dimension, a market economy may be seen as a necessary, indeed desirable, attribute of globalization but its creation of a market society may not be a desirable outcome. If the pursuit of material well-being becomes a dominant, for some an exclusive objective, the culture of materialism, or simply the quest for money, might spread to all spheres of life. A reasonable utilitarianism could then be transformed into Narcissist hedonism (Baudot, 2000). The norms and values which are the foundations of civil society, where individuals have an obligation to society, could be eroded. Social norms and social institutions, so essential for the market economy itself, could be weakened.

In the cultural dimension, the global spread of cultural impulses is at least as important as that of economic impulses (Streeten, 2001). The culture of the young in cities everywhere, across the world, is globalized, manifest in jeans, T-shirts, sneakers, jogging, fast foods, pop music, Hollywood movies, satellite television, 24×7 news channels, Internet and so on. Consumerism is indeed global. Even corruption and crime have become similar everywhere. In all this, the communications revolution and the electronic media have played a key role. But modernity and tradition do not always mesh together. Global integration sometimes accentuates divides within countries, as ethnic, cultural or religious identities capture those excluded from, or alienated by the process, which could create conflict in societies.

TOWARDS AN ANALYTICAL FRAMEWORK

There is an obvious question that arises. How can this process of globalization relate to, let alone influence, the world of higher education? The simple answer is in two factors underlying the process of globalization. For one, globalization is driven by market forces, whether the threat of competition or the lure of profits. For another, globalization is driven by the technological revolution in transport and communications which has set aside geographical barriers so that distance and time matter little. But economic analysis also enables us to provide a more complete, analytical, answer.

In any economy, education is an integral part of the social infrastructure and an essential component of social consumption. And, until not so long ago, education was mostly produced and consumed within national boundaries. It was what economists describe as non-traded. In this attribute, education in general and higher education in particular were not significantly different from services as distinct from goods. Services possess two unique characteristics. First, the production of a service and its consumption are, as a rule, simultaneous, because services cannot be stored. Second, the producer and the consumer of a service must interact with each other because the delivery of a service requires physical proximity.

In principle, it is possible to make a distinction between traded services, non-traded services and tradable services. In the world we knew, just a quarter of a century earlier, education was essentially non-traded across borders. But globalization has changed the world since then. The distinction between traded, non-traded and tradable services, which was always far from clear, has become more blurred on account of the rapid technical progress and the changes in the organization and the production that the world economy witnessed during the late 20th century.

Trade in services may be defined as international transactions in services between the residents of one country and the residents of another country, irrespective of where the transaction takes place. International trade in services so defined can be divided into four categories: (a) those in which the producer moves to the consumer, (b) those in which the consumer moves to the producer, (c) those in which either the producer or the consumer moves to the other, and (d) those in which neither the consumer nor the producer moves to each other (Nayyar, 1988). In the first three categories, physical proximity of the producer and the consumer is essential for the international service transaction to take place. This is in conformity with the characteristics of services. In the fourth category, however, such physical proximity is not necessary and international trade in services is similar to international trade in goods.

It is possible to think of conventional examples of international trade in services in each of these categories. Guest workers, body shopping, hotel chains, and department stores are examples of situations where the producer of a service moves to its consumers. Tourism provides the most obvious example of situations where the consumer of a service moves to the producer. Higher education is the other traditional example as students from all over the world move to study at Harvard or MIT in the United States and at Oxford or Cambridge in the United Kingdom. Entertainers, performing artists and sports persons provide examples of situations where either the producer moves to the consumer or the consumer moves to the producer. Traditional banking, shipping and insurance services provide examples of situations where neither the consumer nor the producer moves to the other, as these services can be disembodied from the producer and transported to the consumer.

In the past two decades, there has been a discernible increase in the possibilities for international trade in services, without any perceptible decrease in the degree of restrictions on such trade, which is attributable to technological change on the one hand and a near-revolution in transport on the other (Nayyar, 1988). Taken together, these developments have had the following consequences: first, non-traded services have become tradable; second, some altogether new services have entered into the realm of international transactions; and third, the possibilities for trade in erstwhile traded services have become much larger. The technological revolution in transport and communications has made hitherto non-traded services tradable either by a dramatic reduction in the cost of transport, which increases the mobility of the producer and the consumer of a service, or by developing a means of communication, such as satellite links or a video transmission, which eliminate the need for proximity between the producer and the consumer of a service. At the same time, the revolution in telecommunications and information technologies has created an altogether new species of traded services.

These developments have transformed not only the possibilities but also the realities of transactions in higher education across national boundaries. For a long time, as a service, higher education was tradable in one category alone where the consumer of a service moved to the producer, as students from different parts of the world went to study in premier universities mostly in industrial societies. Of course, there is a rapid expansion and diversification of this process in terms of student numbers and geographical spread. But that is not all. Cross-border transactions in higher education have entered into each of the other three categories: (i) those in which the producer moves to the consumer, as universities, particularly those in English speaking industrial societies, have established campuses in different parts of the world; (ii) those in which either the producer or the consumer moves to each other, as universities run short duration courses or summer schools either in their own campuses at home or in leased facilities abroad in the home countries of students; and (iii) those in which neither the producer nor the consumer moves to each other, as distance education, satellite television or open courseware dispense with the need for physical proximity between the teacher and the taught.

IMPACT OF GLOBALIZATION ON HIGHER EDUCATION

The spread of markets and the momentum of globalization, during the past two decades, have transformed the world of higher education almost beyond recognition. Market forces, driven by the threat of competition or the lure of profit, have led to the emergence of higher education as business. The technological revolution has led to a dramatic transformation in distance education as a mode of delivery. This is discernible not simply in the national context, but also in the international context with a rapid expansion of cross-border transactions in higher education. It is clear that markets and globalization are transforming the world of higher education. The ways and means of providing higher education are changing. But the process does not stop there. Markets and globalization are shaping the content of higher education and exercising an influence on the nature of institutions that impart higher education.

In reflecting on the content, it is appropriate to make a distinction between higher education, professional education and distance education. These are neither mutually exclusive nor exhaustive. But the distinction is useful for analytical purposes.

In the world of higher education, markets and globalization are beginning to influence universities and shape education, not only in terms of what is taught but also in terms of what is researched. In the sphere of teaching, there is a discernible departure from the liberal intellectual tradition where education was about learning across the entire spectrum of disciplines. Choices of students were shaped by their interest. There was never a perfect symmetry. Even so, universities endeavoured to strike a balance across disciplines, whether literature, philosophy, languages, economics, mathematics, physics or life sciences. But this is changing, as students and parents display strong revealed preferences to demand higher education that makes young people employable. The popularity and the availability of courses are thus being shaped by markets. The employability of students is not simply a force that is pushing to create more places for vocational courses in higher education. It is also inducing universities to introduce new courses, for which there is a demand in the market, because these translate into lucrative fees as an important source of income. Similarly, markets are beginning to exercise an influence on the research agenda of universities as resources for research in life sciences, medicine, engineering or economics are abundant, while resources for research in philosophy, linguistics, history or literature are scarce. There is a premium on applied research and a discount on theoretical research.

The world of professional education is also being influenced by markets and globalization. The obvious examples are engineering, management, medicine or law. For one, markets exercise some, albeit limited, influence on curricula. For another, globalization is coaxing a harmonization of academic programmes. The reason is simple. These professions are becoming increasingly internationalized. Therefore, the context is more global and less national, let alone local.

The world of distance education is somewhat different and could provide a silver lining to the cloud. Market forces and technical progress have opened up a new world of opportunities in higher education for those who missed the opportunity when they finished school or those who did not have access earlier. Of course, these opportunities and access come at a price which may not be affordable for some, particularly in developing countries or transition economies.

MARKETS AND COMMERCIALISATION OF UNIVERSITIES

The preceding discussion suggests that globalization is changing the form and shaping the content of higher education. At the same time, markets are beginning to exercise an influence on the nature and the culture of universities which are the most important institutions in higher education.

There is a discernible commercialization of universities, although it is at its early stages and has not yet spread everywhere. Even so, it is important to analyse the underlying factors (Bok, 2003). The process began life with the resource crunch in governments that led to a financial squeeze in universities. It coaxed universities into searching for alternative sources of income. Entrepreneurial talents, which were rewarded by the market and admired by some in society, legitimized such initiatives in universities. The importance of traditional academic values diminished as competition among universities for scarce resources intensified. This sequence of developments came to be juxtaposed with the emergence of a wide range of opportunities for universities to earn money in the market place, based on their comparative advantage in knowledge that had an enormous potential for applications in management and technology.

Such commercialization of universities has been reinforced by the forces of demand and supply. On the demand side, there is a burgeoning desire for higher education which is driven by a combination of individual aspirations and corporate needs in a changed national and international context. On the supply side, higher education, almost everywhere, is dominated by large public universities which are somewhat inefficient and resistant to change. The safeguards implicit in academic freedom and the security guaranteed by tenure appointments, taken together, often create situations where professors and administrators are not quite accountable to students let alone society. In developing countries, the problem is compounded because the opportunities for higher education in public institutions are simply not enough.

If we read between the lines, the situation in higher education is not very different from the milieu in the health care sector before the advent of private enterprise. Unless correctives are introduced, the world of higher education might be caught in a pincer movement. At one end, the commercialization of universities means business in education. At the other end, the entry of private players in higher education means education as business. There are dangers inherent in such commercialization, but there are also opportunities of learning from markets (Bok, 2003).

It is worth reflecting on the dangers. What can we lose? First, markets should not decide on academic curricula or research agenda. The reason is simple. Teaching and research cannot be simply about use-value and exchange-value. Second, management methods of business are not appropriate for universities. The objectives cannot be efficiency or profits. The practices cannot be incentives or disincentives in the form of rewards or penalties. The performance criteria cannot be fewer teachers per student, higher fees per student or lower costs per student. Third, markets and commercialization could unleash some dangers that may not have surfaced yet in most places. In principle, there is a danger that academic standards may be undermined particularly in admissions which could spill over in appointments and research. Similarly, there is a danger that individual conduct may be driven by self-interest, rather than common cause, where earning more money or exploiting

graduate students becomes a temptation. This could erode the ethos of colle-
giality and the sense of community that are so essential in the teaching-learn-
ing process. The ultimate danger lies in the erosion of values and ethics in the
university community. That could damage the credibility, if not the reputation, of universities which perform a critical role as guardians in open societies. Indeed, the integrity and the independence of intellectuals in universities,
respected by citizens and society, constitute an institutional mechanism of
checks and balances in a political democracy.

It is worth thinking about the opportunities. What can we learn? First, it is
essential to recognize the importance of competition. It is almost always realized in research. But it is sometimes missing in teaching. It must be stressed
that the significance of competition extends much beyond markets or profits.
Universities are not in the business of profit. Yet, competition between universities for academic excellence is essential. Second, it is important to recognize that incentives and disincentives matter, not simply for decreasing costs
or increasing efficiency but also for performance in a qualitative sense. The
moral of the story is not that Presidents, Rectors or Vice-Chancellors should
be rewarded with stock options when their universities do well or that universities should be closed down like firms when they are doing badly. But there
are lessons to be drawn about the importance of incentives and disincentives
that emerge from the experience of corporate entities in the marketplace.
Third, it is critical to accept that striving to improve quality is a continuous
process in higher education as much as it is elsewhere or in the marketplace.
Markets in which firms compete for consumers ensure that product quality
improves over time. But universities are slow to learn and to adapt so that academic curricula and teaching methods change slowly. In fact, the institutional
mechanisms for quality consciousness and quality improvement are few and
far between. Fourth, universities must recognize that it is imperative to be
responsive and accountable to students and society. Ironically enough, tenure
appointments, academic freedom and university autonomy — that are at the
core of the concept of universities — often diminish the accountability of
individuals in the university community to the institution and the accountability of the university as a collective to its students as individuals. The dangers and the opportunities for universities implicit in markets and commercialization are presented in somewhat caricature form if only to highlight their
significance. Universities have continued to provide centres of academic
excellence in spite of their structural rigidities and governance structures.
This is because the nature of incentives in university systems is much more
subtle than in corporate hierarchies (Bok, 2003). The quintessential academic
is motivated by the thought of coming up with an original idea, writing an
influential book, publishing a much cited paper in a refereed journal, discovering the unknown, or inventing something. Similarly, recognition in the

form of invitations to conferences, or awards and honours based on peer review, is also perceived by traditional academics as more important than material incentives or rewards. Alas, this world has changed, slowly but surely, in the past quarter of a century. The very same structures that produced academic excellence are doing so less and less.

It is clear that dangers and opportunities are closely intertwined in this process of change. We cannot afford to ignore these emerging realities because the world of higher education is at some risk. The culture of markets and the advent of commercialization could erode both values and morality that are the life blood of higher education. Universities must endeavour to create a milieu — by rethinking procedures, systems and governance — that reinforces intellectual standards and rejuvenates the quest for academic excellence.

GLOBALIZATION OF HIGHER EDUCATION

There can be little doubt that the process of globalization is exercising a significant influence on the world of higher education. But that is not all. At the same time, there is a globalization of higher education that, in turn, has significant implications. It has implications for people and for countries. It has implications for higher education and for development. Consider each in turn.

In considering what the spread of globalization into higher education could mean for people and for countries, there are three important manifestations that are worth noting (Nayyar, 2002).

First, the *globalization of education* has gathered momentum. This has two dimensions. The proportion of foreign students studying for professional degrees or doctorates in the university system of the major industrialized countries, in particular the United States, is large and more than two-thirds simply stay on. The situation is similar in Europe albeit on a smaller scale. At the same time, centres of excellence in higher education in labour-exporting developing countries are increasingly adopting curricula that conform to international patterns and standards. Given the facility of language, such people are employable almost anywhere.

Second, the *mobility of professionals* has registered a phenomenal increase in the age of globalization. It began with the brain drain. It was facilitated by immigration laws in the United States, Canada and Australia which encouraged people with high skills or professional qualifications. This process has intensified and diversified. It is, of course, still possible for scientists, doctors, engineers and academics to emigrate. But there are more and more professionals such as lawyers, architects, accountants, managers, bankers, or those specializing in computer software and information technology, who can emigrate permanently, live abroad temporarily, or stay at home and travel frequently for business. These people are almost as mobile as capital across borders.

Third, the reach and the spread of *transnational corporations* is worldwide. In the past, they moved goods, services, technology, capital and finance across national boundaries. Increasingly, however, they have also become transnational employers of people. They place expatriate managers in industrialized and developing host countries. They recruit professionals not only from industrialized countries but also from developing countries for placement in corporate headquarters or affiliates elsewhere. They engage local staff in developing countries who acquire skills and experience that make them employable abroad after a time. They move immigrant professionals of foreign origin, permanently settled in the industrialized world, to run subsidiaries or affiliates in their countries of origin. They engage professionals from low-income countries, particularly in software but also in engineering or health care, to work on a contract basis on special non-immigrant status visas, which has come to be known as "body-shopping". This intra-firm mobility across borders easily spills over into other forms of international labour mobility.

The professionals, at the top of the ladder of skills, are almost as mobile as capital. Indeed, we can think of them as globalized people who are employable almost anywhere in the world. And the world, so to speak, is their oyster. In a sense, it is a part of the secession of the successful. The story is similar but not the same for contract workers or those part of body-shopping, for they are somewhere in the middle of the ladder of skills. In either case, however, it is the globalization of higher education that has made it possible. But there is a crucial asymmetry. The investment is made by the home countries. The returns accrue to the host countries. This process is associated with a privatization of benefits and a socialization of costs. For the home countries of these people, there is an externalization of benefits and an internalization of costs.

The WTO regime and the General Agreement on Trade in Services have important implications for higher education which need careful consideration. This multilateral framework embodies the most-favoured-nation clause and the national treatment provision. The right of establishment, or commercial presence, for service providers is also integrated into the agreement. This is not yet universalized but allows for sector-by-sector negotiations. Higher education is on the agenda. Therefore, a multilateral regime of discipline for international trade in higher education services is on the anvil. It would mean too much of a digression to enter into a discussion about higher education in the context of the WTO. But I would like to highlight two possible implications and consequences for higher education in the wider context of development, which relate to the quality of education and to the nature of education.

In developing countries, the globalization of higher education is influencing the quality of education in two ways. It is striking that there is a proliferation of sub-standard institutions which charge high fees and provide poor education. There is little, if any, accountability to students because, in most developing countries, there are no laws for consumer protection or regulators for this market. Such adverse selection of service providers in higher education is a real problem. Of course, there are some good institutions that enter this domain to provide higher education across borders but these are few and far between. Unfortunately, even these institutions are susceptible to the practice of double standards: the global and the local. It might be unfair to cite examples but it would be instructive to compare the academic content and standards of the programmes run by such reputable institutions through campuses at home, through distance education and in campuses abroad. Clearly, unfettered markets without established regulators in higher education are bound to have an adverse effect on the quality of education.

The globalization of higher education is also changing the nature of higher education in the developing world. Its links with and relevance to the society in which the higher education is provided are somewhat tenuous, because the content and scope is determined in industrial societies. What is more, there is a clear and present danger that an internationalized higher education system may stifle rather than develop domestic capabilities in the higher education systems of the developing world, particularly the least developed countries.

CONCLUSION

In a world of unequal economic and social opportunities, higher education provides the only access to faring better, whether we think of people or of countries. Theory and evidence both suggest that the development of a physical infrastructure and a social infrastructure, particularly in education, are the necessary *initial conditions* for a country to maximize the benefits and minimize the costs of integrating with the world economy in the process of globalization. Thus, for countries that are latecomers to industrialization and development, a premature market-driven and passive insertion into the world economy, without creating the *initial conditions*, is fraught with risk. It is not just about an unequal distribution of costs and benefits between people and between countries. The spread of education in society is critical. So is the creation of capabilities among people. In this, higher education provides the cutting edge. It is at the foundations of development in countries that are latecomers to industrialization. This is the essential lesson that emerges from the success stories of Asia in the second half of the 20th century.

At the beginning of the 21st century, it is clear that the wealth of nations and the well-being of humankind will depend, to a significant extent, on ideas and knowledge. In the past, it was land, natural resources, labour skills, capital accumulation or technical progress that were the source of economic growth and economic prosperity. In the future, knowledge is bound to be critical in the process of economic growth and social progress. Without correctives, the widening gap between the haves and the have-nots could then be transformed into a widening gap between those who know and those who know-not. The most appropriate conclusion is provided by an old Buddhist proverb which says that "the key to the gate of heaven is also the key which could open the gate to hell". Markets and globalization provide a mix of opportunities and dangers for higher education. I have not provided an answer to the question I posed at the outset: what is to be done? But a simple prescription would be appropriate. We should not allow markets and globalization to shape higher education. Instead, we should shape our agenda for higher education, so that we can capture the opportunities and avoid the dangers unleashed by markets and globalization.

REFERENCES

Baudot, Jacques. (Ed). (2000). *Building a World Community: Globalization and the Common Good*, Copenhagen Seminars for Social Progress, Copenhagen.

Bok, Derek. (2003). *Universities in the Market Place: The Commercialization of Higher Education*, Princeton University Press, Princeton.

Nayyar, Deepak. (1988). "The Political Economy of International Trade in Services" *Cambridge Journal of Economics*, Vol. 12, No. 2, pp.279-298.

Nayyar, Deepak. (2002). "Cross-Border Movements of People", in Nayyar, D. (Ed) *Governing Globalization: Issues and Institutions*, Oxford University Press, Oxford.

Nayyar, Deepak. (2006). "Globalization, History and Development: A Tale of Two Centuries", *Cambridge Journal of Economics*, Vol. 30, No. 1, pp. 137-159.

Streeten, Paul. (2001). *Globalization: Threat or Opportunity?* Copenhagen Business School Press, Copenhagen.

World Commission on the Social Dimension of Globalization (2004), A *Fair Globalization: Creating Opportunities for All*, ILO, Geneva.

CHAPTER 2

Reinvigorating Universities in an Entrepreneurial Age

Carl Schramm

INTRODUCTION

The global economy stands at a moment of extraordinary potential. The last three decades have produced steep gains in worldwide economic growth, led by a surge of innovative, entrepreneurial activity rooted in advanced science and technology. Nations around the world have an opportunity to capitalize on efficiencies and optimize economic potential on a global scale, thereby building wealth and spreading its benefits as never before.

Recent history has proven the far-reaching benefits of economic growth. The creation of wealth has improved global living standards, alleviated poverty and contributed to the eradication of disease. The market forces that accompany growth have reinforced the essential role of free individuals in directing resources to their best uses.

Though the precise formula for economic growth differs from nation to nation, the most successful economies have shown that innovation and entrepreneurship are essential to expanding the potential for economic output — allowing people to extract greater output from any given level of input. But how can nations accelerate the pace of innovation and entrepreneurial activity in their economies? While there are a variety of methods, we know that higher education plays an integral role. As centres of innovation and research, and producers of human and intellectual capital, institutions of higher education have helped to build the foundation on which worldwide economic growth rests. And universities have generally been eager to support economic growth, seeing it as complementary to their philosophical mission of improving the overall welfare of mankind.

There is troubling evidence, however, that universities in the developed world are failing to adapt to the needs of the modern global economy. As the pace of economic change accelerates, and the need for graduates who are skilled in wealth creation and technological innovation grows, universities are erecting roadblocks to innovation and producing graduates who are better prepared for careers in wealth administration than in wealth creation. Furthermore, far from being centres of pro-growth theory, many top universities have developed into centres of anti-growth ideology, perpetuating a belief that economic growth is somehow inimical to human welfare. The unfortunate result is that other actors in the economy are beginning to distance themselves from universities, locating research and searching for talent elsewhere. If universities remain estranged from the broader economy, nations will not be able to maximize their potential for economic growth.

Interestingly, this trend appears not to have infected universities in the developing world — those nations which stand to benefit the most from increased global economic growth — where higher education institutions are fast becoming international centres of research, innovation and scientific advance. Yet the responsibility for worldwide economic growth does not rest exclusively (or even primarily) with the developing world. Given the importance of economic growth to global living standards, the need for universities in first-tier economies to contribute to the acceleration of growth has never been more urgent. Universities must respond to this challenge by shedding relatively recent habits and practices that prevent them from contributing to economic growth and renewing their traditional mission of producing the human capital, research and innovation, and philosophical leadership that make growth possible.

In short, universities need to adopt many of the entrepreneurial, innovative practices that have transformed economies — particularly the economy of the United States — into engines of growth over the last 25 years. Only when universities fully participate in the effort to generate economic growth will the global economy achieve its potential to improve livelihoods around the world.

THE DYNAMIC NATURE OF CAPITALISM

The importance of globalization and worldwide economic growth today is rooted in the end of the Cold War, which saw capitalism emerge as the prevalent system of economic organization throughout most of the world. Rather than settling the question of how economies should be organized to maximize growth, the end of the Cold War shifted the question. Instead of asking whether capitalism was best, nations asked how to make capitalism function best in their own societies, with their own political systems. The result has been a patchwork of capitalist models at work in countries around the world.

In our recent book, *Good Capitalism, Bad Capitalism*, William Baumol, Robert Litan and I describe four main models of capitalism — oligarchic capitalism, state-directed capitalism, big-firm capitalism, and entrepreneurial capitalism — and determine that some forms of capitalism are better than others at generating economic growth, promoting freedom and individual rights, maintaining predictability and contributing to world stability.

Oligarchic capitalism is the system that reigns in Russia and many third-world economies today. This is the most negative form of capitalism in the sense that it depresses the probability of individual risk-taking. A system that channels wealth into the hands of a few disincentivizes the individual, stunting further growth.

State-directed capitalism is the system in which we place modern China. One of the things that China teaches is how liberalization and freer markets can help achieve what has been a long-time worldwide goal: the alleviation of poverty. In the last 25 years, figures indicate that global poverty has been reduced by at least 20%, and most of that reduction has been in China. Unfortunately, few economists cite China's achievement as laudable. Instead, in foreign policy and academic circles the achievement is given polite nods with the presumption that economic growth and the reduction of poverty cannot happen.

Big-firm capitalism characterizes almost all of western Europe and also characterized the United States throughout much of the 20th century. Three major players emerge in a big-firm capitalist system: large companies, which are responsible for most of the economic activity and job creation in the economy; government, which provides certain guarantees and protections that insulate the big firms from competition; and unions, which collaborate with the other two players to produce maximum job stability. The key flaw in this system is that by focusing on stability — the stability of the major companies on which the nation depends for jobs and income, the stability of the labour market — the system becomes bureaucratic and resistant to change, sacrificing growth in the process.

Entrepreneurial capitalism characterizes the US economy since roughly the mid-1980s and with its focus on risk-taking, lightly regulated markets (including the labour market), and encouragement of business formation and wealth creation, it seems best-suited to driving innovation, efficiency and productivity. These qualities have become increasingly important given the nature of global competition today.

The choice we made to look at capitalism was not a political choice, and it brought to light two overarching perspectives that help us consider the university's role in the new global market ecosystem. The first is that wealth is achievable around the world. Today that sounds like a pedestrian observation. But 25 years ago, the presumption was that growth was the province of the west. In fact, it may have been a particularly western myopia, but it was presumed that several countries that have since taught the rest of the world about growth could not in fact produce growth.

For example, the presumption in the early 1980s was that India's contest over population was such that growth would never take central position. It was inconceivable to imagine India as a net food exporter, as it has been for a decade. Today, India continues to impress the world with its economic growth and its development as a global high-tech centre.

China also was considered a country with limited growth potential. The presumption in the west was that the existence of a Confucian culture that was antithetical to individual enterprise would prevent growth in China apart from the socialist system that prevailed. Today, rapid growth in China has lifted hundreds of millions in that country out of poverty.

The second overarching observation in *Good Capitalism, Bad Capitalism* is that the variants of capitalism we have identified do not represent the end of the story. Ours is not a taxonomy that is necessarily stable. In fact, we argue that it will be dynamic and it is likely to be dynamic at an increasing rate. Nor do we presume that the American system — even with its substantial benefits in an innovation-driven global economy — will somehow be triumphant. Indeed, many of the lessons of this taxonomy suggest the fragility of the relationship between US-style liberal democracy and capitalism.

But it is important to note that the US entrepreneurial system boasts the best record of producing wealth at a pace that yields tangible benefits on a global scale. The contributions the US economy has made to global growth and poverty-reduction are something of a surprise in the sense that the evolution of America's entrepreneurial economy was quite accidental. Over 70 years ago, the US economy organized itself around Keynesian principles (associated with the big-firm capitalist model). Big government, big unions and big business co-managed an economy where interests were balanced and regulated in pursuit of equilibrium (avoidance of recession) and predictable growth. This system, described by economist Joseph Schumpeter and others as bureaucratic capitalism and celebrated by Harvard economist John Kenneth Galbraith in *The New Industrial State*, failed in the late 1970s and early 1980s. At that time, two phenomena emerged that had been thought to be antithetical — high unemployment and high inflation.

Several actions by the US Congress (including pension reform, deregulation of several industries as well as capital markets, and the privatization of ownership of government-sponsored research), unexpectedly set in place an economic revolution. In the 1980s the flow of venture capital increased, labour mobility expanded rapidly, the cost of business risk assumed by individuals was attenuated, and the expense of converting technological innovation into commercial applications fell significantly.

The resulting explosion of entrepreneurial activity has transformed the US economy, and the fruits of this transformation extend beyond America's borders. The United States has set the pace for economic growth and productivity increases. It is persuasively argued that China grows at 9% per year because the United States grows at 3%. Even areas that have experienced less growth than hoped for – Africa, for example – have begun to be transformed by technology and stand poised, given the right conditions, to access the wealth of global markets. At the same time, the tremendous wealth produced by private-sector enterprises has made possible unprecedented commitments of aid to underdeveloped regions of the world.

Having witnessed the example of US economic growth, other nations — notably Ireland and Israel — have reshaped their economies to focus on entrepreneurial activity and have realized strong growth. Ireland has become Europe's economic pacesetter; Israel has more companies listed on the NASDAQ than any country except the United States. And Nicolas Sarkozy was elected President of France in 2007 on a platform of introducing more flexibility and even unpredictability (key markers of entrepreneurial economies) into France's static economy.

UNIVERSITIES' CHANGING RELATIONSHIP TO ECONOMIC GROWTH

The US transformation toward an entrepreneurial economy would not have happened without the modern university playing a central role. While the challenge of supporting growth from a university perspective affects nations around the world, the US experience offers a helpful overview of how universities can contribute to growth and how they have been falling short of the mark.

For much of the nation's history, American universities recognized that their existence and success were intertwined with the economic fortunes of the nation. Scholarly study and discovery can only occur systematically in an expanding economic environment. Economic growth, in turn, has been inexorably tied to the increase of new knowledge and an educated population. To that end, American universities have historically framed their role as a pragmatic one, helping to facilitate wealth creation in the interest of knowledge and discovery, and adapting to the changing economic and social conditions of the country.

In 1824 Steven Van Rensselaer developed a new template for the creation of an institution: personal endowment. The polytechnic school that bears his name became the US's first university focused on engineering and science. And in forming the university that bears his son's name, Leland Stanford attempted to imbue a liberal arts education with explicit commercial and engineering purposes. "I attach great importance to general literature for the enlargement of the mind and for growing business capacity," he said. "A man will never construct anything he cannot conceive."

Celebrated entrepreneurs (e.g., Hopkins, Rockefeller, Eastman, Cornell, Carnegie, Mellon, Duke) who saw the practical importance of education created many of America's private research universities. Public land-grant universities also had as their vision both practical and scholarly contributions to the nation. And whether the institutions were public or private, one founding intent was everywhere: universities were expected to be *useful*, to provide the necessary human capital and essential research support for the country, including the expansion of the American economy.

Closely related to their efforts to promote economic growth, US universities traditionally advanced liberal democratic ideals — free thought, free speech, individual rights — as the foundation for market-oriented growth and thus a main contributor to US economic success. This was especially so when the nation was locked in ideological struggle with communism in the post-World War II era.

In the decades prior to the 1980s American universities collaborated with US government scientists and corporate researchers in the quest for technological breakthroughs, while also educating workers who possessed strong critical thinking skills and were well-versed in the important connection between innovation and economic growth. Thus, when the US economy shifted in a more market-oriented, competition-driven direction in the 1980s, the human and intellectual resources were in place to launch an entrepreneurial revolution.

Today, however, American universities are underperforming the central role they must play: 1. providing flexible, inventive talent trained and skilled at innovation; 2. conducting advanced research vital to the expansion and enrichment of life and civilization; and 3. promoting the liberal democratic values that direct capitalism to its best ends and produce its best results, namely raising standards of living through growth and productivity.

NEGLECTING HUMAN CAPITAL

The question of what college students should study will likely always be with us. Nonetheless, today this issue takes on a different cast because of the astoundingly wide chasm between what growth-oriented economies need students to learn and the new alternatives universities provide. In this way, today's educational shortcomings differ from those in the past. When William Whyte wrote in 1956 of a "generation of bureaucrats", he fretted that business degrees were crowding out the liberal arts. Those students who studied business, however, were precisely what the American economy (and thus American society) needed at the time — this was the era of large firms that required managers skilled in financial administration and analysis. As before in an industrial age, universities established specialized graduate schools in a wide variety of sciences and engineering, readying generations of graduates for innovative roles where they could expand the nation's technological capacity and economy.

Such adaptation in response to the social and economic needs of the country appears to be the exception today. America's future standard of living depends on not only professions such as computer science and geophysics, but also the generalists who, economist Edward Lazear has argued, are crucial for entrepreneurial expansion. Unfortunately, the nation's universities now offer an astounding array of vocational fields of study that meet neither of these needs. Examples include parks and leisure studies, talent management, sports medicine and entire disciplines focused on schooling students in the finer points of government regulation (e.g., forensic accounting, a post-Sarbanes-Oxley development).

At the same time, the productivity of the US education establishment is in decline: as American schools produce less, they cost more. In the period 1993 to 2004, 30 of the United States' leading research universities experienced budget growth of over 70%. In the same institutions, the number of students during the period was only 8% greater, with five of the schools experiencing a decline in their student populations.

In an analysis of the composition of rising costs in universities, data for the period 1976 to 2003 show that the growth in non-instructional employees in universities far outpaced either the growth of students or faculty. Non-faculty professional staff alone (lawyers, compliance officers, budget personnel, development staff) grew nearly 250%.

This bureaucratic growth stands in sharp contrast to other sectors of the economy. In the US private sector we find that while the top 25 corporations account for a larger percentage of GDP than they did 30 years ago, they do it with 40% fewer workers. These firms have realized tremendous productivity gains and demonstrated a very highly conscious attempt to expel bureaucratic culture.

DECLINE OF RESEARCH PRODUCTIVITY

Research productivity presents a yet more troubling problem. Despite an enormous expansion in research support, mostly from the US federal government, the generation of breakthrough ideas likely to produce practical applications leading to faster economic growth, longer life, safer products, cheaper energy or healthier foods appears to be slowing.

Over the past 25 years the United States has seen a dispersion of academic research and development funding, away from the concentration in a handful of elite institutions, as in the two decades following World War II. Yet, at the same time, output of patents and licences in many fields has remained concentrated in a handful of schools. Moreover, despite the increase in academic R&D, the growth of patents has recently slowed. Similarly, the National Science Board has noted a "flattening in the output of US S&E [science and engineering] publications" (academic institutions account for three-quarters of American S&E article output). And over the past two decades America's share of the top 1% of highly cited S&E articles has dropped.

One reason may be classified as a failure of good intentions. The newly developing interest among universities in formally transferring discoveries into commercial applications has, in many instances, dampened innovation. During the last decade, more than 200 universities have established offices to manage "technology transfer", a process by which the university seeks to enrich itself by controlling intellectual property developed by faculty. These bureaucracies too often slow the commercialization process, setting unrealistic values on their intellectual property that result in long and frequently fruitless negotiations. Consequences have included several titanic struggles between universities and industry arising in cases where a company has supported specific research over which the university later asserted ownership. The problem lies not in attempts to commercialize academic discoveries (these often enhance human welfare), but the bureaucracy universities have built around the process.

The uncertainty and cost accompanying this bureaucratic build-up have helped encourage the migration of research to commercial laboratories. Over the last 50 years, industry-funded basic research in universities generally kept pace with all categories of research and development, even outpacing industry's own performance of basic research. In the mid-1990s, with the explosion of trans-disciplinary fields such as biotechnology, corporations began funding university-performed basic research at a blistering pace: such investment grew 45% from 1995 to 2000, much faster than the growth of total R&D funding. In 2000, however, industry abruptly reversed course, funding more basic research in its own laboratories than in universities. Commercially-funded research in universities, a vital piece of American economic success, has steadily declined since the beginning of the century.

ERODING SUPPORT FOR LIBERAL DEMOCRATIC VALUES

Finally, quite in opposition to their traditional role as advocates of liberal democracy, American universities today seem to be the epicentre for anti-growth theory for the rest of the world. Many academics speak about growth, capitalism and liberal values almost as if they are unconscious of what the words mean to the rest of the world. Listening to conversations about hyper-protection of the environment, anti-globalism and anti-growth, it is as if

American and many European academics believe that, in the name of preserving the environment, it would be best if developed nations didn't grow anymore at all and others didn't grow much either. Growth is rarely associated with its potential to reduce poverty. The United States has a bipolar debate about growth versus redistribution, and in the academic community the redistributionists far outnumber the proponents of growth.

*

*   *

Taken together, these three factors — the decline in output of human capital prepared for the modern global economy; the fall-off in university-sponsored research leading to market innovations; and academia's increasing hostility toward economic growth — have diminished the ability of universities to contribute to global growth. In fact, it may be said that today's American universities offer a model of how *not* to behave in an increasingly competitive, entrepreneurial economy. As a result, the US government and private industry have begun isolating universities, attempting to work around their defects rather than draw on their strengths.

RESTORING THE LINK BETWEEN UNIVERSITIES AND ECONOMIC GROWTH

Given the importance of the US economy to growth throughout the world, it is imperative that the United States re-establish the link the between universities and the wider economy that contributed to economic growth through much of the 20th century. In the 1950s, for example, a number of universities, such as the Massachusetts Institute of Technology (MIT), pursued pioneering research and development that planted the seeds for later economic growth. If the United States can establish an effective model for creating more entrepreneurial, market-connected universities, this model will not only stimulate growth, but also serve as a template for universities in other nations.

Reform will be a complex process, and several areas of action should receive high priority. Above all, universities should impose on themselves the discipline American corporations did in response to increasing global competition in the 1980s. Companies underwent a painful process of restructuring, which involved reshaping their products, processes and labour forces. In many ways they reinvented themselves from the inside out. Among other transformations, they became singularly focused on improving quality and reducing costs.

Better educational quality at the university level will require in many, perhaps most, institutions a fundamental refocusing of the curriculum. At exactly the moment when we should see growth in the number of students ready to engage in wealth creation, we are watching the proliferation of courses aimed at wealth consumption. In place of such narrow programmes, universities should encourage students to undertake courses that prepare them for highly mobile careers, giving them the capacity to respond to shifts in the dynamic world economy. Critical thinking skills (which emerge from courses such as history and literature) coupled with empirical knowledge that form such fields as mathematics, the physical sciences, economics and business, which result in broadly trained generalists, should be required everywhere.

To provide better educational value for students (in the United States) and taxpayers (primarily in Europe), ancillary services and activities should be eliminated, excessive overhead reduced, and management empowered to develop new models of delivering instruction and research. Because universities operate insulated from market forces, pressure for reform must be instigated externally as well as created internally through the efforts of trustees, presidents and students.

Competition, the prime motivator of most of the world's successful enterprises, is a word unfamiliar to most universities, except as it relates to capturing students through admissions. Greater competition among universities on the basis of their outputs — including the strength of graduate performance and the significance of research contributions — would help differentiate schools on the basis of measures central to economic growth, thereby providing an incentive for universities to engage in education and research activities that demonstrate clear utility to the larger economy.

WHO'S GETTING IT RIGHT?

Some nations are already taking action that the US and Europe would do well to emulate. Universities in the Asian Rim, among other places, have no confusion about their mission. They see themselves providing highly qualified graduates to take up the task of innovation and discovery within an explicit context of making valuable new commercial advances. In the space of a generation, Chinese universities established since the Cultural Revolution have produced much larger numbers of science and technology graduates than the United States. Moreover, these schools also seek to build strong liberal arts curricula to complement their science programmes to produce the generalists needed for an entrepreneurial economy. This remarkable expansion of university graduates reflects official policy based on the premise that the emergence of successful modern, market-based economies relies on the productivity of each country's higher education establishment.

Institutions that emphasize innovation-centred economic growth are reaping dividends. American and foreign companies that once supported advanced research in US universities have created robust partnerships with universities in England, India, Russia, and China. Many of these offer not only lower costs but also fewer bureaucratic disputes over intellectual property. As a result, a survey last year found that most global firms anticipate their expansion of R&D to take place in China and India: by the end of this year, 31% of R&D employees worldwide will work in one of these two countries. In 2004, the percentage was 19%.

This is notable not because of any perceived competition between the United States and emerging Asia, though surely that exists, but rather because it illustrates how nations can be effective in achieving a closer union between universities and economic growth. As the United States has watched its universities slip further from economic relevance, other countries have been more ambitious about establishing the vital link between university research, student education, and economic growth.

CONCLUSION

Historically, universities have been critically important to the growth of entrepreneurial capitalism in the United States, and developing countries properly place enormous hope on the contribution that their universities will make to the growth rates of their economies — particularly in the development of human capital and discovery. Whereas economists once sought neatness in the US economic system, the reality today is that the US has a profoundly messy economy, but one that has produced record-setting rates of annualized growth and productivity, and propagated waves of economic growth that have raised living standards around the world. There is no better recommendation for entrepreneurial, innovative capitalism than the visible results it has produced.

In the effort to continue the extraordinary progress made in reducing global poverty over the last two decades, the United States and Europe must make economic growth a centrepiece of their national and international agendas. In a global economy, the actions of every nation and every institution are crucial to achieving widespread growth. The role of educated people who see clearly how economies and values operate together, and how they are accelerated by discovery and critical thinking, is central to the achievements that await us in the development of humankind. We need all available resources, including universities, to work collaboratively to achieve what is at once a very simple and profound goal: to increase the rate at which the world's economy grows, so that all people benefit.

CHAPTER 3

Partnering on a Global Scale

Wayne C. Johnson [1]

INTRODUCTION

The past decade has brought tumultuous change to industry, effectively rewriting the assumptions and rules of how global business is conducted and of where to locate one's operations and why. The advancement of information and communications technology, the ready access to a global delivery infrastructure, the pervasiveness of worldwide supply chains, the easy access to new and undeveloped markets, and the ability to move thought, information and materials around the globe quickly and easily have contributed to a leveling of the playing field which was once thought to be the exclusive purview of larger companies. With ready access to information, materials, capabilities, other people (human capital), specialized talents and markets (both developed and undeveloped), and with today's infrastructure, it's possible for any individual to become a product designer, a service provider, a systems integrator, a solution provider, a marketer or even an e-commerce channel, and literally create the enterprise of their dreams, large or small. The power of many is rapidly on the way to becoming the power of one.

Yet this shift in capability has not come easily, nor without significant disruption and cost. To get to this point, companies have struggled mightily with their structure, growing explosively in some regions while shrinking in others. They've been engaged in downsizing, rightsizing, rebalancing, offshoring, onshoring, outsourcing, insourcing and just about every form of restructuring as they attempt to adjust their work flows and processes to the new rules of globalization. In recent years, almost every form of value creation and service

1 The author would like to acknowledge, with gratitude, the assistance of Mr Lou Witkin, of HP's University Relations Worldwide, and Mr Ron Crough, of Vosara, Inc., in the preparation of this chapter.

delivery has been disintermediated — and if it hasn't been changed already, it will be soon. The form and structure of just about everything we know is changing, and the question of how not only to survive, but to thrive while all this is going on remains a challenge.

At the highest level, we know from experience that the three pillars — education, entrepreneurship and innovation — can bring lasting success and prosperity to societies. They are built upon a strong partnership between government, universities and industry that takes years to put into place, and can pay many benefits and dividends far into the future. This partnership must be cared for, invested in, shepherded, optimized and moved forward into the future if continuing benefits are to be derived from the investments made.

Yet not all three partners have fully adapted to the global world, and the opportunities and perils that it presents. To date, industry has largely been leading the charge with respect to globalization. Whether this is advantageous or not seems to be a side discussion. No one in industry believes that they can resist the forces of globalization. They must understand what it means to operate in a "flattened world", and they must figure out how to adapt, to take advantage of the benefits, to mitigate the limitations and risks, and, in short, they must learn how to be global companies and citizens in order to bring their unique value to an ever-increasing range of potential markets and customers. It's particularly interesting to note that at a recent meeting of innovation and thought leaders in Silicon Valley and the San Francisco Bay Area, we've noted that even new start-up companies are starting out their lives as global firms. Companies with a mere handful of people (5-10) have employees located in multiple countries and regions of the world, for a variety of reasons that make sense to their particular enterprise and what it's trying to achieve. The new notion is that global does not necessarily equate with big, but global is necessary for survival, from the outset.

Universities are not nearly as far along in their adaptation to a global environment. While they do possess many of the raw building blocks and values to be globally situated (communities based on open inquiry, the free exchange of ideas and knowledge, philosophically, politically and religiously agnostic, etc.), they are still fundamentally a local enterprise. What does it take to achieve cohesion in a university setting? And what does it mean to have multiple locations or sites, in different cities, regions and cultures of the world? How does all this enhance the learning experience and the pursuit of new knowledge? And how can higher education institutions navigate the minefields of legal and regulatory requirements, governmental support, taxation advantages and other hurdles as they grapple with the challenges of globalizing?

We will begin by looking at some of the factors that motivate their need to become increasingly global in a flattened world.

TRENDS AND DRIVERS OF GLOBALIZATION

Unprecedented Levels of Networking & Interconnection

The internet, together with the information and communication technologies, the global materials delivery infrastructure and the worldwide supply chains have brought us into contact with our colleagues and partners at the far reaches of the planet with merely the click of a mouse or the dialing of a phone. Individuals, companies, industries and ecosystems all move "stuff" about the planet, with little or no concern for its ultimate destination, or even where it might be located at the present moment.

It could be argued that universities were the forerunners to globalization. They began the whole process of building interconnections and linkages by using their abilities to attract students from far and wide, with their exchange programmes, their sabbaticals and their gatherings (conferences, symposia, etc.) to support the free exchange of knowledge and ideas. One could argue that the whole networking and interconnection movement began with the actions of universities throughout our global society.

It could also be argued that universities are communities, based on an open attractor model. They are communities, yes, but of what? Are they communities of individuals? Or of departments? Of faculties? Of schools? Or of colleges? At what level do the elements of a university federate into an overall cohesive whole? For decades, companies have been asking similar questions to these about their own sub-structures, as they attempt to locate branch offices and satellite operations in other regions apart from the parent location. Yet the old notions of branch offices and satellite locations are far removed from the present-day models that underlie a global company. What are the equivalent structures for the modern university enterprise, for higher education delivery, and for the interconnected network of global community elements? And how will the present-day knowledge delivery systems become disintermediated and reformed as the universities explore, adapt and discover the models that work for them in the globalized flat world?

The one thing that we know for sure is that just because universities were the forerunners and early beachheads to linking with others in remote regions and countries of the world does not necessarily guarantee them any leverage or special position with respect to conquering the challenges in present-day global operational models and knowledge delivery systems.

Global Talent and the Flow of Ideas

Universities have traditionally been founded on the premise of knowledge creation and a continuous flow of new ideas. They have long been in competition for the "best and brightest minds" (both students and faculty members) to attract to their institutions, to further its outputs, amplify its impact and to enhance its reputation.

In a flattened world, the access to new minds, new people, new ways of thinking, new ideas, new modes and models of operation, new philosophies, new orientations and new knowledge grows significantly. One could easily argue that not to take advantage of the radically enlarged supply of talent and ideas would be to put one's institution at a disadvantage. For that reason alone, access to the wider supply chain of knowledge, ideas and people would be a compelling argument to adapt one's university into a more global enterprise.

Globally Nuanced Offerings

On the other side of the supply chain are the outputs. What are the outputs of a university (thoughts, ideas, students, knowledge), and how are they perceived and received in other regions and countries, apart from the home soil?

Companies have long ago realized that the products and services they design and deliver in one region of the world don't exactly work well and aren't necessarily well received in other areas. To provide compelling value globally, they must increasingly nuance and tailor their offerings at least regionally, perhaps even locally.

One of the outputs of the university is new knowledge. Yet, is new knowledge creation truly universal? Or is it situational and cultural? What are the trends in this area, and what does our experience reveal to us? We would argue that specialization and nuance are the elements that make knowledge and the application of knowledge both academically interesting and impactful to society. Without nuanced outputs and regional application of its work, the higher education institution runs the risk of being recognized for valuable contributions in its locale of origin only.

The Disintermediation of Innovation

Innovation can be described as the process whereby new ideas are converted into tangible value and benefit to society. Traditionally, this has been accomplished through a complex interplay of processes — research, development, commercialization and delivery of products and services into both new and existing markets of those who would enjoy the benefit of the work. This complex interplay has been achieved through a combination of investments in infrastructure, and through government, university, and industry actions and initiatives to enable new value nets to be formed.

Today, the word innovation is on the lips of most every thought leader, seminal thinker, government official, industry leader and academic visionary in the quest to find and apply new knowledge to the situations and opportunities at hand. Yet how we innovate today is quite different from 5-10 years ago. The flattened world has simultaneously brought us access to orders of magnitude, more ideas, knowledge, talents and people, as well as to many more both undeveloped and existing markets and opportunities than can possibly be imagined.

As a result, the form and structure of our one-dimensional value chains are being totally transformed into multi-dimensional value nets. The old vertically-integrated value chains were optimized to have a few inputs (materials, technologies, components) and a single set of outputs (identified markets and targeted customers). These one-dimensional value chains were typically embodied within a single company, and the intermediate, middle nodes in the chain were opaque and hidden from view. They served only to fulfil their roles in a single, one-dimensional value chain, optimized for the contribution that a single company could make.

Ideas, R&D,   Products,
Technology   Services

The new open, multi-dimensional value nets (multi-dimensional networks of multi-input and multi-output value-creating nodes) are flexible, dynamic, reconfigurable, and robust — they adjust and adapt as technologies and materials (inputs) come and go, and as markets and customers (output destinations) shift expectations around what is desirable and wanted. Intermediate nodes no longer create value for a single value chain only, and are sub-optimized within the organization they serve. In the value net model, they have the potential to become independent agents who draw their inputs from multiple cross-industry, even cross-regional, value nets, and contribute their unique outputs to multiple other value-nets across the globe.

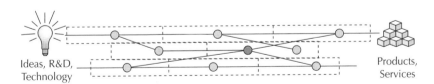

Ideas, R&D,   Products,
Technology   Services

Thus, the old value chain has effectively become disintermediated, reformed and re-linked, and has become one level deep in both directions. Consider the example of the IBM personal computer, created and developed inside the walls of a single, vertically-integrated company (IBM of the 1970s, for example.) Graphics chips designers (intermediate value-creation nodes) inside the company would design and develop graphics chips only for this particular product line. The skill development, the R&D investment, the production costs, etc. for graphics chip design would be limited to that which could be apportioned out from the sales of this particular product line, and its success in the marketplace.

In today's value net model, there are whole companies built around the creation of graphics chips. NVIDIA, ATI and numerous others create graphics chips for many PCs — IBM, DELL, HP, as well as games consoles by SONY, MICROSOFT, NINTENDO, etc. The graphics chip companies build competencies, conduct research, advance their field and move it ahead, reduce costs, and compete with each other to achieve success and excellence. And the market has rewarded their efforts with increased opportunities to employ the results of their work (inexpensive, highly sophisticated graphics processors) in many more places than were originally thought.

The pattern repeats, recursively. Even graphics chips companies (of late) have been disintermediating and restructuring — outsourcing and partnering with research houses in algorithms research, collaborating with CPU makers on pipeline design, and extending their reach into other nodes of the network where they can source inputs and market their outputs.

This disintermediation and restructuring even applies to a "company of 1" (the limit case). With today's infrastructure, a single individual can do complex research and aggregation of knowledge and ideas, without ever leaving their house. Similarly, the potential customers or consumers of what that individual might want to create are one click in the other direction. Consider eBay and the markets and opportunities it has created for literally millions of people.

As a result, we would argue that the very form and structure of innovation are totally changing, and the contributions that individuals and companies can make are accelerating with breakneck pace. The processes of innovation are rapidly unforming and reforming into a network of relationships and interconnections that were previously impossible to envision.

During the past decade, industry has been working in the restructuring of their processes and work flows, making them more suited to a globalized world, while universities are only at the beginning of their comparable journey. Academics should now look deeply and insightfully at their knowledge creation and delivery processes, as well as their value delivery networks. What does it mean for an individual researcher to access the world's knowledge base and to build interesting relationships with others of similar interest? What impact does globalization have on the "input-side" of the equation? And how does a research contribution or knowledge element get used, to provide impact and benefit to others? How is that range extended in a global, flattened world? Looking at both of these areas would provide some useful leverage points in re-architecting the global knowledge enterprise of the future.

The Open Model

With a robust infrastructure, and together with the advances of the past decade, it's now possible for new knowledge to be created at every single node in a value network, intermediate or otherwise. Previously in the older, more closed and proprietary value chains, new knowledge and new value were more likely to be created only at the ends of the net — at the research and development end (more closely tied to discovery and basic science), and at the application end (more close to what customers are experiencing and how the contribution will be actually used).

With today's value nets becoming effectively a collection of value chains one level deep, innovation can now radically increase at each and every node in the network. The pervasive creation of new information and new knowledge leads to a shift in perception as to what constitutes value. When knowledge and information were limited, the value was more apt to lie in its availability, driven by scarcity. Once knowledge and information become abundant and pervasively available, the value lies elsewhere. It shifts to become more rooted in how knowledge and information can be connected, aggregated and combined with other knowledge and information. As a result, interfaces (the language that knowledge is expressed in) and connection standards (the cultural expectations and values surrounding its use) now play a much more important role to enable this next level of value migration.

One could argue that value will move from the aggregated and linked knowledge/information, to its first derivative — how quickly can one evolve and adapt the knowledge connections and make it situationally applicable and useful for some purpose. As a simple example, consider how quickly the trillions of web pages that exist in cyberspace are relinked, reformed and repurposed every minute, as people evolve their thoughts and their creations in real time. The value of a single web page is not as dependent on what's in it, but as to what it links with, and how it enables one to navigate the global thought space of the web. Rather than hold one's own few paragraphs of precious thoughts and insights private, it's more valuable to put them out there, and enable others to build on them, link them, utilize them, tailor them, nuance them, abstract them and develop them into building blocks upon which others can also build.

MODELS OF PARTNERSHIP

As we travel around the world, we see a variety of models for partnership among governments, universities and industry in their national innovation ecosystems. At this time, it's unclear which of these will be more successful than others. However, it is clear that the participants in these partnerships are committed to learning and adapting their models over time to make them be successful.

2-Pole Partnerships

2-pole partnerships are the classic models of interaction between two of the three stakeholders — universities, industry and government. Yet even the classic form of collaboration between a university researcher and their industry counterpart is changing. New structures are emerging and old boundaries are being broken down, as research work begins to become disintermediated in the global ecosystem.

3-Pole Partnerships

In the 1940s, an Argentinean physicist named Jorge Sabato invented a theory describing the necessary relationships between academia, industry and government, along with feedback loops for constant improvement as prerequisite to an optimal system of innovation. He correctly said that if any of these paths in "Sabato's triangle" were weak, the national system of innovation would function poorly.

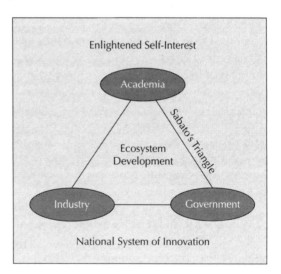

This arrangement of relationships works best against the backdrop of "enlightened self-interest" — a motivation where relationships are built on shared interests and mutual objectives, and where investments align to produce multiple, significant outcomes. This idea of "enlightened self-interest", not just self-interest, creates the foundation for partnerships that last, and have resilience and durability.

Megacommunities

A new type of structure for addressing complex situations is the megacommunity — a large, ongoing joint initiative among organizations that share a complex problem, the resolution of which defies unilateral solutions and depends instead on collaboration among multiple organizations to achieve a mutual goal. The megacommunity grows through informal networks of people with commitments that they act on together to make a difference. Organizational charters, structures and hierarchies matter much less than people's individual commitments. These communities of shared intent grow out of personal relationships and informal networks and enable the pursuit of comprehensive, multiyear, sustainable work.

The megacommunity approach has several notable qualities. "First, it takes advantage of self-interest. It doesn't require leaders of organizations to give up their drives for personal wealth, power, status, or recognition. Nor does it require organizations to forfeit their own objectives. Individuals and organizations come to megacommunities when they recognize that the problems facing them are more complex than they can solve alone."

Second, a megacommunity enables stakeholders to take on larger social goals. At one meeting, a senior finance manager of one corporation said: "War is now obsolete. War in any country harms our company because we do business in every country."

Third, a megacommunity helps a region deal effectively with the goals of global competitiveness and the need for local quality of life and equity. As the megacommunity work raises awareness among the leaders of a region's organizations, they become better equipped to pursue these objectives.

EXPERIENCES IN GLOBAL PARTNERING

2-Pole Partnership Example

For those of us who grew up in the '60s and '70s, the idea of thinking globally and acting locally became engrained and second nature. Today, things have turned around and, in light of globalization, we really must think locally but act against the global landscape. Clearly over the past five years, the emergence of China and India alone has changed economic expectations, opportunities and success criteria. Beyond that are the activities going on in Singapore, Taiwan, Korea, Ireland and a number of other countries. Clearly the balance of power is changing and it seems to be in direct relation with technical human resources and national systems of innovation that work.

One model that China is using involves universities like Peking University partnering with various companies. In this example, the university takes the role of R&D while the companies perform marketing, sales and manufacturing. Professors can hold executive positions in the companies, and students move easily between the campus and the company offices. This provides real-world experience to both graduate and undergraduate students.

Interestingly, although this close symbiotic relationship between the university and company is supported and encouraged in China, it is looked at with discomfort and even alarm in the US and Europe. The R&D involvement of the university with the company is looked at as violating the objective, arm's-length relationship that typically exists between US universities and companies. Also, the role of professors in the company's management is viewed as a potential conflict of interest, where this occurs.

Because of these concerns, partnering between US and European entities and their Chinese counterparts can present some interesting challenges: If you partner with a Chinese university, would you have an inadvertent interaction with a company that is your competitor in global markets because of the R&D being done at the university?

What is not in contention is the clear benefit to students who are able to do real-world applied work. Because some companies choose to locate their R&D function in universities, students can now perform their internships within the university environment, as opposed to having to do an internship in a company.

Another example of a 2-pole partnership is Tsinghua University and its relationship to the Tsinghua Holdings Company. The university owns this holdings company, which has capital of RMB 2 billion yuan (approximately US$260 million). Tsinghua Holdings provides a platform for science and technology development, research commercialization, startup incubation, and international cooperation. Tsinghua Holdings has invested in 80+ portfolio companies in areas including IT, energy and environment, and life sciences. This represents another relationship model which has been successful (during the period from 1991 to 2001, the total revenue of Tsinghua companies increased 100× to $1.2 billion). Several global companies are present at Tsinghua's Science Park. This type of relationship is not common in some countries, yet global participants need to be able to work with all of these kinds of relationship models.

3-Pole Partnership Examples

In Taiwan, the Hsinchu Science Park was founded in 1980 and is administered by the National Science Council. Its purpose is to attract investment in high technology industries and to stimulate local high-tech companies, focusing on employment and wealth creation.

Illustrating Sabato's Triangle, there are multiple companies, universities and government agencies engaged in supporting HSIP. Significant government investment includes Executive Yuan Development Fund of $8 billion, Chiao Tung Bank of $12 billion and government investment of $520 million in land and infrastructure. There are aggressive corporate, shareholder and individual tax incentive programmes. There is a broad collaboration of academics, including partnership with Chiao Tung University, Tsinghua University and the Industrial Technology Research Institute.

Over 20 years, HSIP has grown from 17 companies to 312 companies. Nearly 90,000 people are employed in science and engineering based businesses in HSIP. HSIP is growth-oriented, and continues to attract private investment.

Another example of a 3-pole partnership is Singapore, where government, industry and universities have all aligned their efforts to create partnerships in science and engineering. Long-term thinking and top-down design have been the hallmark of Singapore's efforts to create an economy and infrastructure to foster government-university-industry collaborations.

In 2000, Singapore started an ambitious drive to become the Asian hub for biomedical research. This effort has received significant government funding, including US$2.7 billion in research funding by the Agency for Science, Technology and Research (A*STAR). Also, the Biopolis complex, a $190 million project, has been started.

Singapore has designed incentives into its structure that promote collaborative activities, and has worked hard to design out the kind of in-your-face competition that is characteristic of US and Europe, as well as to mitigate the forces and factors that foster corruption.

Singapore is one of the most technology-intensive nations in the world. Singapore Science Park is a government-sponsored initiative designed to provide a focal point for high-quality infrastructure for R&D. This has become a significant location for state-of-the-art research and development, and has driven significant economic growth, creating about 300 technology companies between 1982 and 2000.

Yet another variant of a 3-pole partnership is exhibited by TR Labs, a non-profit organization in Canada involving a consortia of companies and relationships with five universities in Edmonton, Calgary, Saskatoon, Winnipeg and Regina. TR Labs receives financial support both from the Canadian government and member companies. TR Labs embraces an open innovation model for itself and its member companies, bringing together both internal and external sources of technologies. One unique aspect of this organization is that it also acts as an integrator of these technologies, as opposed to a point-source distribution channel which is commonly found in these types of structures. TR Labs endeavours to provide value to its government, university and industry partners in support of their various missions, such as economic development desired by government, and relevant experiences for students and faculty.

Megacommunities Example

In 1998, a group of colleagues from Raytheon, ISTEC, NSF, the University of Puerto Rico Mayaguez and PUC Rio met at the ICEE Conference in Brazil and began developing a vision for better preparing engineers to address the economic development needs of Latin America. In 2001, this same group visited Hsinchu Science Park in Taiwan to gain a better understanding of the global technical competitive landscape and envisioned how the lessons learned from Taiwan could be transferred. In 2003, the group held a workshop of like-minded thought leaders in Brazil where the idea of "Engineering for the Americas" (EftA) was endorsed. This expanding core group, now including HP, then established a partnership with the World Federation of Engineering Organizations (WFEO) and the Organization of American States to focus on quality assurance for engineering education. World-class engineering education, developed with industry partnership, attracts investment that helps a region or country retain its graduates, rather than lose them to emigration.

In nine years, projects led by Lueny Morell, HP's University Relations director for Latin America, Luis Scarvada from PUC Rio, the accreditation bodies from Canada, Mexico and the US, and by Russ Jones, chair of the Capacity Building Committee of WFEO, grew to involve multiple stakeholders from industry, universities and both governmental and nongovernmental agencies, including engineering education and accreditation agencies. This EftA megacommunity now includes the Organization of American States Ministers of Science and Technology, funding bodies such as the Inter-American Development Bank and the World Bank, and various organizations that support programmes for the innovation of engineering education and the establishment of quality assurance mechanisms in the region.

NEW MODELS OF INNOVATION

It's clear that everyone continues to struggle with and adapt to the forces of globalization, and to find their particular "place in the sun" in this ever-changing landscape. While universities have provided some of the initial connections and beachheads in building relationships with those in other locations on the planet, during the past decade companies have focused intensely on disintermediating and reforming their structures to allow them to take advantage of the benefits of a flattened world, while simultaneously being able to mitigate the disadvantages in order to stay competitive.

It's also clear that emerging and developing nations are working hard to lay the foundation for increased prosperity for their citizens, and increased participation in the global landscape with their own forms of government-industry-university partnerships, and the infrastructure and societal investments they are making.

Of late, it has become more and more apparent that the models of innovation are disintermediating. They are changing shape and scope, crossing boundaries and contexts, and are unforming and reforming into new structures. And these new innovation paradigms and processes are crossing over the boundaries that have traditionally provided government, university and industry separation.

Innovation Becomes Pervasive

In the industry space, it used to be that in order to deliver a significant product or service, one had to perform work inside a large or at least mid-sized company, in order to have access to the resources, support and infrastructure needed. As was argued earlier, today literally anyone can become a product designer, a service provider, a systems integrator, a solution provider, a marketer, or even an e-commerce channel, and literally create the enterprise of their dreams, large or small.

Yet what are the equivalent roles in the university space that have traditionally provided value inside large and mid-sized institutions? In a globalized, flattened world, and with a pervasive infrastructure, is it possible for literally anyone today to become a researcher, an instructor, a teaching assistant, a professor, a dean or an administrator? Setting aside for a moment some of the immediate issues at a model level — what is the value proposition and advantage that a large or mid-sized institution provides to those individuals performing those roles? And how has it changed, and how will it change as universities struggle to adapt to the forces of globalization?

Recently it has come to light that many companies are now out-sourcing even their executive talent — it's possible to "rent a CEO or a CFO" for 3-6-12 months, if one needs a particular skillset or uniquely experienced leader to navigate a company through a near-term transition. Will we see part-time multi-institution professors, or part-time deans who have allegiance to more than one institution, and who can make their unique contributions in multiple value nets simultaneously? And how will they be recognized, rewarded and compensated?

The New Cohesion

Universities have traditionally been communities of individuals who come together around the joy of new knowledge discovery and the satisfaction of passing along the skills of learning to the next generation. Intrinsic rewards have included the freedom to pursue areas of interest and to be associated with the prestige and reputation that goes along with a particular institution, their faculty and staff, and their place in the community. Also, faculty and researchers have typically foregone the more near-term, monetary rewards normally associated with for-profit companies.

Yet this is changing dramatically in recent times. Witness the entrepreneurial spirit that is now growing within universities, and the desire of professors and faculty to be entrepreneurial and to become founders of companies apart from their university duties. Witness also the battles over research sponsorship, intellectual property ownership, licensing and commercialization, and who should receive the monetary benefit from ideas that spawn some interesting marketplace contribution in later years. As the roles, positions and structures in university systems and higher education disintermediate and disaggregate, and as individuals become more flexible, accomplished, and migrate between institutions, what will be the values that create cohesion in the new order, and how will power shift from the brand-reputation of institutions to the brand-reputation of a single individual? Questions such as these will undoubtedly be answered in practical experience terms, as universities struggle with issues similar to what industry has experienced over the past decade.

Models of Globility

It has been said that: "In order to be a truly global company, we must look more like the world in which we operate." This statement evidences a radically different kind of deep understanding than was at the root of the branch offices and satellite locations that companies typically operated in the 1970s. Much of the previous motivation was based around "selling our products and services to a much larger audience". Unstated assumptions centred around "ours is the right way" and "exporting our models to other regions of the world" motivated behaviours which failed to respect the cultures and values of the other regions, as well as to ignore the nuances that would be required in order to successfully serve customers in distant markets.

Today, it's commonplace for executives and boards to be aware of and concerned about the social good in all the regions in which they operate. There's recognition of the unique facets and aspects of every region, as well as a commitment to satisfying latent customer needs and situational factors in those locales. To succeed at being global, one has to succeed at being local many times over, developing differentiated value, cultivating customer loyalty, bringing products and services which make a contribution, and being responsible corporate citizens and stewards of both the physical resources and human capital that are available. Every company must literally become a local integrator with global knowledge perspective.

The model of creating multiple "mini me's" simply no longer works. This was aptly described in a recent IBM article "Hungry Tiger, Dancing Elephant" that appeared in the *Economist*. In this article the global model that IBM is pursuing was outlined — one of instantiating multiple IBMs in every location on the planet, while federating those regional entities into a global network of a single company that is built upon the success of regional accomplishments.

Along with the IBM model, there are undoubtedly many other models that will struggle to find success in a globalized world. So what would a global university structure look like? Will universities have to go through the "branch office" and "satellite operations" structures, or will they be able to leap ahead, benefiting from the 10+ years of struggle and learning that corporations have accumulated, as they have dealt with similar issues in their own arena?

SUMMARY

At one level — the structures and locations level — we know that everything must and will change. The elements of our institutions and our companies will disaggregate and disintermediate — they will change form and new structures will emerge. These will, in turn, go away and give rise to yet newer structures as we attempt to adapt to and thrive with the forces of globalization.

Yet, at another level, there is much stability. Here we find agreement in what we know philosophically, and uncover commonality in our discoveries from experience. We know that there will simply not be one model of innovation. There will be multiple, and they will grow, develop, and adapt over time. We must not only allow for and design for multiple models of innovation. We must anticipate them.

We know that in order to be a truly global entity, that entity must more closely match the world in which it exists. It must have multi-disciplinary, multi-cultural, multi-dimensional aspects, and be diverse, networked and connected, locally optimized, flexible and situationally adaptive, yet able to draw from the knowledge and resources available throughout the world.

There is also an irreversible trend towards openness. Contributions, achievements, and processes that are rooted in closed or proprietary architectures ("control points") will ultimately give rise to more general, flexible structures. Value will migrate more along the lines of human learning, discovery and evolution, and static, proprietary approaches will become obsolete and no longer offer the compelling value they once had.

A surprising discovery with our ever-shrinking world is that one no longer has to be big in order to be global (either companies or universities). In past, being global was once thought to be the privilege of large, profitable, well-established companies. With the pervasive infrastructure, and with the newly flattened world, it's now possible for start-up companies of only a few people to be global, to have people, markets, supply chains, etc. in multiple countries, even in their fledgling state.

Finally, advances in infrastructure require all three elements of Sabato's triangle. The achievement of a flattened world and pervasive infrastructure today is the result of investments and partnerships between government, universities and industries in our past. We truly do stand on the shoulders of giants. Many nations and countries are recognizing this, and are working hard to instantiate their own particular versions of the 3-pole partnerships to make their future success happen.

Globalization is here to stay. But no matter how we globalize, we get to choose how we go about it. Our philosophical orientation can be one of self-optimizing, self-maximizing, and self-interest promotion, usually rooted in scarcity. Or it can be one of openness, collaboration, and partnering, rooted in a win-win-win-win-win philosophy, and drawing from unlimited abundance, creating the future that all can share. The choice is ours.

REFERENCES

Friedman, Thomas L. (2005). *The World is Flat, A Brief History of the Twenty-First Century*, Farrar, Straus, and Giroux, New York.

Gerencser, Mark. Napolitano, Fernando & Van Lee, Reginald. (2006). "The Megacommunity Manifesto", strategy+business, Booz Allen Hamilton, McLean, VA.

Johnson, Wayne C. (2007). "Innovation 3.0: Creating the Next Level Twenty-First Century Innovation Ecosystem Platform", *Kauffman Thoughtbook 2007*, Ewing Marion Kauffman Foundation, Kansas City, MO.

Johnson, Wayne C. (2006). "The Collaboration Imperative", in Weber, L.E. & Duderstadt, J.J. (Eds), *Universities and Business: Partnering for the Knowledge Society*, Economica, London.

Johnson, Wayne C. (2006). "Challenges in University-Industry Collaborations", Weber, L.E. & Duderstadt, J. J. (Eds), *Universities and Business: Partnering for the Knowledge Society*, Economica, London.

Special Report. (2007). "Hungry Tiger, Dancing Elephant: How India is Changing IBM's World", *The Economist* (Print Edition).

Thursby, Jerry Thursby, Marie, (2006). *Here or There*, The National Academies Press, Washington, D.C.

Waugh, Barbara. (2007). "HP Engineers a Megacommunity", Art Kleiner & Michael Delurey (eds), *The Megacommunity Way: Mastering Dynamic Challenges with Cross-Boundary Leadership*, strategy+business Books.

Yarris, Lynn. (2007). "Bay Area Innovation Network Roundtable: Identifying Emerging Patterns of the Next Wave of Innovation", to be published, Menlo Park, California.

PART II

•••••••••••••

Global Strategies for Established Universities

CHAPTER 4

Developed Universities and the Developing World: Opportunities and Obligations

Robert M. Berdahl

INTRODUCTION

A mong the scores of books written during the past decade about globalization — so many, in fact, that some by different authors bear the same title [1] — none has captured as many readers as Thomas L. Friedman's *The World Is Flat: A Brief History of the Twenty-First Century* (2005). It has sold several million copies and been on the *New York Times* bestseller list for well over 100 consecutive weeks. Friedman's discovery that the world has flattened, which he compares to Columbus' voyage to the new world, came to him as he visited the campus of Infosys Technologies in Bangalore. Globalization, Friedman believes, has come about as a result of the convergence of a number of political and economic phenomena, but the underlying cause is technological change. He is, he admits, a technological determinist. He is also a cheerleader for the process of globalization, with an optimistic, neo-liberal confidence that free markets are the basis of human freedom and that global free trade, with its global supply chain of production, produces collaborative and thereby amicable relationships.

In this flat world, relatively devoid of boundaries, driven by knowledge and technology, victory lies with the swiftest and the smartest. Friedman writes: "If you are a knowledge worker making and selling some kind of idea-based

---

1 See, for example, Joseph E. Stigliztz, *Globalization and Its Discontents* (New York, 2002), and Saskia Sassen, *Globalization and Its Discontents* (New York, 1998).

product —consulting or financial services or music or software or marketing or design or new drugs — the bigger the market is, the more people there are out there to whom you can sell your product. And the bigger the market, the more new specialties and niches it will create. If you come up with the next Windows or Viagra, you can potentially sell one to everyone in the world. So idea-based workers do well in globalization, and fortunately America as a whole has more idea-driven workers than any country in the world... That is why America, as a whole, will do fine in a flat world with free trade — provided it continues to churn out knowledge workers who are able to produce idea-based goods that can be sold globally..." (Friedman, 2005, p. 230).

The reason that Friedman's book has attracted so much attention in the United States is the nagging concern that we are in fact *not* continuing "to churn out knowledge workers". The deep concern is that our schools are not preparing students adequately, and that our colleges and universities are not producing enough scientists and engineers for the country to remain competitive in the global economy (NAS, 2007). Americans thus have read Friedman's book with some alarm, aware that a globalized economy means more competition and more outsourcing. Not everyone is so sanguine about the positive effects of this new reality. Harvard's Michael Sandel calls the Friedman's flat world, "just a nice name for the ability to hire cheap labour in India" (Friedman, 2005, p. 205).

Whether or not one agrees with Friedman's optimism about the positive and peaceful consequences of globalization, it is difficult to dismiss his assessment of its inevitability as it pertains to higher education or any other aspect of the knowledge-based global economy. Nothing provides clearer evidence of global competition in igher education than the fact that we now have, for the first time, a worldwide ranking of universities. [2]

GLOBALIZATION VALUES

In the discussion of globalization, I believe several things need to be noted. First, globalization is not a value-free concept. Although it is viewed by many, like Friedman, with optimism and a strong sense of inevitability — Globalization 3.0, as he refers to it — globalization is laden with ideology. The technological revolution in communications, the internet and large-scale computerized information systems make it possible to conduct business on a planetary scale in real time. This is the essence of a global economy. This technological transformation happened at the same moment as socialism collapsed in Eastern Europe and the Soviet Union, and free market capitalism, increasingly

---

2 See the ranking of universities compiled by Jiao Tong University in Shanghai.

deregulated in Western Europe and the United States, emerged triumphant. Globalization thus has taken place in the framework of neo-liberal economic theory, with its confidence in the efficacy of the market, and its call for the privatization of public goods. The logic and ideology of globalization are an unfettered world market for labour, finance and goods.

Second, globalization is thus a new phenomenon, different in form from internationalization. Internationalization presumes the agency of the national state, it presumes an international market or a structure of exchange mediated and, in varying degrees, controlled by the national state. Globalization presumes a world market, one which is beyond the reach of the nation state. Global manufacturing, for example, is determined by the location of cheapest labour costs, which nation states are relatively powerless to regulate because regulation would simply result in the manufacturing moving elsewhere. When markets were largely national, the state had the ability to soften their harshest effects; with global markets, the force of the state is much more attenuated. Even immigration policy, presumably within the sphere controlled by the nation state, is increasingly difficult to regulate in the context of a global market for labour.

These same economic and political transformations have shaped higher education. The logic of the free market has profoundly altered the role of higher education virtually everywhere. Whereas for much of the 20th century, higher education was viewed as a public good, worthy of public investment because of the broad benefits it yields for society as a whole and the importance to democratic institutions of a well educated populace, higher education is now viewed primarily as a private good, with those who receive the education the primary beneficiaries. It is the logic of the market of individual competitors that those who gain should also be the ones who pay. In the United States, where educational fees at public universities were historically relatively nominal, state support has declined and fees have increased. Universities have adopted cost-centred budgeting mechanisms that resemble market-driven business systems. At some public universities, those segments which are capable of generating their own revenue, especially business schools and law schools, have been largely or completely privatized. Colleges of engineering, whose graduates are deemed to be in higher demand in the employment market, often charge higher fees than other undergraduate programmes in their universities. In fundamental ways, the social contract that had governed public higher education in the United States has been re-written, making it conform more fully to the logic of the market.

These changes have been accompanied by the effort to provide financial support for those unable to afford the increased costs. But within the framework of high-tuition, high-aid, the primary increase in aid has been in the form of guaranteed loans, so that the cost of education is still borne by those who benefit individually, not by the society at large.

The United States has not been unique in this process. Throughout most of the OECD, this phenomenon has occurred, beginning with Thatcherism in Britain, Reaganism in the United States, and the re-introduction of fees in Australia in 1986 and the legislation of the 1990s that enabled Australian universities to set their own fees and generate their own revenue.

The "privatization" of public universities, especially in the United States, has proceeded in other ways as well. Public universities began to emulate private universities in their pursuit of private gifts and the building of endowments. The passage of the Bayh-Dole Act in 1980 allowed universities to license the patents their researchers developed with federal grant funds, increasing the collaboration of universities with industries dependent on the intellectual property they created. Although industrial support for basic research in universities remains a relatively small percentage of the whole, it is growing. An example is provided by the agreement of British-Petroleum with the University of California, Berkeley, Lawrence Berkeley National Laboratory, and the University of Illinois in Urbana-Champaign. The process of privatization has made universities increasingly entrepreneurial.

The logic of the market has affected universities in another profound way: it has defined the purposes of universities largely in terms of their role in economic development. Knowledge-driven economies require education systems that produce new technologies, but, more importantly, that produce a workforce to serve these technologies. This is not entirely new, of course; nor is it, in and of itself, a bad thing. Universities have long played an important role in the economic development of their societies; the land-grant university, arguably the most significant American contribution to the development of universities, clearly anticipated this role for universities. Clark Kerr defined the mid-20th century research university as a "multiversity", in service to the corporate world. But universities have never been so essential to economic development as they are today. Economic growth has become the primary justification for improved public investment in higher education.

The problem with the overwhelming use of this economic justification for universities is that it ignores or overrides their other fundamental purposes. The role of the university as a centre for free and open debate about the values of society or the nature of social justice is overlooked. The role of the university in preserving and critiquing its national culture or understanding other cultures is treated as secondary importance. Education as the process of self-discovery and preparation for meaningful life is of less importance than education as preparation for economically productive life. Higher education as the foundation for citizenship in a democratic society, expressed in countless engraved walls of public universities across the United States, is seldom mentioned as a fundamental objective. The report of the Commission on the Future of Higher Education, known as the Spellings Commission, the assessment of the current role of higher education in the United States, concentrates almost exclusively on the need to prepare students for a competitive labour market.

OPPORTUNITIES AND OBLIGATIONS

All of these changes form the context for the primary topic of this paper, the opportunities and obligations of universities in the developed world toward their counterparts in the developing world.

The global knowledge-based economy has generated an enormous growing demand for university graduates. The World Bank estimates that the number of students seeking university degrees will grow from about 100 million today to roughly 160 million in 2025; others estimate that the number could reach a quarter of a billion, with most of that enormous growth taking place in the developing world. This growth, which can be of tremendous benefit to countries undergoing development, provides remarkable opportunities for the mature universities in the United States, Europe and Australia. One response of the developed countries is to recruit students from the developing countries, primarily from Asia. American graduate programmes in science and engineering would be severely handicapped were it not for the flow of students from abroad, and American high tech industries increasingly depend on a supply of Indians and Chinese who have received graduate degrees in the United States. The CEO of the second largest bio-technology company in California, with a market cap of $29 billion, recently commented that last year his company had hired only one native-born American Ph.D. last year. [3] Australian universities have turned to international students as a revenue source for sustaining their universities.

A significant number of universities are working to meet this global demand for education by developing constructive programmes in developing countries. Cornell, Carnegie Mellon, Case-Western, SUNY-Buffalo and the University of California at Berkeley and San Diego have entered into a partnership with AMRITA University and other Indian universities. The American universities will encourage members of their engineering faculties to spend a sabbatical term at AMRITA, while AMRITA will extend its e-learning centre, making it possible to transmit educational programming to educational institutions throughout India. While expanding educational opportunities in India, this programme also aims at reversing the decline in the number of Indian students coming to the United States for graduate education. Other major American universities have also developed affiliated programmes in India, virtually all of which have a primary focus on engineering.

---

3 Conversation with the author, April 2007.

Collaborative programmes between US institutions and China have also grown in recent years. Johns Hopkins' Paul H. Nitze School of Advanced International Relations offers two programmes with Nanjing University. Yale has a joint undergraduate programme at Peking University in Beijing and, in what may be one of the most creative collaborations of all, has built a graduate-research Institute of Developmental Biology and Molecular Medicine with Fudan University in Shanghai. A recent proposal by the ministry of education in Pakistan seeks international partners for the building of ten new universities in Pakistan, all of which would be institutes of science and engineering. The list of these joint ventures or proposed joint ventures could go on.

It is difficult to find fault with these ventures. Most are high quality, contribute to the educational resources of the countries in which they are located, and help build the capacity of these developing countries. It is important to note, however, that the primary concentration of virtually all of the programmes is in technical and professional disciplines, especially engineering and business. This is, of course, where the demand is. It is also the case that only the very technical courses or specialized business or professional programmes are capable of producing the level of revenue necessary to maintain the programmes without government subsidies or substantial support from private donors.

Because of the costs involved for traditional universities, the rapidly expanding demand for education worldwide is also being addressed by a large number of for-profit institutions. The for-profit sector represents the fastest growing element in American higher education, with dozens of for-profit educational companies having been launched over the past decade. Seventy for-profit institutions of various kinds are listed on the web, some with a single location, others with multiple locations. The best known of these, of course, is the University of Phoenix, which, in addition to the centres it has established in the United States, is also in Brazil, Chile, China and Mexico. Sylvan Learning Systems, Inc., a Baltimore-based company, has built a network of eight universities with over 100,000 students in nine countries in Latin America. Sylvan Learning Systems now has nearly one-tenth of the college students in Chile enrolled in its campuses. Scores of for-profit educational enterprises have sprung up in recent years, with many now listed on the stock market. Hundreds of thousands of students in 20 countries are enrolled in these kinds of programs.

A safe prediction is that for-profit education will play a significant role in meeting the growing demand in developing countries or in countries in which the higher education system is underdeveloped. Traditional universities are also developing for-profit, web-based subsidiaries; last fall, the University of Illinois announced the creation of an on-line, for-profit, degree programme. Its business model, like that of the other on-line, for-profit ventures, is to employ part-time faculty who will not be eligible for tenure or research support from the University. Even universities in the developing world, strapped for resources, are beginning to explore for-profit programmes; in April of this year, the University of Mumbai announced the unusual step of looking at the possibility of a stock market listing. (*Financial Times*, 2007)

For-profit education is a profitable business, sufficiently profitable, in fact, that groups of American investors have, in at least two recent instances, bought struggling colleges for their "academic assets", which they do not define as the faculty, all of whom were quickly dismissed after the acquisition; "academic assets" refers to the accreditation these colleges had received by the North Central Association of Colleges and Universities, which was initially transferred to the new entities. For-profit education is also powerful, having built a significant lobby working Congress and exercises a powerful influence in the current US Department of Education.

These enterprises do fill an educational void when they provide quality training for skills enabling people in the developing world to improve their opportunities in a global economy. Technical education is essential to development. But we should also be aware of the more adverse consequences of a process that treats education largely as an export commodity, subject primarily to the demands of the marketplace (Altbach, 2006). It underscores the private and utilitarian import of education at the expense of its public and intrinsic value. It does not impart the values that are essential to the development of universities and it is less willing to provide those less marketable elements of education that contribute to aspects of life beyond the workplace. It does not ground education in local culture and habit or build a local self-sustaining capacity, but imposes what some consider a "neo-colonial" system of higher education. [4]

HUMAN CAPITAL

As developmental economist Amartya Sen has stressed in his various works, however, development involves considerably more than economic growth alone. Development, he has stressed, must be concerned with advancing human well-being and human freedom. Although rising income levels are a necessary condition, they are not a sufficient condition for achieving development; a market society does not lead inexorably to expanded human freedom. Sen considers globalization an important potential source of improved living conditions, but the introduction of the market economy alone will not suffice. Development for Sen is a consequence of rising human "capabilities", human

---

4 Comments by Ahmed C Bawa, of the University of KwaZulu-Natal, Durban and Pietermaritzburg, South Africa, at a conference, University of California, Berkeley, March 26-27, 2007.

capacities to exercise a wide range of freedoms. Sen comments specifically on the role of education in achieving human freedom:

If education makes a person more efficient in commodity production, then this is clearly an enhancement of human capital. This can add to the value of production in the economy and also to the income of the person who has been educated. But even with the same level of income, a person may benefit from education — in reading, communicating, arguing, in being able to choose in a more informed way, in being taken more seriously by others and so on. The benefits of education, thus, exceed its role as human capital in commodity production. The broader human-capability perspective would note — and value — these additional roles as well. The two perspectives are, thus, closely related, but distinct (Sen, 1999, pp. 293-94).

While Sen's definition of "capabilities" is relatively flexible and situational, others have defined the capabilities essential to development in more concrete ways. The philosopher Martha Nussbaum defined the "central human capabilities" necessary for development as (1) Life; (2) Bodily health; (3) Bodily integrity; (4) Senses, imagination and thought; (5) Emotions; (6) Practical reason (7) Affiliation; (8) Other species; (9) Play; and (10) Political and material control over one's environment (Nussbaum, 2000, pp. 72-75). What is interesting about this list is the fact that much of it calls for an educational system that goes well beyond the development of skills that can be employed in an advanced, technological labour market. It calls for discernment, reason, the capacity to understand complex issues from different vantage points, the capacity for what Sen as has referred to as "public reasoning". It calls for what has traditionally been known as liberal education.

If the interest, or indeed the obligation, of mature universities in the developed world toward the developing world is to assist in development, as I believe it should be, rather than simply to exploit a market, this perspective on development is important to bear in mind. It can, in fact, define the agenda that mature universities can take for themselves as the process of globalization moves forward. It seems important, therefore, that mature universities work with their counterparts in the developing world based on a set of principles that are aimed at enhancing the scope of human freedom. I would summarize some of these principles in the following manner:

One, universities should stress the fundamental purpose of education is to enlarge human freedom. Education is a "liberating" force in every sense of the word. This will require the development of marketable skills that will improve income and the standard of living, but it should not be exclusively defined in these terms. Education, to enlarge freedom, must also enhance tolerance, citizenship and the capacity for contributing to social discourse.

Two, to enhance human freedom, universities must themselves be free institutions, free from government interference or control, places where the principles of academic freedom are understood and protected. Universities are disruptive institutions, often inspiring criticism of the societies in which they are located. Indeed, most disruptive and revolutionary movements historically have originated in universities. Oppressive regimes may find virtual universities preferable to universities as places where students and faculty gather. They may also wish to censor curricula. But if universities are to play a proper role in any society, they should foster the critical skills that will reject control and oppression.

Three, in mature universities, the faculty have a central role in the governance of the institution, the development of its curriculum, and the selection of other faculty. This feature, too, is missing in virtual, for-profit universities, but it should be an aspect of any process of quality assessment or accreditation for institutions operating in the developing world.

Four, mature universities should have the goal of building the capacity of universities in the developing countries. The asymmetrical relationship between developed universities and developing universities, between North and South, East and West, often results in a brain drain from the developing world. Bilateral partnerships should be of mutual benefit to both parties and have as one goal building an educational and intellectual infrastructure in developing countries.

Five, the quality standards for education transmitted to developing countries should not be inferior to those of developed countries. The principles of self improvement and accreditation should be equivalent. This does not suggest the requirement of uniformity of outcomes, but it does suggest close scrutiny of the equality of education from whatever source it is delivered.

There are undoubtedly other principles that should guide the relationship between developed and developing universities, but these five at least are essential to the development of universities that enhance human capacities and freedom.

REFERENCES

Altbach, Philip G. (2006). *International Higher Education: Reflections on Policy and Practice*. Center for International Higher Education, Lynch School of Education, Boston College Publication, pp. 23-28; 33-42.

Financial Times (2007). *Financial Times: Asia-Pacific, India*. 16 April 2007.

Friedman, T. (2005). *The World Is Flat. A Brief History of the Twenty-First Century*. Farrar, Straus and Giroux Publishers, New York.

NAS. (2007). Report of the National Academies of Science and Engineering, *Rising Above the Gathering Storm*.

Nussbaum, M. (2000). *Women and Human Development: The Capabilities Approach*, Cambridge University Press, Cambridge.

Sen, A. (1999). *Development as Freedom*. Knopf, New York.

CHAPTER

The Challenge to European Universities in the Emerging Global Marketplace

Howard Newby

Although the topic for this paper implies a focus on Europe, the issues I want to address are by no means limited to that continent. Without wishing to minimize the significance of national differences and continental contexts, it is possible to discern a set of generic issues facing higher education systems around the world which bear a distinct similarity.

My justification for this bold statement rests upon the findings now beginning to emerge from a major OECD programme, the OECD Thematic Review of Tertiary Education. (Reports and updates are available from www.oecd.org/edu/tertiary/review). This is a collaborative project to assist countries in the design and implementation of tertiary education policies which contribute to the realization of their social and economic objectives. It is based on an acknowledgement of the fact that the tertiary systems of many OECD countries have experienced rapid growth over the last decade and are experiencing new pressures as the result of a globalizing economy and labour market. As a result, in late 2003 the OECD agreed to establish the review, whose principal objective is to assist countries in the understanding of how the organization, management and delivery of tertiary education can help them achieve their economic and social objectives. The principal focus is on policies and systems, rather than the detailed management and operation of institutions.

The review encompasses the full range of tertiary programmes and institutions as defined by international statistical conventions. The project involves two complementary approaches: an Analytical Review strand; and a Country

Review strand. The Analytical Review strand uses several means — country background reports, literature reviews, data analysis and commissioned papers — to analyse the factors that shape the outcomes in tertiary education systems and possible policy responses. All of the countries involved in the programme are taking part in this strand. In addition countries can choose to participate in a Country Review, which involves external review teams analysing tertiary education policies in those countries. There are 24 countries involved in the programme, of which 13 have opted to undertake a Country Review. Not all OECD member countries are participating (there are currently 28 OECD members, with plans to add to this number); but, contrarily, some non-OECD members have sought to participate (e.g. Chile, China, Croatia).

The programme is expected to run until 2008 and is therefore not yet completed. I have been involved in the programme in a number of ways (including participating in the Country Reviews of Japan and China) as an external expert. It is clear to me already that it is providing a rich source of both statistical and non-statistical information from which certain common themes have begun to emerge. It is a discussion of those themes which form the basis of this paper.

MACRO-SYSTEM CHALLENGES

In some respects the challenges facing higher education [1] policy-makers around the world are remarkably similar and can be stated quite simply:

There is a common move towards expanding the proportion of the population achieving higher education qualifications. This produces a common desire to shift from an "elite" to a "mass" higher education system — known in Europe as "massification". This is occurring because governments all around the world accept that higher education is a major driver of the global knowledge-based economy and that the quality of human resources is, long-term, a major source of global economic competitiveness. Hence there is a desire to raise skills levels, including higher education skills. In many countries there are also strong social pressures to expand the opportunity to participate in higher education.

Governments all around the world not only wish to expand the sector, they also wish to achieve this expansion without any dilution of quality. Indeed, they wish to enhance quality at the same time as engage in expansion.

And finally governments all around the world wish to expand the sector and enhance quality while simultaneously reducing — if not in absolute, then certainly in proportional, terms — the burden of resources this requires from

---

1 For simplicity's sake I focus on the higher education sector in this paper, rather than the tertiary sector as a whole.

public finances. In the face of other public spending priorities — health, welfare, schools, security — higher education must take its place in the queue. So governments all over the world are seeking ways to reduce the burden on the taxpayer when it comes to defining their higher education policy goals.

These three public policy polarities — massification, quality enhancement and reducing the burden on the taxpayer — create a kind of force field which puts higher education systems around the world in a state of some considerable tension. It is apparent that it is difficult, if not impossible, to achieve all three of these macro-policy goals simultaneously and so different countries have sought different solutions, within differing socio-political contexts, in an attempt to reconcile these tensions. In some countries the pace of massification has been held in check — producing an increase in international student mobility. In other countries teaching quality has been allowed to slide, and even more the quality of the student experience has declined. In many countries the attempt is being made to shift the burden of financing from the taxpayer to the student (via tuition fees) and from the public to the private sector (by encouraging the entry of private, including for-profit, providers). All of this adds up to a highly diverse and complex policy mix at the national level. But what is ironic is that most countries see their own policy challenges as unique to themselves, when in fact the dilemmas they face are common to most others.

NATIONAL POLICY CONSIDERATIONS

Of course, at the national level the considerations outlined above express themselves in a variety of different ways. I am certainly not implying a level of homogeneity in higher education policy which can take no account of national, or even regional, factors. In recognizing this, it is also important to stress that different activities in universities have different geographical frames of reference. For example, research — especially basic research — is globally competitive and has been for several decades, especially in science and engineering. Undergraduate learning and teaching are more nationally-oriented (although this is beginning to change, especially in Europe). And knowledge transfer activity tends to be regionally, or even locally, focused. It follows from this that the competitive forces operating on research-led universities are predominantly global; while those operating on predominantly teaching institutions are mainly national.

This degree of complexity and diversity clearly presents a number of challenges in developing a consistent and coherent set of policies across the higher education sector. This is compounded by the multi-functional nature of modern universities. No longer are they limited to just teaching and research as they were just a generation ago. Today's universities are expected to engage in lifelong learning (not just "teaching"), research, knowledge transfer, social inclusion (via widening participation or "access" for non-traditional students), local and regional economic development, citizenship training and much more. No university is resourced sufficiently to perform all these functions simultaneously and in equal measure at ever-increasing levels of quality. Moreover as competitive forces increase, universities must identify their areas of comparative advantage and focus on them. This "massification" has engendered an increasing diversity of institutions, both in terms of their mission and, as a result, their geographical focus.

How are national governments seeking to grapple with this level of diversity and complexity? It is apparent that the pace of higher education policy reform has accelerated in the last decade across the OECD countries, probably propelled by these factors among others. This is particularly the case in Europe, where the Bologna Process has provided the excuse — as opposed to the reason — for reform in several European countries. But the same features are observable outside Europe — in Asia, Australasia and even, in an emerging form, in the United States. Thus, at the national level, the generic issues of massification, quality enhancement and public affordability overlay an almost kaleidoscopic set of geographical, institutional and functional features which make it difficult to discern general trends.

For the OECD studies some common themes do, however, emerge. Three, in particular, stand out.

System-level Planning and Mission Differentiation

Since the 1990s there has been a tendency across most OECD countries to reduce the level of direct management from Ministries of Education or their equivalent. Granting greater "autonomy" to universities (see below) has been viewed as a necessary feature of developing a more flexible, dynamic and entrepreneurial higher education sector. This has been regarded as particularly appropriate for the development of leading research-intensive universities which, it is often observed, need to be imbued with a level of innovation, enterprise and dynamism which requires a level of institutional autonomy which centralized regulation can easily stultify. However, there is a recognition that, in certain other respects, too much de-centralized autonomy may work against the public interest. For example, most countries apply constraints to the variation in teaching quality which is considered acceptable.

For most OECD countries the major dilemma at the system level relates to how far mission differentiation should be encouraged, or even planned. As noted above, mission differentiation is emerging anyway under the impact of the twin trends towards massification and market competition. In the academic community there is general opposition to explicit forms of mission differentiation. Governments, however, are more ambivalent. Given that the primary mission differentiator in most countries relates to research performance, and given the increasing public and private investment required to sustain global competitiveness in leading-edge basic science, then it is perhaps not surprising that many governments are increasingly prepared to countenance a planned, or at least managed, level of mission differentiation based upon the selective allocation of research funds.

In many countries this has engendered a lively debate about how far the sector should be strategically planned to achieve the optimum level of mission differentiation — optimum, that is, from the perspective of multiple policy goals: cost-efficiency, teaching quality, research excellence, business innovation, social inclusion, regional equity, and so on. The debate, however, is not usually as sophisticated as this implies. It tends to revolve around the desire to create and sustain a small number of "world-class" research universities whose relationship to the rest of the sector is, in the absence of any coherent strategic planning, not clearly specified. The advent of global "league tables" based on research excellence has also given these debates the flavour of a kind of higher education Olympic Games. Policy reforms in countries as diverse as China (Project 211), Japan (the university reforms of 2004), Germany (the Federal Finance Ministry's proposals — now abandoned — to designate five "world-class" research universities) and the UK (via the Research Assessment Exercise) have each included this as part of their objectives. And there are many other examples. In the United States it is interesting that an essentially competitive research economy at the federal level can coincide with a highly planned public university system at the state level — the epitome being, of course, California, but in reality virtually all states plan, strategically and operationally, their public university systems in a way which would not look out of place in post-war Europe.

By comparison with the debates around research selectivity, other drivers of mission differentiation are less vigorously debated. Following the Humboldt tradition of universities in Europe and elsewhere, for example, there is hostility to the notion of "teaching-only" universities being bona fide universities at all. Indeed this is the European Universities Association's declared policy stance. Once upon a time universities existed to provide teaching and learning, and research was a residual: now it sometimes seems as if the reverse is the case: students are the unfortunate necessity — a teaching "load" — whose presence detracts from research time. Be that as it may, teaching excellence, no more than other activities in the modern university, does not engender mission differentiation to the extent that research does. There is no widespread adoption of the American model of the "liberal arts" college elsewhere in the world, for example. Nor has knowledge transfer been embraced as a mission focus by any but a small minority of universities. Thus if world-class research is to be concentrated in a small minority of universities, few governments have explicitly set out their vision for the role of the remainder, even though they constitute the numerical majority. To regard them as "merely" teaching-only is surely not good enough. They, too, need to be invested with the same elements of innovation, creativity and enterprise. Given that the status hierarchies of the academic community consistently rank research excellence above teaching excellence, these universities need to be incentivized to excel in their non-research choice of mission focus. In most OECD countries there is insufficient strategic planning capacity to "steer" their higher education systems in response to these issues.

In some respects this is understandable. Teaching provision is principally demand-led and so student choice is the main driver of what is taught and where. It is, of course, not an entirely unrestrained choice, but notions of manpower planning have, in almost all countries, not only been abandoned, but even discredited, certainly at the level of individual degree programmes. But do the choices of millions of students in thousands of universities add up to supplying the needs of the labour market? Politicians, employers, and even some academics worry about this constantly. For example, outside South-east Asia there is a long-term, consistent decline in the demand for degree programmes in mathematic, physics, chemistry and engineering. Conversely there has been a massive growth in business studies, media studies and cultural studies. Whether or not the market will eventually clear in response to supply and demand in the labour market remains hotly debated. In the meantime there is a reluctance to second-guess student choice. My point is not to advocate a return to manpower planning, but rather to indicate that beyond the particular example of mission differentiation via research selectivity, more OECD countries have no strategic planning capacity to steer other essential elements of the sector.

Autonomy vs. Regulation

In the debate on higher education policy, planning and regulation are often conflated. But they are not the same. Arguably in most OECD countries higher education is over-regulated, but under-planned. This is probably the most common tension at the national level. In most countries mission differentiation cries out for a strategic planning framework that will support it and allow it to flourish. Meanwhile in most countries the scale of public investment in a mass higher education system has, under the guise of "accountability", produced greater centralized regulation — audit, evaluation, quality assurance, transparent reporting. Yet, at the same time, there is a recognition, as indicated above, that universities flourish in a state of at least relative autonomy from the overbearing presence of centralized government regulation. In today's fast-changing world, universities, in common with other organizations, need to be agile, flexible and unencumbered by bureaucratic controls.

This presents dilemmas for all governments. Publicly-funded universities must be publicly accountable. As one former English cabinet minister once put it: "Universities can have medieval levels of autonomy if they are prepared to accept medieval levels of funding." So autonomy is not to be equated with laissez-faire. There is a public interest in higher education that needs to be reconciled with the benefits which institutional autonomy can bring. This is most obvious in areas such as guaranteeing academic quality and standards, ensuring the equity of student admission procedures, securing accessibility for students from poor families and/or remote regions, and so on. An appropriate balance therefore needs to be struck between securing the public interest on the one hand and encouraging institutional autonomy on the other. This implies allowing greater autonomy to institutions that have demonstrated their capacity to govern their own affairs effectively — but within a regulatory framework which constrains this autonomy in order to ensure that the public interest is secured.

There are no formulaic solutions to this problem. Different countries have attempted to deploy different mechanisms to reconcile these policy imperatives according to local history and circumstances. For example:

Some countries (e.g. the United States, Japan) have developed what might be termed a "managed market" approach. This admits market forces into higher education, including a substantial private, for-profit sector, but within a public-sector regulatory framework.

Other countries (e.g. UK, Ireland, Hong Kong, New Zealand) have developed so-called "buffer bodies" — non-governmental agencies which mediate the relationship between the government and the higher education sector, implementing regulation and distributing funding in one direction, while offering policy advice and quality control in the other.

Most countries, however, encourage competition between universities, but fall short of creating a genuine market. But in the quest to reduce the burden on public finances there is a greater willingness to contemplate a real, rather than a shadow, market in higher education.

The Role of the Private Sector

In many countries the burden on the public purse of higher education expansion has been mitigated by drawing upon private contributions to the cost, either from the students themselves through tuition fees and/or by encouraging the establishment of private institutions. In this respect the oft-cited example of the United States is unusual among OECD countries. It is comparatively rare for private universities to predominate in the elite segment of the sector. More commonly private universities cater for the excess student demand which cannot be accommodated in the more prestigious public institutions and where governments are unwilling or unable to expand provision at a rate which will satisfy increasing public demand. This phenomenon can be observed over much of Eastern Europe, Asia and Latin America. Globally, higher education is now becoming big business, with several stock market-listed companies involved which are international in their scope. Many, somewhat confusingly, are established and controlled by affiliated public universities, providing a useful income stream (for example, many leading Chinese universities have established their own "minban"). Some are vertically integrated into the schools system (common all over Asia).

In many OECD countries the establishment of private universities is a potentially sensitive, if not contentious, policy issue. However, the private sector is increasingly prepared to respond to the social demand for higher education where the public sector does not have the fiscal capacity to do so. Looking forward this could apply to an increasing proportion of OECD countries. Even where private institutions are absent, more governments have been prepared to contemplate the introduction of tuition fees in order to sustain investment in higher education at a level which will both fund expansion and assure quality. Most economic analysis would support a high-fee, high student support, and therefore "needs blind", system of funding. But those countries which have moved in this direction (England, Australia, Japan — even China) have found it politically impossible to both charge fees at a sufficiently high level to sustain both growth and quality and to support a fees regime which is completely needs blind. Most existing systems are the reverse — fee levels too low to provide the necessary investment and still providing public subsidy to affluent households.

The issue, it seems to me, is less whether the necessary resources are publicly or privately generated than whether these resources can be brigaded in a socially equitable manner to assist in the achievement of public policy goals for higher education. In other words, can private institutions be encouraged to develop via a regulatory framework which complements, rather than conflicts with, state-supported access — especially with respect to quality assurance and widening participation. Unregulated expansion of the private sector (not a serious policy option in any OECD country) will be contrary to the public interest. But so, too, will be a policy which excludes the private sector and thereby restricts both access to higher education and innovation within it.

CONCLUSION

This brief overview of the challenges facing higher education policy is perforce perfunctory and very generalized. Nevertheless, reading many of the OECD Country Reviews, it is striking to see how many of these challenges are regarded as unique by the country under consideration, but also how striking are the commonalities amongst otherwise diverse nations. In terms of the "force field" described in the opening section of this paper, it is clear that different countries' higher education policies come to rest closer to some polarities than others; but common observations suggests that all are grappling with the same sets of issues. Even those countries (e.g. in Scandinavia) with a long and deep tradition of state-provided, free-at-the-point-of-use higher education are questioning the level of public investment required in the face of other claims on public finance, not least because of predictable demographic trends. Adherence to this model represents a gamble on long-term political support if those university systems are to be internationally competitive in the long term.

Higher education is both a public and a private good. There are returns both to society and to the individual. This alone suggests that the way forward will involve a mix of public and private resources if universities are to continue to thrive. However, there needs to be greater clarity of policy in determining what the purposes are of public funding and a focus of resources on these purposes. Having established this, there needs to be less emphasis on detailed regulation and more emphasis on providing a strategic planning framework within which autonomous universities can be incentivized to excel — not just in research, but in all the other functions of the 21st-century university. The public interest rests not on creating a Gosplan for higher education, but in performance managing a sector which collectively achieves the multiple public goals which are expected of it, while allowing each university individually to focus on what it is best at delivering. The individual vested interests of universities will not add up to an overall national interest, but neither can a simplistic national interest be imposed on an increasingly diverse sector in a centralized way.

CHAPTER 6

Comprehensive Universities in Continental Europe: Falling Behind?[1]

Georg Winckler

INTRODUCTION: THE GRAND HISTORY

U niversities in continental Europe have a long tradition of nearly one thousand years, incorporating the idea of the "Greek academia". The foundation of universities spread rapidly throughout medieval Europe, with Bologna (1088) and Paris (1150) as the first, acting as models for the others to come. The university started as a "universitas magistorum et scholarium", a corporation of teachers and students, enjoying legal and financial privileges.

In the early 17th century the European concept of a university reached North America and, thus, began to spread around the globe. Today, the world is witnessing another triumph of the university idea, especially in the developing world. India, for example, aims to increase the number of universities from about 300 in the year 2005 to 1,500 in the year 2015 (*Times Higher Education Supplement*, "Bids invited for mutual gain", 27 April 2007).

However, there were also periods of decline. E.g., during the French Revolution, universities were regarded as outdated and impeding social progress. Universities were replaced with "écoles spéciales" (today France's grandes écoles; see De Talleyrand-Perigord [1791]). Many technical universities throughout continental Europe were founded as an "école polytechnique" in

1 I wish to thank Martin Fieder for helping me with the statistics on university rankings and for valuable suggestions and comments.

the first half of the 19th century. Responding to this radical and utilitarian challenge, and after many universities had been closed (Langewiesche [2005] reports that more than 50% of the universities in continental Europe were closed during the Napoleonic period), Humboldt designed the concept of the "Humboldtian" research university, a comprehensive university ("universitas litterarum") in quest of scientific truth and, idealistically, not geared to societal demands. The idea of freedom of research and teaching was stressed by Schleiermacher. This philosophically legitimized rejuvenation of the idea of a university originated in continental Europe, in Prussia, around 1800. As a consequence, universities abandoned bachelor and master programmes and started to concentrate on doctoral studies only. The success of the Humboldtian research universities reshaped Ph.D. education all over the world.

When Johns Hopkins University initiated Ph.D. programmes in the late 19th century, the US system of colleges and universities converted to a hybrid one: On top of the medieval, still British college education, Humboldtian Ph.D. programmes were laid. This hybrid system facilitated the "massification" of the higher education sector in the late 20th century. It comprised a three-tier system allowing universities to adopt a diversity of missions and profiles and, thus, to cater effectively to the various educational demands of society.

The three-tier system is now being taken over in continental Europe through the Bologna Process, but, of course, continental Europe can claim to be the originator of this study architecture.

Continental European universities have been falling behind since the 1930s. Concerning research and teaching performance, the Anglo-American university system seems to dominate worldwide, particularly if peak performance is considered. This domination is most easily visible in international rankings and league tables. Although the relevance of league tables and international rankings is disputed (Bowden, 2000), they seem to be highly relevant, especially when providing a broad overview for primary customers — students, their parents (Dill & Soo, 2005) and the public.

In the following section, I describe three international rankings in more detail: i) the *Times Higher Education* Ranking 2006; ii) the Shanghai World University Ranking 2006; and iii) the *Newsweek* 2006 University Ranking (a methodological mix of *Times Higher Education* Ranking and the Shanghai Ranking). This description will be supplemented by an analysis of the most "Highly Cited Researchers (ISI)" in the fields of mathematics, physics and molecular biology in respect to the geographical region of their workplace (i.e. continental Europe, UK and US). In sections 3 and 4, I will discuss various reasons why continental Europe is apparently falling behind. Reform issues of continental European universities are presented in Section 5.

INTERNATIONAL RANKINGS

Methodologically, the *Times Higher Education* Ranking and the Shanghai Ranking differ considerably. The former uses six indicators contributing with different weights to the overall score: Peer Review Score (40%); Recruiter Review (10%); International Faculty Score (5%); International Students Score (5%); Ratio Faculty/Students Score (20%) and Citations/Faculty Score (20%). The Shanghai Ranking also uses six, but different indicators: Number of alumni winning Nobel Prizes and Fields Medals (10%); number of staff winning Nobel Prizes and Fields Medals (20%); highly cited researchers (20%); articles indexed in SCI and SSCI (20%); articles published in *Science* and *Nature* (20%); performance in respect to size of institution (10%). In applying these indicators, the Shanghai Ranking is clearly biased towards the sciences. In addition, the use of Nobel Prize winners can be contested, although it represents an unequivocal indicator (Braun *et al.*, 2003).

Without discussing these issues further, the following results appear when comparing continental Europe, the UK and the US using the rankings mentioned above:

University Rankings

Times Higher Education Ranking (THES) 2006

- Among the **top 20** universities in the world, there is only one university from continental Europe (Ecole Normale Supérieure, Paris). Yet four universities are located in the UK (Cambridge, Oxford, Imperial College, LSE) and 11 universities in the US.
- Among the **top 100** universities in the world, there are 27 continental European universities, 16 universities from the UK and 35 universities from the US.
- Among the **top 200** universities in the world, there are 55 continental European universities, 28 come from the UK and 55 universities from the US.

Shanghai World University Ranking 2006

- Among the **top 20**, there are no continental European universities, yet two from the UK (Cambridge, Oxford) and 17 from the US.
- Among the **top 100**, there are 22 continental European universities, 11 from the UK and 53 from the US.
- Among the **top 200**, there are 49 continental European universities, 22 from the UK and 87 from the US.

Newsweek 2006 University Ranking
(methodological mix of THES and Shanghai)

- Among the **top 20**, there is no continental European university, but three universities come from the UK (Cambridge, Oxford, Imperial College) and 15 from the US.
- Among the **top 100**, there are 16 continental European universities, 17 universities from the UK and 42 from the US. (There is only a list of 100 universities).

The outcomes in the three rankings are not identical, but similar. There is an extremely high concentration of the very best in the US. Only UK universities are able to compete globally. Yet among the top 200, just counting entries in the ranking tables, continental Europe is nearly on par with the US (on par according to THES, less so according to Shanghai).

Ranking of individual researchers ISI —
Highly Cited Researchers (as of 10 May 2007)

Mathematics

- Among the top 20, there are seven researchers from continental Europe, two from the UK and 10 researchers come from the US.
- Among the top 100 researchers, 18 researchers come from continental Europe, 10 from the UK, 66 from the US.
- Among the top 200 researchers, 32 researchers come from continental Europe, 16 from the UK, 136 from the US.

Physics

- Among the top 20, there are six researchers from continental Europe, one from the UK and eight from the US.
- Among the top 100 researchers, 32 researchers come from continental Europe, 10 from the UK, 50 from the US.
- Among the top 200 researchers, 51 researchers come from continental Europe, 15 from the UK, 101 from the US.

Molecular Biology

- Among the top 20, there are seven researchers from continental Europe and 13 from the US.
- Among the top 100 researchers, 17 researchers come from continental Europe, five from the UK, 75 from the US.
- Among the top 200 researchers, 35 researchers come from continental Europe, 10 from the UK, 144 from the US.

Examining the results in these three subject areas, the outcome is at first glance surprising: Among the top 20 most highly cited researchers, continental Europe seems to be nearly on a par with the US; however, the gap widens between continental Europe and the US when it comes to the top 200 researchers. It seems that US top universities excel not so much by employing the few very top stars, but by engaging the bulk of the top 100 of the top 200 researchers. Obviously, continental European universities lack critical mass at the top.

IS CONTINENTAL EUROPE FALLING BEHIND?

Concerning international rankings, continental Europe is clearly situated behind the US; this is particularly the case if considering the first 20 places in the overall university rankings and the first 200 places with respect to individual researchers. In contrast, the UK manages quite well and keeps her position, although mainly through the flagship "Oxbridge" and some other universities.

Continental Europe's position deteriorates if the placement is corrected by population figures. Continental Europe, the EU member states in continental Europe taken as a proxy, counts about 420 million inhabitants, the US 300 million and the UK 60 million. If the numbers of inhabitants are considered, continental Europe is clearly not efficiently using its enormous human capital relative to the US and UK. In fact, Europe seems to be wasting its human capital, if the constant brain drain over the Atlantic in the last 70 years is taken into account.

Another interesting question is whether the positions of continental European universities are stable. Does the trend point up- or downwards? Unfortunately, the time span available in international ranking is too short to yield accurate trend estimates. Changes in the ranking positions, as they appear during the last two or three years, are not so much due to a changing performance of universities, but to varying assessments of performance by ranking institutions. Counting Nobel Prizes is not a very serious business.

Given the fact that the developing world, especially Asia, is increasingly recognizing the importance of research and higher education for economic development (Siannesi, 2003), we can expect the developing world to invest ever more in higher education and research, and hence in universities. This might cause continental European universities to lose further ground, not because of a widening gap to US universities, but through intensified competition induced by additional competitors outside North America and Europe.

University reforms, of course, may change overall teaching and research performance. Yet, improved performance due to reforms should not be expected quickly, as Australian examples demonstrate (Gamage & Mininberg, 2003). Among the top 20 most highly cited researchers (in the fields of mathematics, physics and molecular biology), continental Europe is better positioned than continental European universities per se. This gives cause for hope that building critical mass around strong research by individuals in continental Europe may be the best strategy to boost the performance of these institutions within a short period.

WHAT ARE THE REASONS FOR THE CURRENT POSITION OF CONTINENTAL EUROPEAN UNIVERSITIES?

The dominance of English and national fragmentations

In and after the 1930s, the centres of scientific communities clearly shifted to Anglo-American countries, making English the dominant scientific language. For example, until the 1930s, the main language of academic communities in physics was German. Around and after the Second World War this changed dramatically. Now, the main language in physics is English. If members of the international scientific communities meet at congresses, English is often the only language spoken. This shift of scientific centres to Anglo-Saxon countries is impressively documented when looking at the editorial boards of influential science journals.

The shift of centres has consequences on the scientific development in continental Europe. Blau (1994) argues that debates on the state of scientific progress and the competition among scientific communities for new results — now mainly conducted in US (and UK) universities — have an important side effect: they spur the development of new scientific fields. Yet, this lack of positive feedback is not the sole factor which disadvantages continental Europe.

Another factor is that, in continental Europe, the university system is diverse, but this diversification is mainly the result of national fragmentations, and is not an outcome of a division of labour by competing and cooperating universities. These national fragmentations reflect the heavy impact that the emergence of nation states with national bureaucracies has had on universities.

The national differences within continental Europe are large. France, for example, has a highly centralized university system with national recruitments of its staff and specific borderlines between the university system and the research system (dominated by the CNRS). Germany, in contrast, has a decentralized university system that is too strongly governed by regional interests and by "strong local personalities", also within the universities (Blau, 1994). Moreover, much of the efforts in basic research are conducted outside the university system (Max Planck Society, Helmholtz Society, Frauenhofer Society).

The competition among continental European universities of different national origins is weak with respect to students, staff and ideas. Language borders and national regulations (e.g. pension systems) are still responsible for low mobility rates of students and staff between universities across borders. As the Rector of the University of Vienna, I can confirm this: Almost all professorial positions are advertised internationally, but most applications still come from German-speaking countries only.

However, continental Europe could turn its multiculturalism and multilingualism (although not an ethnic diversity) to an advantage, especially when communicating with the developing world.

Positive scale effects

The US university system is characterized by an enormous expansion and diversification in the 20th century. Mobility of students and staff and common quality standards have created a large area of knowledge. The diversification of higher education and research in the US is less dependent on state borders, but is driven by the demands of the society and the market. Private institutions compete with public entities. Currently there are about 4,000 colleges and universities in the US: these institutions differ tremendously in size, mission, constituencies and funding resources (Gamage & Mininberg, 2003; Duderstadt, 1999). There are only 200-300 research intensive universities. In addition, the US introduced a highly competitive and diverse grant system (NSF, NIH). The US development is in line with what Peter Blau suggested: expansion enables diversification and diversification in turn facilitates the changes for innovation (Blau, 1994).

In Australia as well, diversification with a push for the private sector has taken place since the 1980s. Its integration into global markets of higher education, manifested by an increasing inflow of overseas students, is a good indication for the increasing importance of the Australian university system. Australia seems to be moving in the American direction (Gamage & Mininberg, 2003) and has already become a "new" and strong competitor on global higher education markets.

Compared to the US, the UK lacks a comparable diversification. The UK system, however, has successfully positioned its flagship "Oxbridge" and certain other universities globally. The higher education institutions there are clearly better prepared for an increasingly global competition.

Other factors influencing the overall performance of European universities might be:

- Continental Europe still suffers from the emigration of the 1930s and 1940s and the accompanying shift of intellectual focus towards Anglo-Saxon countries.
- The cooperative governance of universities in the post-1968 era had considerable negative effects, especially on recruitment policies. The obvious consequence of the cooperative governance was an increase

of inner recruitment and, in addition, researchers and teachers quickly reached tenured positions, often irrespective of their performance. As a consequence, the now "young generation of scientists" is confronted with dramatically reduced career opportunities, again fostering emigration of human capital. To overcome such tendencies towards creating "fixed positions", many German universities (respectively their regional governments) introduced an increasingly higher percentage of time-limited contracts (up to 90%). However, these abrupt measures also had negative effects because of increased uncertainties for university careers. The university career became less attractive (particularly for talented candidates).

- The concentration on Ph.D. programmes in the 19th century reduced educational opportunities through the abolition of the Bachelor and Master system. In the 20th century this tendency was corrected by introducing Diploma or Master studies, but only due to the Bologna Process were Bachelor studies re-introduced in continental Europe.

REFORM AGENDA FOR EUROPE: MODERNISATION AGENDA

Europe's Universities still operate mostly in small national systems or sub-systems, which results in a lack of recognition of foreign degrees and in low levels of trans-national or trans-sectoral mobility of researchers and students. To overcome these fragmentations, the creation of the Europe of Knowledge, comprising the European Higher Education Area (Bologna Process) and the European Research Area, is a goal which should be pursued with great efforts at the European level and which should bring first results by 2010. European universities need the scale effects and the competitive pressures of a large area which a Europe of Knowledge could provide.

Although the Bologna Process, an intergovernmental process now comprising 46 European states, is moving on and will likely reach its ambitious goals of enhancing mobility through Erasmus and of introducing a common study architecture with a wave of modern curricula by 2010, and although the European Research Area was given a boost by setting up the European Research Council on 1 January 2007, the university system will not be sufficiently modernized by these activities. Special measures are necessary to move the universities out of the shadows of governmental bureaucracies which still tend to micro-manage the nationally fragmented university systems.

During the informal meeting of the European Council at Hampton Court, at the end of October 2005, and to the surprise of his colleagues, the British Prime Minister Tony Blair emphasized how important a modernized university system would be for a refocused Lisbon strategy. The Commission reacted to the discussion at this meeting ("Hampton Court Follow-Up") by issuing, on

10 May 2006, with input from experts, a communication on "Delivering on the modernisation agenda for universities: education, research and innovation" (COM [2006] 208 final). Since the Hampton Court meeting of October 2005, the discussion of the modernization agenda has centred on the following points for action:

- Universities are key players in Europe's future and for the successful transition to a knowledge-based economy and society. The knowledge-based economy will also dramatically change the role and the manner of research and teaching: scientists will be able to work worldwide, not necessarily located at a particular university and a large amount of data and research tools will be freely available through the net (a good example for ongoing developments are free economic and census data as well as free analysis programmes). In the framework of these ongoing developments, the role and the definition of a scientist will change. More people will be engaged in the "production of knowledge". Universities are well advised to take these developments into account.
- Overcoming the fragmentation in continental Europe — the geographical and inter-sectoral mobility within Europe needs to be increased substantially (e.g., through Erasmus and Socrates Programs). The Bologna Process should also enhance the vertical mobility of graduates in the sense that one earns a Bachelor's degree in country A, a Master's degree in country B and a Ph.D. in country C. The cross-border employability of graduates has to follow the increased internationalization of economies in Europe which can be witnessed by increased foreign direct investment and the high export and import ratios of GDP.
- Cooperation *and* competition among universities within Europe has to increase. So far, Framework Programs and Socrates have strengthened the cooperation among universities. Now, universities have started to compete within Europe: e.g., through grant schemes of the ERC and the forthcoming implementation of the EIT (through the formation of KICs: knowledge and innovation communities).
- The European education and research system should be diversified at all levels, as well as on the grant system level. The diversification should not be ordered from above, but should be the outcome of a bottom-up process, driven by appropriate incentive schemes.
- An attractive Higher Education and Research Area has to be created: attracting scientists and students from over the world — avoiding brain drain. The Bologna Process, supported by the referenced Lisbon Strategy, may make continental Europe particularly attractive for students

and scientists from the developing world by using Europe's multicultural and multilingual "profile". Continental Europe should foster the formation of international scientific communities with the increasing participation of students and scientists from the developing world.

- Dialogue with society and the economy has to be strengthened so as to better legitimize more investments in the university system, in order to overcome the funding gaps of the European university system.

CHALLENGES AHEAD

Evidently, continental European universities need to do a lot in order to be able to compete globally. Alas, there are additional challenges ahead:

- Continental Europe should be better prepared for the demographic developments in the next 20 years. There will be an increased competition for resources between health care, care for the elderly on the one hand and higher education and research on the other hand (Schuller, 2005).
- Continental European universities must give young, performance-oriented scientists a realistic chance to work independently and to advance in the university system. University systems in Continental Europe are still characterized by feudal professorial positions.
- Searching, finding and supporting new ideas have to be backed by more risk-taking investments.

REFERENCES

Bowden, R. (2000). "Fantasy higher education: University and college league tables", *Quality in Higher Education*, 6, pp. 41-60.

Blau, P.M. (1994). *The organization of academic work*. Transaction Publishers, New Brunswick (US) and London (UK).

Braun, T., Peresztegi-Szabadi, Z.S. & Nemet-Kovacs E. (2003). "No-bells for ambiguous list of ranked Nobelists as science indicators of national merit in Physics and Medicine", *Scientometrics*, 56, pp. 3-20.

De Talleyrand-Périgord, C.M. (1791). *Rapport sur l'instruction fait au nom du comité de constitution a l'assemblée nationale, 10.9.1791*. Archive parlementaire, première série, 1787-1799, Vol. 30 (Paris 1888, Reprint: 1969), pp. 447-480.

Dill, D.D. & Soo, M. (2005). "Academic quality, league tables, and public policy: A cross national analysis of university ranking systems", *Higher Education*, 49, pp. 495-533.

Duderstadt, J.J. (1999). "The twenty-first century university: A tale of two futures", in Hirsch, W.Z. & Weber, L.E. (Eds.), *Challenges Facing Higher Education at the Millennium*. American Council on Education, Oryx Press, Phoenix.

Gamage, D.T. & Mininberg, E. (2003). "The Australian and American higher education: Key issues of the first decade of the 21st century", *Higher Education*, 45, pp. 183-202.

Langewiesche, D. (2005). "Schöne neue Hochschulwelt". *Frankfurter Allgemeine Zeitung*, 23 June, p. 7.

Sianesi, B. & Van Reenen, J. (2003). "The returns to education: Macroeconomics", *Journal of Economic Surveys*, 17, pp. 157-200.

Schuller, T. (2005). *Access, Equity and Outcomes: an international contextualisation.* Presentation at the 15th EAN Annual Conference in Vienna, July 2005.

CHAPTER 7

The Engagement of Australian Universities with Globalization

John Niland

INTRODUCTION

Despite the common image of isolated ivory towers, universities in point of fact have long embraced the world beyond their national horizon. Initially, scholars travelled from country to country in search of a student audience. Now, students in their hundreds of thousands are internationally mobile in search of a university degree and a cross-cultural experience. Researchers often earn their doctorates in other countries and in modern times have drawn on international data and insights in the pursuit of new knowledge. And in what other sector do leading institutions routinely seek to recruit so widely from around the world?

So, in one sense, universities have always been in the global game. But it is becoming clear from the prodigious writings on the topic that globalization is a deeper and more profound phenomenon than its simpler antecedent, internationalization. Internationalization essentially meant a mobility of staff and students and the extensive exchange of ideas. But globalization drives more deeply, forcing fundamental change upon universities about how they operate in a truly borderless world: "Concepts of space and location are no longer constraining factors to either the process of production or the process of exchange… (globalization)… can apply quite easily to many areas of human endeavour, including knowledge production and dissemination". (Marquez, 2002, in UNESCO, 2003).

For Australia, the serious inflow of international students started in the 1960s, consolidated in the 1970s and early 1980s and then grew sharply through the subsequent decades to set the foundations for what we now see to be a more intense phenomenon — globalization. The point at which internationalization gives way to globalization is not clear cut. One marker of the switchover point may be the proportion of overall enrolment drawn from full fee paying international students. The Australian experience suggests this could be around the 15% point, and with that proportion now at 25% for the sector, globalization is the single most powerful influence on university strategies. Another marker is the growing incidence of international students enrolled in offshore campuses of Australian universities (which now exceed 20 in some 15 countries).

Beyond international students, globalization brings to universities elements of competition and standards of efficiency that go well beyond national borders. These touch not just the academic function but also the style and substance of management, as well as strategic relations with staff, government and the business world. Globalization drives change to the very core of how universities organize themselves, and how they operate.

In broad terms (and with some exceptions), public funding to the 38 universities comes from the federal government. The six state governments, on the other hand, carry responsibility for the enabling legislation and its administration, as well as auditing financial affairs and appointing about a third of the typical governing body (although governance is just one area being changed by global influences). Power over the purse puts the federal government in the driver's seat for policy setting, and having at the national level since 1992 a politically conservative, economically reformist government has forced into the university sector a competitiveness borne on the winds of globalization. This is examined in three parts: the international student wave; the regulatory response of government, and the global-related strategies of the universities themselves.

THE PIVOTAL ROLE OF INTERNATIONAL STUDENTS

An enduring feature of the Australian university scene over the past decade has been the remarkable growth in the enrolment of overseas students. From only a handful of universities being active recruiters in 1989, by 2007 only two of 38 universities were inactive on this front (see Table 2). Now, for 80% of Australian universities, 15% or more of their overall enrolments are international; for 40% the international component is over 25%; and for four universities, the figure is beyond 40%. Generally, the larger universities (25,000 students and over) are more internationally intensive by this measure. This is a significant element in the funding strategies of both universities and government, and underscores the pivotal role global influences now play.

Table 1 underscores the strength of the trend since the late 1980s (when data was first reliably collected across the sector), both in terms of absolute numbers and in terms of their growing importance in the overall profile. In

Table 1: International and Domestic Enrolment
in Australian Universities 1989-2005*

Year	International			Domestic	Overall	%
	Onshore	Offshore	Total	Total	Total	Internatnl
1989	18,691	2,241	21,112	419,962	441,074	5%
1990	22,470	2,528	24,998	460,068	485,066	5%
1991	25,820	3,810	29,630	504,880	534,510	6%
1992	29,276	4,800	34,076	525,305	553,381	6%
1993	31,132	6,020	37,152	538,464	575,616	6%
1994	32,374	8,120	40,494	544,941	585,435	7%
1995	35,921	9,843	46,187	557,989	604,176	8%
1996	42,280	10,483	53,188	580,906	634,094	8%
1997	47,713	14,995	62,996	595,853	658,849	10%
1998	52,024	19,812	72,183	599,670	671,853	11%
1999	55,985	26,645	83,111	603,156	686,267	12%
2000	66,188	28,114	95,607	599,878	695,485	14%
2001	112,029	45,179	157,208	684,975	842,183	19%
2002	134,646	50,412	185,058	711,563	896,621	21%
2003	154,578	55,819	210,397	719,555	929,952	23%
2004	164,519	64,020	228,539	716,438	944,977	25%
2005	175,589	63,906	239,495	717,681	957,176	25%

Source: Complied from DEST Student Unit Record Files 1989 to 2005, by Tim Sealey at
AVCC.
* From 2001 DEST reported full-year enrolments whereas previously only Semester 1 enrolments were counted. More recent numbers are drawn from institutions which qualify under the
federal government's fee paying protocols, which overwhelmingly are universities.

1989, 21,112 international students were enrolled, 88% onshore and 12%
studying in offshore programmes. Overall, these represented just 5% of all
enrolled students. By 2005, the number of international students had grown
11-fold, and for those instructed offshore, the growth was 28-fold, mostly from
and in South-east Asia.

Initially, the vast majority of international students enrolled onshore, but
as communications technology changed the parameters on place and time,
and as universities became more adept within a globalized environment, large
numbers of international students began to study offshore for Australian

degrees. A variety of delivery modes are evident, ranging from licensing arrangements with overseas universities through online instruction, to actual branch campuses. As shown in Table 2, over three-quarters of Australia's universities are involved, to a greater or lesser extent, in such offshore delivery, and over a quarter count 10% or more of their total enrolment in this mode.

A sign that offshore engagement is lifting to a new global level was the decision in 2004 by UNSW (the University of New South Wales) to develop a stand-alone campus in Singapore. Amid much publicity, UNSW Asia was promoted as being the first "wholly owned research and teaching institution to be established overseas by an Australian University" (www.unswasia.edu.sg), and Singapore's first private comprehensive university. The campus, planned for a 22-hectare "garden" site at Changi, was to be enrolling some 10,000 students by 2015, up from this year's planned initial intake of 500. The same admissions criteria would apply as for UNSW Sydney and students would be strongly encouraged to complete part of their programme at the Sydney campus. Similarly, Sydney-based students would be encouraged to undertake a semester of inter-campus study at UNSW Asia to round out their regional experience. In its fully developed phase, some 30% of students were expected to be Singapore residents with 70% from elsewhere in the region — a key component of the Singapore Government's "Global Schoolhouse" strategy.

But after just one semester of operation, the University suddenly announced on 23 May 2007 that it was closing UNSW Asia and offering the 147 students then enrolled the opportunity to transfer to placement in Sydney. The University indicated that the numbers enrolling, particularly those coming from outside Singapore, did not augur well for the longer-term business plan. It is too early for reliable conclusions to be drawn about what went wrong and why. Certainly the initial media coverage has been intense and highly negative on UNSW, and possibly on "Brand Australia" in the global sense. Several preliminary observations, however, can be made. First, resources funnelled to offshore developments become a "political" issue on the home campus, particularly if the latter is effecting staff redundancies. On the other hand, to bring international students to the home campus bolsters jobs. Second, if students are going to travel internationally for higher education they probably prefer the home campus, which is usually larger and more vibrant that the branch campus. Third, when a university's leadership and the composition of the governing body change significantly, major strategies (such as the mode of globalization) will inevitably come under critical review. This is intensified where there is general instability at the top: in UNSW's case, the incoming President in 2006 was the fourth in four years to hold that position. Fourth, the forces and imperatives of globalization bring great opportunities for a wider engagement and higher institutional profiles, but they also bring (as in financial markets) greater risks. Finally, the collapse of UNSW Asia will no doubt bring greater

Table 2: Enrolment at All Australian Universities: Total and International (Onshore and Offshore) 2005

University	Actual Enrolment				Percent Distribution		
	Total	International			International/Total		
	Overall	Onshore	Offshore	Total	Onshore	Offshore	Total
Charles Sturt University	33,560	2,537	4,539	7,076	8%	14%	21%
Macquarie University	29,985	8,798	758	9,556	29%	3%	32%
Southern Cross University	13,127	665	1,716	2,381	5%	13%	18%
University of New England	18,146	1,068	686	1,754	6%	4%	10%
University of New South Wales	39,183	8,939	64	9,003	23%	0%	23%
University of Newcastle	25,114	2,642	1,911	4,553	11%	8%	18%
University of Sydney	45,630	8,854	610	9,464	19%	1%	21%
University of Technology, Sydney	31,502	6,854	1,257	8,111	22%	4%	26%
University of Western Sydney	33,309	3,472	1,726	5,198	10%	5%	16%
University of Wollongong	22,124	5,534	3,498	9,032	25%	16%	41%
Deakin University	33,238	5,280	1,205	6,485	16%	4%	20%
La Trobe University	27,208	3,560	1,117	4,677	13%	4%	17%
Monash University	37,450	11,348	5,820	17,168	21%	11%	31%
RMIT University	28,006	7,128	7,889	15,017	19%	21%	39%
Swinburne University of Technology	10,547	3,883	718	4,601	24%	4%	29%
University of Melbourne	27,546	8,848	88	8,936	21%	0%	21%

Table 2: Enrolment at All Australian Universities: Total and International (Onshore and Offshore) 2005 (*suite*)

University	Actual Enrolment						Percent Distribution		
	Total	International					International/Total		
	Overall	Onshore	Offshore	Total			Onshore	Offshore	Total
University of Ballarat	4,953	3,651	1,496	5,147			37%	15%	53%
Victoria University	14,982	3,621	2,732	6,353			18%	13%	31%
Bond University*	1,723	2,282	478	2,760			51%	11%	61%
Central Queensland University	15,145	12,512	1,325	13,837			49%	5%	54%
Griffith University	26,213	7,695	560	8,255			22%	2%	24%
James Cook University	11,180	1,828	841	2,669			12%	6%	18%
QLD University of Technology	29,215	4,993	281	5,274			13%	1%	14%
University of Queensland	26,184	6,333	0	6,333			17%	0%	17%
University of Southern Queensland	13,595	8,963	0	8,963			36%	0%	36%
University of the Sunshine Coast	3,707	1,101	0	1,101			21%	0%	21%
Curtin University of Technology	28,189	7,257	8,835	16,092			19%	23%	42%
Edith Cowan University	17,985	2,866	1,437	4,303			12%	6%	18%
Murdoch University	10,767	1,503	683	2,186			11%	5%	17%
The University of Western Australia	12,842	2,141	915	3,056			13%	5%	18%
Flinders University	10,327	1,692	1,087	2,779			12%	7%	19%
University of Adelaide	12,934	3,660	745	4,405			19%	4%	23%

Table 2: Enrolment at All Australian Universities: Total and International (Onshore and Offshore) 2005 (*suite*)

University	Actual Enrolment				Percent Distribution		
	Total	International			International/Total		
	Overall	Onshore	Offshore	Total	Onshore	Offshore	Total
University of South Australia	22,570	4,189	5,676	9,865	13%	18%	31%
University of Tasmania	13,802	1,806	1,924	3,730	11%	11%	22%
Charles Darwin University	3,643	218	0	218	4%	0%	4%
Australian National University	8,754	3,036	0	3,036	21%	0%	21%
University of Canberra	8,028	1,342	1,231	2,573	12%	11%	22%
Australian Catholic University	8,827	2,069	0	2,069	16%	0%	16%
TOTAL	761,340	175,589	63,906	239,495	19%	7%	25%

Source: DEST Student Unit Record Files. Prepared with the helpful assistance of Tim Sealey of the Australian Vice Chancellor's Committee.
* Privae university.

oversight by government and its agencies when it comes to offshore operations. And countries hosting global expansion may also have reason to review their strategies.

All this is reinforced by the keen awareness in Australia about the economic dimension of international student enrolment. Universities account for 65% of all international enrolments with the remainder going to vocational and technical education (15%) and secondary schools and English language programmes (20%). Overall, education exports accounted for A$10 billion in 2005-06, just behind tourism and well ahead of wool and wheat. In higher education, about 40% of this expenditure went directly to fees and 60% to other elements such as living expenses, entertainment etc. Putting this to scale, "Australia's education exports constitute the largest share of total services exports of any major English-speaking country." (DFAT, "Education without Borders", Economic Analytical Unit). Just as government leaders often talk of international education exports, university leaders now apply a similar language when lobbying for higher education funding. Part of the argument is that better infrastructure funded by government will help generate additional earnings, much as with the mining industry which regularly argues for better rail lines and port facilities to bolster exports.

UNDERLYING PRESSURES AND GOVERNMENT RESPONSES

Just how and why Australian universities grew international enrolments so intensely is something of a jigsaw, with different elements interacting to build the full picture.

History and Geography

The role of the English language, and Australia's particular position on the globe have certainly played a part. Australia's active support in the 1950s and 1960s for the Colombo Plan laid the foundation for subsequent recruitment of Asian students seeking immersion in a Western culture, and an English-language education (Oakman, 2004). By the 1990s quite a few of the political, business and community leaders in South East Asia had held Colombo Plan scholarships 30 years earlier, and were now opinion makers (and aware, if not active, alumni) in their own countries.

But this alone could not account for such a sharp rise in international enrolments. What became pivotal is a mix of demographic, economic and political factors internal to Australia, which revolutionized the landscape of university funding. This went hand in hand with an active, even aerobic, public policy in shaping the university sector and its regulatory framework. While there were some protests along the way, universities by and large adapted, then actively adopted strategies for global engagement.

Demography and Domestic Student Demand

From being once almost entirely funded by governments pre-1980s, public funding of university places has since succumbed to more politically powerful pressures on the federal budget. The demographic reality of an ageing population has been drawing public funding away from the university sector since the mid-1990s, and this is set to intensify. The government's 2007 Intergenerational Report forecasts that over the next 40 years, the age cohort 65 and older will nearly double to 25% of the population while those aged 85 and over will triple to nearly 6%. This brings ever rising demands for medical and hospital care and pensions support, all of which compete with university funding in the "big bucks" league for social infrastructure. Yet at the same time, the income tax revenue base is shrinking: currently there are five people of working age for each person over 65, but by 2047 the dependency ratio will have halved.

The second underlying pressure on government funding of university places is the growing domestic student demand, reflected in the higher and higher proportion of the age cohort completing secondary education and then seeking a university place: the "massification" effect.

Fee Regimes

Over the past two decades the federal government's response to these pressures has been to shift away from public sources of university funding, primarily through student fees paid by both domestic students and international students.

Australia's system of income contingent, deferred liability loans — the Higher Education Contributions Scheme (HECS) — was introduced in 1989 and has drawn considerable interest from other countries; a number, including South Africa, Chile, Thailand and Britain have adopted this approach. This itself is another dimension of globalization — international transfer of public policy settings. Through HECS (now called HECS-HELP), all domestic undergraduates contribute an (increasingly) higher proportion of the true cost of their university education. Essentially, the government provides loans to students which are passed through to their university annually, on the basis that the student will start to repay that loan through the income tax system on entering the workforce. The key variables in this scheme are: the level of the loan which is set in one of three bands, usually reflecting course costs; the income threshold at which repayments commence; the extent the marginal tax rate is adjusted upward; the period over which the loan is repaid; the groups or categories for whom the loan is forgiven; and the implied rate of interest (set at the inflation rate). This provides a rich array of settings the government can rejig in policy reformation.

Throughout the 1990s it became clear that domestic demand was outstripping supply of HECS supported places. A particular point of community grievance and public debate was that international students could gain admission while some qualified domestic students could not. Indeed, many international students moved on to university after completing their secondary study in Australia, itself another element in Australia's marketing advantage. Yet sometimes these students had matriculation exam scores slightly lower than the cut-off for a HECS place, at least in courses where domestic demand drove the cut-off score well above levels actually required to successfully handle the subject matter. In some well publicised cases, the two students (one domestic and one international) were actually class mates in the same secondary school. A difficult political problem for the government was emerging, but rather than increase the number of HECS-funded places as the prime solution, in 2000 it introduced regulations allowing universities to charge full fees to qualified domestic students who missed out on a HECS place, with a cap on the numbers to not exceed 25% of the enrolment in any degree programme (which cap was subsequently abolished). These domestic students were thus put on the same basis as the international students. Even more significant, the HECS eligibility was extended to approved private providers (through the new HECS-HELP scheme). In short, global influences are at the core of quite profound policy changes in higher education.

Quality Assurance

The Australian Universities Quality Agency (AUQA) began operating in 2001. Foreshadowing its establishment in 1999, the Federal Minister for Education said: "Education is now one of Australia's major export industries in an intensely competitive market. While Australian universities compete with each other in this market, they also compete with the rest of the world. Our major competitors have external quality assurance mechanisms and countries in our largest markets look to Government verification of quality standards. To maintain market position we need to be able to advertise that we have quality assurance mechanisms in place, that they are being applied and that they are having a positive effect on outcomes." (Kemp, 1999, p. 5).

AUQA is a not-for-profit company owned by the governments of Australia. From 2005 earmarked funds are being provided for AUQA to strengthen its attention to "transnational education". It conducts overseas site visits of campuses operated by Australian universities, and increasingly is liaising with counterpart bodies in other countries (in a manner not dissimilar to the strategies of regulatory bodies overseeing other areas of global impact, such as in financial markets, agricultural markets, pharmaceuticals etc). By March 2007, AUQA had made 89 visits to overseas partner agencies and offshore campuses of Australian universities: China (13), Hong Kong (20), Singapore (22) and the remainder to Taiwan, Japan, Fiji, Malaysia, South Africa, Vietnam, United Arab Emirates, Indonesia and Thailand.

One sign of how globalization is changing the world of universities is seen in the comprehensive array of questions that shape AUQA's offshore reviews. These probe such issues as: the underlining philosophy of the operation; how the offshore partner is selected and their role; the nature of the formal contract and whether proper host country approvals are in place; governance arrangements; policies on plagiarism and Australian-themed student grievance procedures; processes of curriculum approval, teaching modes and assessment; pastoral care and community links; and the evaluation and review process. There are those who see in this the loss of institutional autonomy and academic freedom.

From its offshore review AUQA has reached various conclusions about the effect of transnational education, including:

Transnational activities are often run as a "commercial" activity rather than an "academic" activity, and there is increasing use by universities of private corporate arms to manage these activities. This changes behaviour.

There is a gradual move from thinking in terms of Australian education overseas, to thinking about locally-relevant education provided by an Australia-based university.

UNIVERSITY STRATEGIES

With the federal government pulling back per capita support for student places from the 1990s, the response by most universities has been to follow strategies that reflect the influence of globalization. There are many signs of the changed mood, but space limits consideration to four in particular: offshore marketing and recruitment; governance reforms; the new management ethos; and competitive world ranking exercises.

Offshore Marketing and Recruitment

The surge in international enrolments could not have been achieved without dedicated support services specializing in offshore marketing, themselves supported by government officers attached to some 19 Australian embassies and consulates in 14 countries. The universities most active offshore also establish offices in key places. UNSW, for example, for the past 15 years has had a substantial presence in Bangkok, Singapore and Hong Kong, for the purposes of liaising with prospective students and their families, but also to provide base support for their researchers when working in the region.

For the sector as a whole, 20% of recruitment is undertaken by IDP (originally International Development Program), a company owned by Australia's 38 universities, with 50 offices offshore in some 35 countries. In 2006 IDP entered into a commercial partnership with SEEK Limited, a publicly listed company, to boost its marketing, sales, technology and business development expertise (www.idp.com). Globalization also brings added competition for topline domestic undergraduate students, evidenced in the growing presence in Australia of recruiters from eminent U.S. and U.K. universities, with a rich array of scholarship offerings. (Ironically, sporting scholarships from U.S. universities have long been available to elite junior athletes).

One important element in the marketing of Australian universities is the offshore graduation ceremony. Australian universities follow the British tradition of running graduation ceremonies of several hundred, structured around particular disciplines or schools/departments, rather than a single omnibus ceremony of thousands, for all graduands. A university graduating some 10,000 students per year would run about 35 separate ceremonies. In the early 1990s Monash University and UNSW were the first to hold ceremonies offshore and most Australian universities have followed suit. Now, in any one year, around 100 ceremonies are held in places such as Singapore, Bangkok, Hong Kong, Shanghai, Jakarta, Seoul and Mumbai. At one level these events cater to the interest of the home families who may not be able to get to a ceremony in Australia: it is not unusual for 500-600 family and friends to attend. At another level, the offshore graduation ceremony, featuring the Chancellor, Vice-Chancellor (i.e. President), Deans and other academics, all robed for the occasion and well reported in the local media, is a highly effective branding and recruitment strategy. Many universities report second- and third-generation graduates at these offshore ceremonies.

Governance Reforms

In the corporate world, governance reform is a particular effect of globalization (e.g. Sarbanes-Oxley in the U.S. and ASX reforms in Australia) and since 2000, these effects have flowed through to Australian universities. In the 1990s a typical governing body comprised 25 to 35 members, around half elected by stake holders such as students, staff and alumni, together with others appointed by state parliaments and/or ministers of education (where party political considerations are not always absent). The resulting culture was one of "representatives" coming from particular "constituencies", with an orientation towards special interest issues, often intent on vetoing change. Governance transformation is well underway, as the federal government makes some funding conditional on the restructuring of governing bodies, serving to reduce their size and expand the proportion of members external to the university and with business or professional experience. The effect, in time, will be profound and should bring forward a stronger support for the new management ethos now becoming evident.

The New Management Ethos

Shifts in the styles and strategies of university management over the past decade, away from more traditional university administration, are another pointer to the influence of globalization. Corporate plans, mission statements and KPIs are one marker; another is the trend for universities to outsource non-core services, such as payroll, security, property management, and staff and student counselling. Indeed, the very scope of the core is being rethought.

Also being rethought as part of the new management ethos are balance sheet strategies and capital raising. In Australia, the physical infrastructure — land and buildings — are vested in the universities themselves and account for up to 80% of balance sheet assets. Since the mid 1990s there is growing inclination to shed "lazy" assets and reassign capital thus released to more strategic purposes. There are now many instances of active capital management strategies. Major equipment acquisition at most of the larger universities is increasingly through lease arrangements with financial institutions. Public/private partnerships (PPPs) and BOOT schemes are no longer rare in areas such as on-campus student housing (www.clv.com.au). In Australia, some 7,000 student beds are owned and/or managed by private providers and this feature will grow as Australian universities begin to face real competition from Asian countries for the international student dollar.

Another sign of the globalization ethos is the growing willingness of university management and governing bodies to take on debt to launch innovation and transformation strategies. A handful of universities have secured credit worthiness ratings from Standards and Poor's to provide access to cheaper capital, the first being Latrobe University in 2002. As the University of Melbourne noted in December 2006, it had "retained its S&P's AA+ credit ranking despite Australian universities experiencing a flattening in the international student market that year". S&P, however, have signalled that the progress of the University of Melbourne in implementing the U.S. model of four-year undergraduate degrees, and its effect on finances, need to be monitored.

These shifts have not been without some angst from staff and students directly affected, and from those on governing bodies with a philosophical objection to the new management strategies; traditional university cultures don't embrace the centralizing pull of management efficiency. There are those who rail at "the terrible viruses of managerialism, relevance, privatization and education in the service of industry". This view laments the passing of happier days when the university was a community of scholars engaged in teaching and research in the spirit of Erasmus of Rotterdam and Cardinal John Henry Newman. The counter argument, which is gaining ascendancy in the post-global period, is that good management should not be a perjorative term. With greater emphasis on revenue generation through fee income and growing pressure on resources, every dollar reasonably saved is a dollar to be strategically spent. There is now awareness of the imperative to maximize returns on investments and other assets; to manage financial and student data for timely and accurate information; to market imaginatively; to build and renovate campus facilities, particularly when pressures are strong for expenditure of a more recurrent kind; and to do well all those prosaic things which teachers and researchers could take for granted in simpler, better funded and less competitive times (Niland, 2007, p. 69).

League Tables and Benchmarking

Globalization has induced heightened attention to how universities are perceived by their many stakeholders. International ranking exercises present an opportunity for internationally alert universities to showcase their attractiveness in recruiting both students and staff. To be ranked in the top 50 or top 100 universities worldwide in the Jiao Tong Index or to do well in the THES Survey (as is the case for five or six of Australia's research-intensive universities) is a quality marker for recruitment of both domestic and international students. Through the effects of globalization, where the old rules of status and standing are changing, much younger institutions can replace more traditional universities as the preferred destination for new generations of students. This affects behaviour in quite fundamental ways.

Benchmarking exercises of the type provided by the Association of Commonwealth Universities (ACU) or Universitas 21 typically involve a cross section of universities from different countries coming together to examine their performance within a specified framework, and to common standards. This may help inform decisions ranging from whether to adopt management software systems from Peoplesolf or SAP, to the costs and benefits of subcontracting and outsourcing, through to setting comparative international metrics on a range of scholarly performance.

While international benchmarking is less controversial, the competitive ranking exercises now familiar in many countries can generate heated debate about methodology, reliability and relevance (Sadlak & Liu, 2007). Yet to "perform" well is an irresistible promotion point when marketing for top students, especially from overseas. What once may have seemed to be unseemly self-promotion is more normal with globalization.

CONCLUSION

Australia provides an interesting case study of the influence on universities of globalization. As UNESCO noted in 2003, "international education and cooperation in higher education have, in the past decade, gained a great deal of prominence" and are most often viewed as higher education's response to the overarching phenomenon of globalization. But this is only part of the story.

The enrolment of students from other countries has provided Australian universities with an enormous opportunity to strengthen their international presence, to widen and deepen scholarship and to significantly expand funding that is independent of government. At the same time, government has seen the opportunity to wind back its real support per student of a growing domestic enrolment. To achieve and sustain this transformation, universities have had to come to grips the greater involvement (some would say intrusion) of government in setting strategic directions. This comes in the form of an active quality assurance process, particularly for offshore operations; the profound redesign of fee regimes for domestic as well as international students; and the steering toward genuine role differentiation and mission among the 38 public universities.

But the Australian experience also highlights that globalization is much more than the inflow of international students. Most significantly, it drives into the corporate world a new management ethos and this in turn (with some lag, to be sure), flows through to the universities. Here, the changing ethos about management systems and strategies brings new styles of governance, balance sheet strategies; and the outsourcing of non-core functions. All this changes the very culture of the university. Whether this is for the better is not without debate.

REFERENCES

Coaldrake, P. & Stedman, L. (2007). "Universities and Australia's Future Workforce", *Proceedings of Higher Education Summit*, Melbourne.

Davis, G. (2007). "Fairness, Fees and Equity in Higher Education", *AFR Higher Education Summit*, 3 April, Melbourne.

Jolley, A. (1997). *Exporting Education to Asia*, Victoria University Press, Melbourne.

Kemp, D.A. (1999). "Quality Assured — A New Australian Quality Assurance Framework for University Education". To Seminar on New Quality Assurance Framework, Canberra.

Marquez, A.M. (2002). "The Impact of Globalisation on Higher Education: The Latin American Context". *Globalisation and the Market in Higher Education*, Stamenka Uvalic Trumbic (ed), UNESCO, pp. 83-94

Milbourne, R. (2007). "Funding Diversity", *AFR* Higher Education Summit, 3 April, Melbourne.

Niland, J. (2007). "The Challenge of Building World-Class Universities", in Sadlak, J. & Liu, Nian Cai (Eds), *The World-Class University and Ranking: Aiming Beyond Status*, UNESCO-CEPES, Bucharest.

Oakman, D. (2004). *Facing Asia: A History of the Colombo Plan*, Pandanus Books, ANU

Sadlak, J. & Liu, Nian Cai. (Eds). (2007). *The World-Class University and Ranking: Aiming Beyond Status*, UNESCO-CEPES, Bucharest.

Woodhouse, D. (2007). "The Role of AUQA in Transnational Education Quality Assurance", March 2007.

UNESCO (2003). "Internationalisation of Higher Education: Trends and Developments since 1998", for Meeting of Higher Education Partners, 23-25 June, Paris.

CHAPTER 8

Japanese University Reform seen through Bureaucratic Reform and Changes in Patterns of Scientific collaboration

Yuko Harayama and René Carraz

INTRODUCTION

In order to understand the radical changes that Japanese universities have been undergoing in recent years, the observer has to keep in mind three essential facts: the demographic factor as an engine behind the changes, the ongoing political drive to a reorganization of the university management structure and the need to improve and facilitate the link between university and industry. On a wider perspective, we can add the challenge induced by global competition. Whichever view you take — fearful, constructed by the political sphere or based on real facts — you have to keep in mind the role that global pressure plays on the idiosyncrasies of the Japanese system. The reasons Japanese universities are increasingly facing global competition are that students are increasingly mobile (even though, as for 2005, there were only 79,000 Japanese students studying abroad and 120,000 foreign students in Japan [MEXT, 2006]), that professors and ideas can travel, and that industries choose the best colleges worldwide to cooperate with.

To begin, here are a few figures in order to visualize essential aspects of the Japanese university system. In 2005, there were 726 universities and junior colleges, of which 87 were public national universities. The number of national universities is down from 99 in 2001 due to the merging of several institutions. A large majority of the students are enrolled in private institutions, but the lion's share of the research is conducted in public institutions. This is the reason why we will mainly focus on the national university reform process as a major element of the Japanese effort to reform its scientific system. Historically, while the private universities have been responsible for the massification and extension of the higher education system, national universities have provided academic research and graduate education.

As for education spending, Japan is below the OECD average. It corresponds to 1.1% of growth domestic product of which 0.5% comes from public expenditure and 0.6% from private spending, mainly from households through tuition fees. Households bear a considerable share as scholarships and grants are relatively small compared to the OECD average (OECD, 2005).

Furthermore, one has to keep in mind the demographic downfall pressure on the Japanese higher education system. Indeed, enrolment is doomed to decrease; the total fertility rate has been in decline since the 1970s. As of 2005, it stood at 1.25 [1]. In addition to a matured rate in higher education (Japan's entry rate to higher education is high at 74.1%, with 49.8% of students going on to universities, junior colleges or colleges of technology [four-year institutions]), these factors are pushing the universities to review their recruiting methods through modifying entrance exams, enriching curriculum and finding new kinds of students (for instance, foreigners or working people).

The aim of this article is to consider whether the changes that the Japanese universities have undergone in recent years are responding to the challenges entailed by global competition or are a mere ritual reform. We will also focus on the reinforcement of university-industry links induced by the change in the pattern of scientific endeavours, specifically the expansion of knowledge-intensive investments and activities [2].

This article is organized in two parts. First, we will analyse the major organizational changes that the national universities have undergone. Second, we will examine how major changes in Japanese Science and Technology policy have implied reciprocal transformations in the universities.

A REFORM AND GOVERNANCE CHANGES

A process of administrative reform

One of the anchoring points of the university reform is the Toyama Plan, 2001, named after the Minister for Education, Culture, Sports, Science and Technology (MEXT) Atsuko Toyama. This plan proposed three major reforms: the reorganization and incorporation of national universities, the development of

1 http://www.stat.go.jp/English/data/handbook/c02cont.htm
2 See Foray (2003) for a seminal contribution to the subject.

universities that conform to the highest international standards by using third party evaluation, and increasing the proportion of competitive funding.

We will first explain the sequence of events that led to the reform and then state legislative changes. Our intention is to investigate whether the reform was intended to downsize or to enhance the autonomy of national universities.

In 1996, the Liberal Democratic Party (LDP) made a campaign pledge to incorporate or agentificate public service. After their re-election, the Hashimoto Administration set up a Council for Administrative Reform, chaired by the Prime Minister. As a result, a new organizational structure was created to comply with the agentification process: Independent Administrative Institutions (IAI), a structure created with relative autonomy from the government. During the discussions the Ministry of Education [3] defended the view that national museums and training centres for the youth should be transformed into IAI, but that national universities should remain under the Ministry's jurisdiction. This was a sensible move as the budget for national universities amount to ¥270 billion, compared to ¥5.5 billon for national museums. It can be assumed that the Ministry had a preference to maximize or at least preserve its budget and its realm of power (Yamamoto, 2004). In April 1999, a cabinet meeting decision made the transformation of national universities into independent administrative institutions an urgent matter. In July 2000, the Ministry established a study team concerning the transformation of national universities into IAI. The MEXT led the reform process. The study team was composed of members from academia, business people and experts. The majority of the team members were from national universities.

The launch of the Koizumi Cabinet in 2001 caused the Ministry to lose the leadership: the Prime Minister asked the Minister for Higher Education, Ms Toyama, to hasten the university reform process. This was part of Koizumi's actions to reform the public sector. In parallel, the Ministry of Economy, Trade and Industry (METI) called for greater flexibility in university management, and recommended the restructuring of the university system [4]. This led to the Toyama Plan, officially entitled "The Policy of Structural Reform of University". The main points of the plan are the following:

- The plan recommended that national universities should be transformed into national university corporations (NUC), a legally separate institution from the government.

---

3 In 2001, the Ministry of Education, Science, Sports and Culture (*Monbush*) merged with the Science and Technology Agency to become the Ministry of Education, Culture, Sports, Science and Technology (MEXT).

4 Priority Plan towards Creating New Markets and Jobs, see http://www.METI.go.jp/english/information/data/c2001polie.html

- Universities should prepare mid-term plans (6 years) to be submitted to the Minister.
- Universities should be evaluated by an independent institution, the National University Evaluation Committee (NUEC).
- Personnel matters should be carried out independently and autonomously by the university itself.

Following these lines, in April 2004, the Japanese government incorporated the national universities as "independent administrative entities". We can comprehend this move as double-edged; on one side appears the rhetoric for reform of the public sector coupled with downsizing elements, and on the other side this reveals a move towards more autonomy of the universities in order to achieve excellence and favours internationally competitive universities. To visualize this move towards more autonomy and excellence, we will take three examples. First is the Center of Excellence (COE) program, which is based on a MEXT report entitled "A Policy for the Structural Reform of Universities". The COE program was established in 2002 to cultivate a competitive academic environment among Japanese universities by giving targeted support for the creation of world-standard research and education. It aimed to promote through competitive funding a first-rate academic environment among Japanese national, public [5] and private universities. The project applications are screened by a committee outside the MEXT: namely the Global COE Program Committee, a structure within the Japan Society for the Promotion of Science (JSPS). The funds are given for a period of five years, and the scale of the funding ranges from ¥100 to ¥500 million a year per project. In FY2003, 113 projects of 50 universities were selected, 133 projects of 56 universities in FY2004, and 28 projects of 24 universities in FY2005. The eligible fields of research are defined by the government on a year-to-year basis (life science, interdisciplinary fields, material science, etc.) [6].

On a similar ground, the FY2004 budget allocated to the national universities (operational grant) was unchanged from that of FY2003. Furthermore, resulting from negotiations between the Ministry of Finance and the MEXT in winter 2003-2004, it was agreed that the operational grant would subsequently be reduced by 1% each year except for the component provided for faculty members' salaries. This could be seen as an indirect way to push the universities to look for alternative revenue sources, such as from industry.

---

5 Public universities are different form national universities as they are managed by local governments and not from the State.
6 See for an exhaustive list of the fields: http://www.jsps.go.jp/english/e-21coe/02.html, http://www.jsps.go.jp/english/e-globalcoe/01_outline_eligible.html

Finally, the management structures of universities are supposed to be centralized around the newly empowered university presidents. They are responsible for the management of the organization, including appointment of staff, as well as education and research matters. They are supported by the Management and Academic Councils. This gives the universities a potentially strong leadership to implement coherent educational and research policies. However, the level of their real power is still under scrutiny as the MEXT keeps considerable influence through the dispatch of former MEXT senior bureaucrats to the universities. In addition, the new members of the councils may lack management skills as they are mostly university professors.

We could refer to Goldfich (2006) to propose a critical assessment of the reform. Indeed, he argues that the university reform is rather symbolic. "Despite the rhetoric of independence and autonomy, MEXT has not given up its control over the university system — rather it has adopted the rhetoric of agentification to enable it to exert control through other means, with the mechanism of control changing largely to indirect ones." (Goldfich, 2006, p. 599). Yamamoto (2004) argues that the corporation process has a dual meaning, enhancing autonomy of the universities and a downsizing of the public sector.

In terms of global performance, we still have to wait to see whether or not the new law will improve governance and subsequently performance. The new structure is still difficult to read as the president's realm of power is still up for debate. What the effect of the evaluation system will be is another question. In order to conclude upon the reform, we will have to judge on how universities will use the newly available tools provided to them. For instance, the incorporation of national universities in 2004 meant that they would own all inventions made subsequently by their employees under commissioned and joint research. This gives the universities a strong policy instrument to manage their own knowledge base.

Epitaph or Epilogue

The reforms have just been enacted, and it is still not known exactly how it will affect university governance. However, some voices have already been rising for more changes. The new Abe Government wants to push for new reforms of the university system. The Council on Economic and Fiscal Policy (CEFP [7]) on its fourth meeting (27 February 2007) has enacted a plan to boost productivity in Japan by 50% within five years. The idea is to enhance Japanese growth potential. This will be done in three ways: developing growth areas, increasing venture capital, and university reform. According to experts of the CEFP, Japanese universities have been left far behind in the global trend. In order to

---

7 The Council on Economic and Fiscal Policy is a consultative organ placed within the Cabinet Office.

improve the university system they favour three reform paths. First, universities should concentrate on selected research areas. Second, funding should focus on the selected research areas. Finally, the CEFP is proposing to increase the proportion of competitive funds and reform rules concerning allocation of administrative expense subsidies for national university corporations.

Looking at the different waves of legislative reforms, the university looks like a sheep sacrificed on the altar of change. Different layers of reforms are overlapping. In a world where science and technology are taking an ever-increasing importance, universities are major players in societies based on science. The question is whether all the reforms are helping to create an institution that nurtures talent, technology and invention. This leads us to the broader picture of the Japanese Science and Technology (S&T) policy. We will in the next section examine how the S&T field has become central in the policy debate and what the implications are for universities.

A CHANGE IN SCIENCE AND TECHNOLOGY POLICY

A Big Bang

The most radical change in the Japanese S&T policy is without any doubt the 1995 Science and Technology Basic Law (hereinafter referred to as "the Basic Law"), and the subsequent changes it brought about. In the previous section we have mainly looked at the university reforms' political push; now we will focus on the S&T drive. Our aim is not to be exhaustive on the subject, but rather to highlight the implications of this S&T shift on university structures and missions.

The Japanese government has emphasized the need to promote basic research since the mid-1980s. The general guideline for science and technology policy, which expresses an agreement of all ministries in the Japanese government to promote science and technology, was adopted by the Cabinet in 1986 and reiterated in 1992. This general guideline for science and technology was defined by the Council of Science and Technology (CST), which was composed of cabinet ministers and agency heads, as well as representatives from university and industry. The enactment of the Science and Technology Basic Law on 15 November 1995 symbolized a firm commitment towards the promotion of research and development, determined its basic principles, and required the Japanese administration to raise science and technology related spending for five consecutive fiscal years. In response to the Basic Law, the Japanese government was required to develop and implement two successive five-year Science and Technology Basic Plans: the first effective from FY1996 through FY2001; the second from FY2001 through FY2006. The third one was drafted by the Council for Science and Technology Policy (CSTP) and enacted by the government — it will be effective from FY2006 to FY2010.

The Basic Law had some major policy implications for the universities as it shapes the formulation of the basic plans. Below are summarized the main implications for the universities of the successive plans:

1st Science and Technology Basic Plan

- Expansion of R&D Investment by the Government.
- Expansion and financial support for international exchange programs.
- Achieving a program to support 10,000 post-doctoral students by FY2000 (achieved).

2nd Science and Technology Basic Plan

- Doubling the amount of competitive funds and allocating funds (increase by 30%) for indirect expenses.
- Reinforcement of industrial technology and reform of industry-academia-government collaboration.

3rd Science and Technology Basic Plan

- Suppressing the rate of inbreeding within universities.
- Enhancing the human resource development functions of universities
- Human resource development by industry-university partnership.
- Developing smooth intellectual property (IP) activities.

We can see that the measures of the first and second plans are mainly clustered around the improvement of infrastructures and important financial efforts toward research. But we can only consider this as a first step, many scholars of the innovation process stress that the interaction of people, structures, and properly designed incentives are at the centre of the innovation matrix. Fortuitously, the 3rd Plan goes a step further, as it beckons universities to an improvement of their human resource and IP management. The human resource side is an important issue that Japanese universities will have to face if they intend to be internationally competitive. Improvement of women's opportunities, increasing the share of international staff, and the diversification of the recruitment procedures to stifle inbreeding practices within the universities are major issues for the university to face. Indeed, the incorporation of national universities gave them new prerogatives on their human resource management. The incorporated universities can decide who they will recruit, and how they will pay them, as the salary structure of the personnel is no longer directed by the National Public Service Law. Hence, presidents of universities and the board of directors, whose powers have been reinforced, have an important role to play in shaping the research potential of their universities. The third plan reveals a shift from a perspective centre for infrastructures and financing to the one based on human resources.

Together with the Basic Law, three other laws reshaped the face of Japanese transfer technology framework.

- The 1998 Law to Promote the Transfer of University Technologies (the TLO Law) legitimized and facilitated transparent and contractual transfers of university discoveries to industry.
- The 1999 Law of Special Measures to Revive Industry (the Japan Bayh-Dole Law).
- The 2000 Law to Strengthen Industrial Technology established procedures, through which university researchers can obtain permission to consult for, establish and even manage companies. It also streamlined the procedures for company sponsored commissioned and joint research.

This leads to the next section which will focus on the university-industry link's gained momentum.

The strengthening and officialization of University-Industry linkages

Japan, among other countries, is aiming to increase its national competitiveness by establishing new Industry-Science relationships. Japan tries to move out from in-house R&D type of organization to a more decentralized system. It is often seen giving strong support to "private" companies' science laboratories and minor encouragement to academic science (Nakayama & Low, 1997). One of the initiatives to attain such a goal is to improve the quality of the research done in Japan and strengthen university-industry linkages. American successes in the fields of IT and biotechnologies and the relative failure in these fields of Japan is one of the reasons to ameliorate the industry science relationship.

Fransman (1999, pp. 245-247) interviewed six biotechnology companies in order to assess their different sources of external knowledge. He found that Japanese universities are the most important source of external knowledge for these firms, more than other companies or non-Japanese universities. On the same token, Cohen et al. (2002) argue that open publication of university research results is important for private sector innovation.

The two original missions of universities are to provide education and to conduct research, a third one is now emerging: establishing a spirit of entrepreneurship [8]. We will now focus on the third emerging mission while looking at the technology transfer mechanisms of Japanese universities.

---

8 See Etzkowitz (2002) for further discussions on the subject.

University-Industry technology transfer

University-Industry collaboration has evolved recently in order to facilitate interaction between the two entities. Until 1980, restrictive government regulations have caused low level of university-industry collaboration. In 1983 the Ministry of Education relaxed its rules through which national universities could cooperate with industry. However, it is only after the S&T Basic Law and the TLO Law that we have seen real changes.

The important thing to note is that there is an ongoing change in the technology transfer procedure. Up until recently the links have been mainly informal; a teacher basically having networks of client companies he deals with. The pattern was the following: in exchange for donations, professors would inform donors of their research progress and let the donors file patent applications. They would also encourage qualified students to consider the donors as future work places upon graduation [9]. The system was fast and low-cost, but was lacking incentives for the industry to develop all the technologies given by the university, and missing the transparency necessary for global technology transfer management by a university. The TLO Law was one of the steps towards a more coherent policy.

In 1997, the MITI (now METI), in coordination with the Ministry of Education, proposed to extend the support of university-industry cooperation. A major element of this initiative was the creation of TLOs. The Technology Transfer Law authorized universities to establish semi-independent TLOs that could sell or license inventions and distribute royalties to inventors and the university. However, academic inventors are not obligated to assign their inventions to the TLOs and can continue to transfer their inventions directly to companies. Kneller (2003b) suggests that inventors often turn to the TLOs only when an invention has no takers. In order to boost the efficiency of TLOs, the MEXT went a step further.

In 2003, just before the incorporation of the national universities, MEXT established and began to subsidize 34 IP Management Offices within universities in order to bolster the TLOs and to give universities in-house IP management expertise. But their responsibilities overlap those of the TLOs, and they have final authority over patenting and licensing decisions. In some universities, relations between the IP Management Offices and TLOs have been managed smoothly, but in others there has been friction. The problem is that there is a conflict of interest between the two structures. The inventor has many people to deal with, and the delimitation of power is not clear between the TLO and IP management Offices. An important issue for the newly incorporated universities to address is to resolve these problems of competency between the two structures in order to create synergies.

---

9 See Kneller (2003b) and Kneller (2007) for a discussion on the subject.

Another policy initiative designed to encourage university-industry linkages was the "Hiranuma Plan", initiated by the METI in 2001. This plan included a goal of establishing 1,000 university start-ups in three years (as well as subsidies designed to foster that goal), sending a clear signal to universities. This movement was salutary as the number of start-ups increased from 26 in 1998 to more than 1,000 in 2005. METI has budgeted ¥47.6 billion (2002), ¥47.4 billion (2003) and ¥61.7 billion (2004) for the Hiranuma Plan.

This initiative can be seen as a way to increase the chances of talented young scholars. Indeed the relation between university and industry in Japan is biased towards big companies. As an example, the data show that big companies account for around 70% of joint research projects (MEXT, 2005). Therefore, as some evidence shows [10], if you buy the argument that small companies are needed to develop certain kinds of technologies, nurturing start-up from universities becomes essential.

Overall, the scale of the cooperation between industry and university has been magnified, for instance the number of joint research contracts jumped from 1,139 in 1991 to 9,378 in 2004, the amount of these contracts increased from less than ¥4 billion to ¥20 billion in 2004. Through different means the interactions are increasing, creating a new research environment for conducting scientific research at universities.

CONCLUSION

To conclude, we will take the case of Tohoku University to illustrate two points we have discussed in this paper: the changes in IP policy, and the organizational *millefeuille* of the newly created university structure.

Tohoku University was founded in Sendai in 1907 as Tohoku Imperial University. It was the third Imperial University in Japan. It is located in Sendai, the most important city of the Tohoku Region (North-East of Japan). It is known as a strong research university; the 2006 Shanghai academic ranking put it in the 4th place among Japanese universities and 76th in the world. The Thomson ISI list of most cited papers in the world ranked Tohoku University 2nd for material science, 13th for physics and 22nd for chemistry [11].

The graph below shows the three steps upward hike of the university's patenting activity. The activity was very low up to 1999, in 2000 the trend started to increase slowly and from 2004 onward the numbers skyrocketed.

We can relate these trends with the different policy changes; we see a huge surge of patent applications after 2004 and the introduction of the incorporation of Japanese national universities. The upward trend is following the

---

10 For instance, see Motohashi (2005).
11 Figures collected from Tohoku University internal documents.

Figure 1: Tohoku University patent application

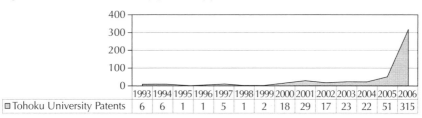

	1993	1994	1995	1996	1997	1998	1999	2000	2001	2002	2003	2004	2005	2006
▣ Tohoku University Patents	6	6	1	1	5	1	2	18	29	17	23	22	51	315

Figures compiled by the authors

major policy changes regarding the push to market of Japanese inventions: TLO Law (1998), Japanese Bay-Dole Act (1999), and the Corporatization of National Universities (2003). Anecdotally, Tohoku University became the university which patents the most in Japan in 2006.

Moreover, we can notice an important change of structure of the applicant's profile before and after the incorporation. Indeed, previously, the majority of applicants were not the university itself, but were rather faculty members, but this pattern changed after 2005, and the number of applications by the university started to increase. Before the reform national universities did not have a status distinct from the government, and they could hardly apply for a patent by themselves; with the incorporation they became an independent legal entity. The universities' change of status gave them more power to manage their IP. Since 2004, the inventor has to transfer its IP rights to the university property rights centre which decides whether to apply for a patent. An identical trend can be seen in all the former national universities, with a jump of the number of patent applications starting from 809 in FY2003 to 4,171 in FY2006.

The figure above shows the complexity of the cooperative research structure at Tohoku University. At the centre, there is the Office of Cooperative Research and Development; it is at the centre of a nexus of supporting institutions. The links between all the elements are not straightforward, and the powers and prerogatives are entangled. The reform of the university and technology transfer system opened a Pandora's Box. Many supporting structures, often overlapping, have sprouted.

To illustrate our argument, looking at Figure 2, we could consider merging the missions of the TLO and the Intellectual property division. Simplifying the structure would make more flexible supporting activities and could promote a further promotion of technological transfer from industry to university and vice versa. Such relation should be based on our view on three concepts:

- Favour local and small entrepreneurial companies.
- Encourage mobility and creativity of the university personnel.
- Support the poles of excellence of the university and have a redistributive strategy among the faculties.

Figure 2: Tohoku University cooperative research structure

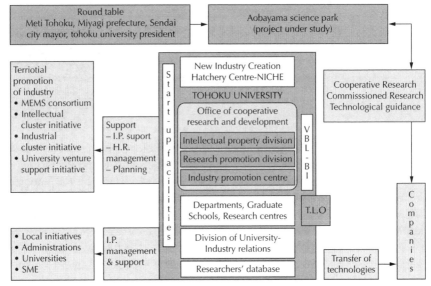

Source: Tohoku University internal documents, translated by the authors.

The Japanese university system is at a crossroad. It is therefore an adequate time to scrutinize the process of change; squeezed between a politically driven agenda and the urge to adapt to the changes of the scientific enterprise. It is at a crucial point in time, and the university has to adapt its structure and to respond to new scientific ethos. The difficult choices lie here and it is like facing the two mythological monsters Scylla and Charybdis on the way to progress. The university has to confront them to continue its journey towards modernity.

REFERENCES

Cohen, W.M., Goto, A., Nagata, A., Nelson, R.R. & Walsh, J. P. (2002). "R&D spill-overs, patents and the incentives to innovate in Japan and the United States", *Research Policy*, 31, pp. 1349-1367.

Etzkowitz, H. (2002). *MIT and the Rise of Entrepreneurial Science*. Routledge, London.

Foray, D. (2003). *The Economics of Knowledge*, MIT Press, Cambridg.

Fransman, M. (1999). *Vision of Innovation: the Firm and Japan*, Clarendon Press, Oxford.

Goldfinch S. (2006). "Rituals of reform, policy transfer, and national university corporation reforms in Japan", *Governance: an International Journal of Policy, Administration and Institutions*, 19(4), pp. 585-604.

Kneller, R.W. (2003). "Autarkic drug discovery in Japanese pharmaceutical companies: insights into national differences in industrial innovation", *Research Policy*, 32, pp. 1805-1827.

Kneller, R.W. (2003b). "University-industry cooperation and technology transfer in Japan compared with the U.S.: Another reason for Japan's economic malaise?" *University of Pennsylvania Journal of International Economic Law*, 24(2), pp. 329-449.

Kneller, R.W. (2007). "The beginning of university entrepreneurship in Japan: TLOs and bioventures lead the way", *Journal of Technology Transfer*, 32(4), pp. 435-456.

MEXT. (2005). "University-industry cooperation: The actual situation in universities in 2004". In Japanese, available at http://www.MEXT.go.jp/b_menu/houdou/17/06/05062201.htm

MEXT. (2006). White paper on Science and Technology. See http://www.MEXT.go.jp/english/news/2007/03/07022214.htm

Motohashi, K. (2005). "University-industry collaborations in Japan: The role of new Technology-based firms in transforming the National Innovation System", *Research Policy*, 34 (5), pp. 583-594.

Nakayama, S. & Low, M. (1997). "The research function of Universities", *Japan Higher Education*, 34, pp. 245-258.

NISTEP (2004). *Science and Technology indicators: 2004*, Ministry of Education, Culture, Sports, Science and Technology, Japan.

Oba, J. (2005). "Development of the autonomy in French and Japanese universities: a comparative study on the French contractual policy and incorporation of Japanese universities", *Higher Education Research in Japan*, Vol. 2, RIHE.

OECD. (2005). Education at a glance. OECD indicators at a glance. OECD, Paris.

Yamamoto, K. (2004). "Corporatization of National Universities in Japan: Revolution for Governance or Rhetoric for Downsizing?" *Financial Accountability & Management*, 20(2), pp. 153-181.

CHAPTER 9

Russian Universities in the Global World

Vladimir Troyan

INTRODUCTION

Modern knowledge, economy and social development are creating a new, rapidly changing intellectual labour market. Institutes of higher education should constantly modify and upgrade educational programmes and technologies, update equipment and support lecturers' professional development. Institutes of higher education should react adequately to external environment challenges, switch to innovative development, follow the market and even create it in a number of cases.

Now, institutes of higher education in developed countries are being challenged by changes in the external environment, loss of former stability, reduction of government financing and, at the same time, prompt expansion of requirements from consumers wanting their primary activity products — scientific research, technological developments, educational services and qualified experts. In Russia the delayed stage of social and economic reforms intensifies these factors influencing the whole higher education system and every institute of higher education.

Experts note a significant asymmetry and imbalance of relations in institutes of higher education with the external environment which give rise to dissatisfaction of the institute of higher education with the organizational management and prompts demand for reforms.

Analysis of adaptation by leading US and Europe universities to the changes of social and economic conditions of external environment in the 1990s has shown that basic transformations of institutes of higher education were caused by changes in economic structure, in the role of the state and the demographic situation, all connected to the development of technologies and the processes of globalization. Russian institutes of higher education are going the same way, with diminishing delay.

The changes in age groups, the ageing of populations in the world's developed countries, the internationalization of education, increase in academic mobility and expansion of need for continuous education, all lead to varying contingents of trainees entering institutes of higher education. This necessitates continuous perfection of programmes, professional development of lecturers, updating of teaching and methodical support and use of new teaching technologies.

The changes in technological development, in particular in the field of information and communication technologies, require the same. The wide application of new high-level technologies in modern production necessitates intensive fundamental scientific research in the institutes of higher education, performance of applied developments and the organization of technology transfer and use of the newest results for the educational process.

Economic globalization intensifies the specified changes in the external environment of the institutes of higher education as factors influencing their behaviour. Emerging global markets of high-technology products, intellectual labour and educational services create new competition conditions for universities, stimulating them to change the organizational management with a greater focus on the needs of people and society, under conditions of adherence to state interests.

The results of monitoring and inspection of the higher professional education system in Russia show that the processes of transformations connected to changes in the external environment can also be observed in Russia's institutes of higher education.

The institute of higher education is continuously interacting with its environment — it communicates, studies society's needs, obtains financing, attracts resources, develops cooperation, gains experience, delivers products, renders services and so forth. In order to hold and consolidate the position of the institute of higher education in the external environment, this interaction should be more and more active, intensive and effective.

In order to gain the competitive advantage in modern markets for intellectual labour and educational services, institutes of higher education should make certain changes which could result in reforms of the institutes themselves and even in a new type of institution of higher education — the innovative, academic university.

All this can be achieved by the modernization of the organizational management system of the institute of higher education as a whole, with the introduction of market mechanisms and the direction of its efforts to ensure that society's needs are met.

In recent years, Russia has confidently taken its place in the global economic environment. Owing to high prices for energy resources, the country has been able not only to pay off its debts — the "legacy" of the Soviet Union — ahead of time, but also to set up the stabilisation fund and the national projects system. One of the top-priority national projects is the "Education" project. A significant part of this project is devoted to the creation of a system of innovative development for Russian universities. The competitive system of prioritizing financial support of the best universities proved to match the global tendencies of development in higher education.

INNOVATIVE RUSSIAN UNIVERSITIES

The first step in this direction was made by the special competition in the scope of the national "Education" project of the leading innovative universities in the Russian Federation in 2006. There were two levels of competition. On the first level, 17 universities were winners, and, on the second level, 40 universities were winners from different regions of Russia. These 57 universities represented the best projects of the innovative development of the universities. Each university has received between 200 million rubles (US$8 million) and 1 billion rubles (US$40 million) for two years. One of the most important conditions of the competition was the financial investment from the university to the project of more than 20% from the common sum of the project. The money from the project will be used for new equipment, for research for raising the qualifications of teaching staff, including scholarships to leading universities in Europe, the US, Japan, Canada, etc.

RUSSIAN UNIVERSITIES IN THE BOLOGNA PROCESS

Russia is making major progress towards globalization in the higher education system, together with Europe within the framework of the Bologna Process which it joined in 2003 in Berlin. Russian universities are closely connected historically with the European system of higher education.

The Russian system of higher education originates from Peter the Great's Decree of 28 January 1724 on the institution of the Grammar School, the University and the Academy of Sciences. The experience of European universities was made use of in the establishment of this triad. Peter the Great corresponded with prominent scientists of his time and considered various projects for the institution of the University and the Academy of Sciences. The project offered by the outstanding 18th-century German scientist Leibnitz in his letters to the Tsar is worthy of special attention. The statutes of the Academy of Sciences, the University and the Grammar School set out the goals and tasks of these governmental institutions. The grammar school envisaged training under secondary education programmes with advanced studies in mathematics, languages and natural sciences. Grammar school graduates had an opportunity to continue education at university. Upon graduation from the university, the graduates could work as teachers, engage in scientific research or become civil servants and diplomats. Usually capable students had scientific advisors — academicians — and were supervised and trained by them as they prepared for scientific work and further teaching at the university. A specific feature of Peter's university was the active participation of students in research work — an example of the research university close in ideology to Alexander Humboldt's model. At the period of establishment of the university and the academy, brilliant, world-famous scientists such as L. Euler, D. Bernulli, A. D. Kantemir, G. Z. Bayer. V. Lomonosov and many others worked there.

By joining the Bologna Process, Russia not only became a full member of the European educational environment, but also an active player in this field, capable of influencing the process of development while preserving the best traditions of the Russian high school: fundamentality and profound theoretical knowledge (www.bologna.spbu.ru).

One of the provisions of Bologna Process supposes transition to the three-level system of education: Bachelor, Master, Ph.D. This system is totally in line with the Russian Federation Law "On higher professional and post-university education". Apart from this three-stage system, there is mass-scale training in Russia in the categories: qualified specialist — aspirant to the doctor's degree. In the long term, qualified specialists will probably remain in a number of specialities: doctors, some engineering specialities, creative specialities. The advantages of the Bachelor-Master system are connected with the necessity of fast updating of knowledge. The training of graduates supposes that the student gets a broad education and the ability to update knowledge and skills promptly, in accordance with set tasks. In Russia at present the bachelor's course runs for four years, the master's for two years. It should be noted that the bachelor's degree corresponds to a complete higher education. A graduate may work in any establishment, in companies, firms, in the banking system, in small and medium business, in the service industry. Normally a graduate gains the necessary skills and knowledge on the spot, learning at special courses while working. Masters and Ph.D.s, as a rule, find jobs at research institutes or at universities. The inclusion of postgraduate studies in the third stage of training requires the enhancement of the educational component within the postgraduate course: lectures and seminars on the chosen speciality, work in science, and the opening of new scientific fields.

When shifting to the Bologna Process, it is principally important to preserve the essentially attractive features of the Russian system of higher education: fundamentality, scientific/pedagogical schools and preparedness for innovative transformation.

In addition to the document on higher education — the diploma — the graduate at Russian universities will be given a supplement to the diploma containing the following data: information on the diploma-holder, on his qualification and its level, on the contents of the educational programme and the results gained; information on professional and job-related orientation of the qualification, on formal certification of the given supplement in the given country; description of the system of higher education in the country, supplementary information at the discretion of the university. The supplement to the diploma is executed in Russian and in one of the European languages, usually English. At present a number of Russian higher schools, as an experiment, issue the supplement to the diploma to meet all requirements of the Bologna Process.

The next element of the Bologna Process — the mobility of students and teachers — is already being implemented in Russian universities within the framework of bilateral agreements with foreign universities. Certainly, this exchange does not take place as a mass-scale phenomenon, basically for purely economic reasons. In our country, the system of grants provided to students on a competitive basis for training abroad during one semester is insufficiently developed. Further development of the system of state and private funds will enable students and teachers of Russian higher schools to enjoy academic mobility.

For the due realization of the principle of mobility, so that the courses read to the students at another university were deemed as completed within the Russian system, a standard, generally accepted system of test units or assessment marks is necessary. Such a system has been developed — ECTS (European Credit Transfer System). One credit in European countries corresponds to 36 academic hours. The total number of test units (credits) for the bachelor is about 180 hours. As a rule, a student, jointly with his tutor, makes an individual plan including obligatory and optional courses. In a number of universities in Russia, alongside the traditional 5-grade system, a 10-grade system is being introduced. The student is given a corresponding number of test units for a course if he was given a positive assessment mark at the examination in the conditions of 5-grade system — not below 3.

As noted in the concept of modernisation of education in the Russian Federation, the major purpose of the modernisation process is the improvement of the quality of schooling of higher schools graduates. The problem of quality of higher education is central in the Bologna Process as well. As a rule, two models of quality assurance are used: a governmental body (in the Russian Federation, federal service for supervision in the sphere of education and science) or public organizations, professional associations and independent agencies. At present most Russian universities have departments or boards engaged in internal control of the quality of the educational process. Undoubtedly, the principal person responsible for the quality of specialist training is the pedagogue. The issues of quality of education are directly connected with the procedure of accreditation of the university and of particular educational programmes. In Russia the accreditation of universities is made by the Agency for Certification and Accreditation, though the Law "On Education" envisages the possibility of public accreditation in addition to governmental accreditation. Some Russian universities, in addition to state accreditation, are granted international accreditation of the university as such or of particular educational programmes. At present there is a broad network of accreditation agencies in Europe. The internationalization of accreditation procedures will make it possible to achieve competitiveness of the Russian universities in the context of globalization.

One of the most acute problems that are to be solved by the Bologna Process is reciprocal recognition of qualifying documents in higher education and scientific degrees. An important step in this direction was taken in Lisbon in 1997 when the Convention on recognition of higher education qualifications in Europe was signed. The convention was signed by the overwhelming majority of European countries, Russia, US, Canada and Australia. It should be noted that most of the provisions of the convention have a recommendatory character and are not binding. A seminar on mutual recognition of qualifications took place in Lisbon in 2002 within the framework of Bologna Process, where a number of recommendations were developed:

- It is supposed to pay principal attention to the results of education and gained skills (competencies), instead of the time of training and names of courses.
- It is expedient to develop bilateral contacts between the universities and joint educational programmes, with issue of documents on jointly awarded degrees.
- To create conditions for having full-scale knowledge about the educational systems in different countries and in particular universities.
- To provide development of the system of external assessment of education quality, to apply to international accreditation agencies.
- To inform university teachers, administration, undergraduate and postgraduate students of the problems of recognition of qualifications and scientific degrees.

All these recommendations were taken into account at leading Russian universities.

An important aspect of the Bologna Process is the autonomy of the university. Special attention is being given to this issue in the modernisation of the Russian education. The development of autonomy of a university is connected with the processes of democratization and reciprocal responsibility of the university and the state. A number of provisions concerning the autonomy of universities, characteristic of the European universities, totally comply with the present-day Russian conditions:

- Independent management of the university and realization of strategic planning.
- Choice of partners, both Russian and foreign, for research and educational activities.
- Independent adjustment of curricula and syllabi within the framework of state-prescribed standards, that are developed by training-and-methodology associations and are submitted to the Ministry for approval and are further passed to the university where they can be altered and supplemented to some extent (5-10%).
- Settlement of personnel issues — employment of teachers and research workers.
- Independent admission to the university, to fill the allocated state-budgeted positions.

However, the problem of the independent use of finance within the framework of approved budgets involves a number of restrictions connected with the so-called budget funding and excessive custody of the Board of Treasury. There should be more mutual trust between the university and financial bodies, with strict accountancy and transparency of financial matters of the university, not only for the controlling financial bodies, but also for the university public at large.

"The Great University Charter" adopted in Bologna in 1988 states: "The university functions in the societies having differing organisation being the consequence of different geographical and historical conditions, and represents an institute that critically interprets and disseminates culture by way of research and teaching. To meet the requirements of the modern world, it should be morally and scientifically independent of political and economic authorities in its research and teaching activity." The Charter was signed by Rector of St Petersburg State University, S.P. Merkuryev. Within the two last decades St Petersburg University has consistently supported widening the autonomy of universities, especially as concerns development of educational programmes and new specialities demanded by modern society, in the first place, interdisciplinary programmes. The rigorous system of educational standards impedes the dynamics of innovative development of the leading universities of Russia.

The unity of the educational and scientific processes is a cornerstone of higher education in Russia. In the pre-revolutionary period, the scientific research was concentrated in some leading universities of Russia. In the 1930s the situation changed somewhat in connection with the institution of a great number of academic research institutes. However, leading universities continued to preserve the tradition of the unity of educational and scientific processes. It is very important that the Bologna Process is aimed at further development of scientific research at the universities with the obligatory involvement of students in research. In Russia, according to statutory documents, every teacher must devote half his work hours to scientific research. A teacher actively involved in science introduces in his course the spirit of new ideas and due research dynamics. At present conferences and seminars devoted to the development of Bologna Process refer to the integrated European educational and scientific research environment. Therefore participation of Russia in the Bologna Process will stimulate the development of scientific research in Russian universities.

A very important step of the reformation of the Russian science-education sphere will be the transformation of the Russian Academy of Sciences. The main aims of this action will be the integration with the leading Russian universities and the extension of the innovative character of research results. This step is very important for the training of highly qualified specialists.

International cooperation plays a very important role in the Bologna process. Therefore joint master and doctoral programmes between Russian and European Universities are very significant. As an example, I would like to point to joint master programmes run by St Petersburg University with German universities. The Master Programme "Applied polar and marine study" was organized five years ago between St Petersburg University and Bremen, Kiel and Hamburg Universities. Students receive their qualification (Master's degree) from St Petersburg University and Bremen University. The programme is accredited in Germany and in Russia. Students have two supervisors, one from St Petersburg University, the other from a German university. Students do practical work on Russian and German polar research ships. This year is a so-called "Polar Year"; therefore this programme is very up-to-date. The next example is a joint master programme "Applied Physics and Computational Physics" between St Petersburg University and the Technical University of Munich, Technical University of Ilmenau and Leipzig University. This programme is very important in connection with the development of Nano-technology and the Nano-industry in Russia. The practical work for our students will be in the Russian Research Center (Kurchatov Institute) and in the Nanotechnology Center of the Technical University of Munich. An example in the humanities is the joint master programme "Europe Study", organized by St Petersburg University and Bielefeld University.

Our Masters and Ph.D. students are involved in many international research projects, for example, with CERN (Geneva) Ion collider (ALICE project), with BESSY-2 Synchrotron Radiation (Karlshorst, Berlin, Germany), SHELL Research Centre Seismic Processing (The Netherlands), Tokyo Electro-Communication University Earthquake Prediction (Japan) and many others.

The next important element of the Bologna Process is development of the system of continuous education — Lifelong Learning (LLL). The fast development of new technologies and introduction of latest research achievements in practice is leading to the need to update knowledge and gain new skills and competencies. Besides which, the labour market is changing dynamically, which brings about the need for graduates to master a new speciality (second higher education). Sometimes it is enough to attend a short-term course and to implement the gained knowledge by practical classes. Russian universities have been paying more and more attention to these issues recently, especially with regard to the demographic recession expected in Russia.

The Bologna declaration proclaims the necessity of preserving major European values. This thesis is especially important in the context of the globalising world. It should be noted that Russia has made an appreciable contribution to European culture, so Russian universities, being not only centres of science and education, but also centres of culture, naturally advocate the preservation and further development of the spiritual and cultural heritage of Russia and Europe. We should not lose our cultural traditions in the competitive struggle in the market of educational services.

The Bologna declaration draws the universities' attention to their social responsibility in the development of the modern society. The concept of social responsibility is highly multifaceted and includes:

- Accessibility of higher education for capable young people irrespective of their material condition.
- Training of specialists at the level of up-to-date requirements.
- Training of political, economic and cultural elite who will secure the efficient development of the country.
- Development of science and new advanced technologies promoting the progress of the society.
- Reproduction of intellectual resources and human capital.

The modern state of the Russian universities in relation to the major elements of the Bologna Process is presented in the report of A.A. Fursenko, Minister of Education and Science, read in Bergen in 2005 and in London in 2007, at the meetings of Ministers of Education of the countries-participants of Bologna Process. Below are the data published on the Internet by results of the meeting in Bergen (http://www.bologna-bergen2005.no):

- Two-level programmes are introduced in half of all Russian universities for more than 100 specializations, except for medicine, military disciplines and information security (the bachelor training takes place in 681 universities [50.7%], the master training — in 305 universities [22.7%]).

- 752 universities include postgraduate studies as a third stage of training.
- 31 universities (2.5%) are participating in the pilot project of introduction of the system of credits (ECTS) for certain educational programmes (10-15%).
- The issue of appendices to the diploma (Diploma Supplement) under the Bologna Process standards is realized in a number of universities as a pilot project.
- The quality control system is practised in all universities: 568 state-run (federal) universities and their 1,242 branches; 52 accredited (non-federal) universities, 352 accredited (private) universities and their 341 branches.

The analysis of these data shows that Russian universities are in a number of parameters within the framework of introduction of the Bologna declaration principles, for instance the use of credits system and issue of supplement to the diploma remain behind in the meantime from the European universities. At the same time the transition to the two-level system and inclusion of postgraduate training as a third stage in educational process are the positive achievements of Russian universities. If the European universities which started the transition to the principles of Bologna Process plan to complete this process by 2010, the same will take place in Russia approximately in 2014-2015. But, at least, one can already observe good dynamics in the adaptation of Russian universities to the principles of Bologna declaration.

CONCLUSION

At present Russian universities cooperate actively in the world's education and research with leading research and educational centres in the US, Europe, Asia, and Latin America. Joint educational programmes are created, joint research projects are carried out by Russian and foreign Foundations.

Since 2003 Russia is linked to the Bologna Declaration, entering the European educational system as a competent member and receiving the possibility of active influence on its development. The transition to the three-cycle system with all other elements of the Bologna requirement will be evolutionally with the preservation of the best traditions of Russian universities.

The integration of Russia into the world educational space should be accompanied, in the condition of the adjunction to the WTO, foreign economical policy including both the export of educational surveys and its import.

Russian universities will develop the mobility of students, teachers and researchers, invite foreign students to come to Russia and create branches in other countries, developing distance learning.

PART III

••••••••••••

Global Strategies
for Emerging Universities
and Univerity Systems

CHAPTER 10

Response of Chinese Higher Education and SJTU to Globalization: An Overview

Jie Zhang

INTRODUCTION

Globalization means more competition and that a nation's investment, production and innovation are not limited by its borders. Internationalization, according to Levin (2001), is one set of behaviour influenced by globalization processes. These processes are not only political and economic, but also social and cultural, and also include education. Internationalization has become the basic measure for universities on a global level. Universities have been affected greatly by globalization and have seen vast cultural, economic and technological transformations at all levels.

In order to face the challenges and demands of globalization, Chinese higher education institutions (HEIs) have been expanding and strengthening international academic exchange and cooperation, increasing the number of students going abroad as well as the number of foreign students studying in China, encouraging their faculty to constantly improve themselves and to develop research collaboration.

OVERVIEW OF CHINESE HIGHER EDUCATION

The history of Chinese modern higher education could be ascended to the late-19th century. With the arrival of gunboats in the war, Chinese intellectuals discovered the numerous Western advances in science and technology. One of their attempts of learning from Western advances was the building of universities and colleges. Many foreign groups such as French Jesuit missionaries and American Protestants also created a number of higher education institutions (HEIs) in China before 1949. After the foundation of People's Republic of China, in the early 1950s all HEIs were brought under government leadership and the whole higher education system was restructured in the form of the Soviet model. Consequently, every HEI became a specialized institution, and research was separated from higher education. From 1967 to 1976, China's Cultural Revolution greatly devastated higher education, and most HEIs stopped admitting students during that time. From the late 1970s, with the implementation of reform and the opening-up policy, Chinese higher education underwent a series of reforms and began to make new strides.

Nowadays, there are more than 1,800 universities and colleges in China — about 38% of them can award bachelor degrees. In 2006, the total numbers of undergraduate admissions and postgraduate admissions were 5,500,000 and 400,000 respectively. And the total number of students enrolled in various Chinese higher education institutions reached 25 million, becoming the largest higher education system in the world (Ministry of Education of China, 2007).

It has come to our notice that private higher education has developed rapidly in recent years. Approximately 1.5 million students enrolled in 278 private higher education institutions in 2006, about 6% of the national total (Ministry of Education of China, 2007). Almost all of the private HEIs are focused on undergraduate education, most of them awarding only undergraduate certificates, without the power of awarding bachelor degrees.

PROFILE OF OVERSEAS STUDENTS IN CHINA

Statistics of overseas students can give an intuitive impression of the situation of Chinese international education. Figure 1 shows that the number of overseas students enrolled within Chinese HEIs has increased steadily since 2003. The annual growth rate was 21% on average during the period 2001-2006. In 2006, China received 162,000 oversea students from 184 countries, which is the highest number since 1949, and more than 8,000 students obtained Chinese government scholarships (China Scholarship Council, 2007). However, considering the huge gross amount, the proportion of overseas students is still very low (less than 1%).

A majority of overseas students studying within China are from Asia, approximately three-quarters in 2006. Among 184 countries, South Korea makes up the largest proportion (35%), followed by Japan (11%), USA (7%), Vietnam (4%) and Indonesia (3%). Chinese universities and colleges are still less attractive than those of most developed countries since only one third of overseas students are degree-seeking students. In addition, overseas students

Figure 1: Total Number of Overseas Students Enrolled in HEIs 2001-2006

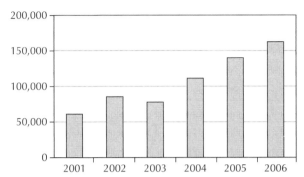

enrolled in Chinese-related subjects are very high, including Chinese Language (60%) and Chinese Traditional Medicine (4%). By contrast, the percentage of overseas students enrolled in all S&T subjects is only 4% (China Scholarship Council, 2007).

INTERNATIONAL COLLABORATIVE PROGRAMMES

China is opening its doors to foreign higher education providers at a time when competition and markets are being expanded domestically. Presently there are five major international collaborative models, including (i) independent campuses in China set up by overseas universities; (ii) joint institutes or schools; (iii) dual degree programmes; (iv) joint programmes or projects; and (v) overseas campuses set up by Chinese universities. These five models are actively impacting Chinese higher education through the availability of high-quality education resources and through the development of international collaborations.

Model I: Independent Campuses (in China)
of Overseas Universities

This model mainly introduces the ideas, teaching methods and evaluation systems of world-class universities to China. The most typical example of this model is the University of Nottingham-Ningbo, which is sponsored by the City of Ningbo and run by the University of Nottingham with cooperation from Zhejiang Wanli College. It opened as the first Sino-Foreign university in China with approval from the Chinese Ministry of Education in 2004. All degree programmes are conducted entirely in English with the same teaching and evaluation standards as in the Nottingham University in the UK. In addition, every student has the opportunity to study at Nottingham UK for a short period in the summer. In 2006, the Xi'an Jiaotong-Liverpool University at

Suzhou was founded, starting up with the subjects of science, engineering and management, and using English as the teaching language. It is a form of cooperation between two prestigious partners, Xi'an Jiaotong University in China and the University of Liverpool in the UK.

Model II: Joint Institutes

Until now, there has been only one example of this model, the Joint Institute of Shanghai Jiao Tong University, China and University of Michigan, USA. The Joint Institute was founded in 2006, which created a unique organizational linkage between a US and a Chinese university by providing a joint governance structure to manage and direct degree-granting programmes offered by both universities to students from both nations. The joint board of directors is made up of people from two universities, five each. The relationship between SJTU and U-M began in 1997, mainly through the exchange of engineering education. In 2001, the Chinese Ministry of Education approved an agreement by the U-M College of Engineering and SJTU that made U-M the first non-Chinese academic institution approved to offer graduate engineering degrees to students in China. U-M has conferred more than 50 degrees to SJTU students since that time. The creating of the Joint Institute formalized the degree-granting process and expanded the programmes to include undergraduate and graduate degrees.

Model III: Dual Degree Programmes

This model is characterized by awarding students both Chinese and foreign degrees. The earliest dual degree programme, an MBA programme, was established in 1987 by Tianjin University of Finance & Economics and Oklahoma University. By the end of June 2004, there were 164 dual degree programmes, involving 54,000 students (Ministry of Education of China, 2005). These programmes mostly focus on professional fields such as MBA. As a result, these programmes are particularly attractive for students who want to gain useful experience for attaining top-level management job positions in China. The scope of international dual degree programmes in China is still narrow, and they usually require very expensive tuition fees, so that development of such programmes is controlled primarily by market demand.

Model IV: Joint Programmes and Projects

This is the most popular model of international cooperation in Chinese HEIs. The joint programmes enable students to study at foreign partner universities for one or two semesters. Students' credits were recognized by their universities of origin. For instance, SJTU has more than 50 joint programmes and projects with universities from USA, Canada, England, France, Germany, the Netherlands, Singapore, South Korea and Australia, etc. And more than 1,500 students have already benefited at SJTU from such schemes, including both Chinese and foreign students.

Model V: Overseas Campuses Set up by Chinese Universities

This is a rather new model in China. Opening overseas campuses requires economic strength. Consequently, Chinese universities seldom actualize this model. As a pioneer, SJTU set up a graduate School in Singapore in 2002, in collaboration with Nanyang Technology University. The school has already granted 250 MBA degrees in total.

Implementation of these five models can be expected to help expand international cooperation, foster talent and aid universities in global development. Cooperation programmes in particular can be used to promote university brand. The students do not need to pay the high fees normally required to go abroad to study, and they can take advantage of world-class university educational resources, learn English, and strengthen international communications. In many cases, students can also obtain degrees from foreign universities. Compared to students in Chinese universities, such students have a lot more opportunities to develop and obtain employment domestically and abroad. Through these models, Chinese universities can improve their own level of international cooperation and increase their impact on the world.

NATIONAL INITIATIVES

Laws and Regulations

After China joined the WTO, foreign universities and international companies began to directly invest in the running of schools. However, according to the WTO convention, foreign institutions are not allowed to run schools independently in China. The Chinese government issued policy documents based on protecting Chinese education and culture that were designed to moderate the external opening of the education field. On 19 February 2003, the Chinese government adopted "Regulations of the People's Republic of China on Chinese-Foreign Cooperation in Running Schools". The regulation applies to the activities of the cooperation between foreign educational institutions and Chinese educational institutions within China, and it clearly prescribed steps and requirements for setting up, organizing, managing and supervising teaching in cooperatively run schools (Ministry of Education, 2003). Chinese overseas cooperation has obtained good results since the implementation of the regulations. By 2004, the Chinese government had approved nearly 800 programmes designed to conduct collaborations between Chinese HEIs and their foreign partners. Among them, about 270 were degree programmes involving about 100 universities and colleges (Zhou, 2006). At present about 1,400 foreign higher education institutions have been approved by various education authorities in China to operate in the country (Altbach, 2006).

The '985 Project'

At the 100th anniversary of Peking University (in May 1998), the President of China declared that China should have several world-class universities, which resulted in the "985 Project". The main goal of the project is to help China's top universities improve international competitiveness, and finally become world-class universities. The total funding for the 34 universities was 28.3 billion RMB for a period of three years, of which 15.0 billion RMB was from the central government. For Phase II of the "985 Project", 33.0 billion RMB has been allocated to 38 universities for the period of 2004-2007. Nine universities received the largest amount of support from the governments in the "985 Project". They are Tsinghua University, Peking University, Shanghai Jiao Tong University, Fudan University, Zhejiang University, Nanjing University, Xi'an Jiao Tong University, University of Science and Technology of China, and Harbin Institute of Technology. In terms of the performance as percentages of all Chinese HEIs, these top nine universities account for 44% of the State Key Labs, 42% of articles indexed in SCIE and SSCI of Thomson Scientific, 42% of the academicians of Chinese Academy of Sciences and Chinese Academy of Engineering, 20% of the research income and 20% of enrolled doctoral students (Liu, 2007).

Projects to Attract Overseas Scholars

Another major national strategy in responding to globalization is to launch special initiatives and projects to attract overseas scholars. For example, the "Changjiang Scholar Incentive Program", initiated by Chinese Ministry of Education and funded by Jia Cheng LI, a very successful Chinese entrepreneur. In order to attract world famous scholars, the "Changjiang Scholar Incentive Program" provides significant amount of research funding to selected scholars, and gives them a special bonus besides their normal salaries. From 1998 to 2006, more than 1,200 professors have been appointed, including 309 adjunct professors working abroad (*People's Daily Abroad Edition*, 2007). Other initiatives of such kind are "The Fund for Returnees to Launch S&T Researches", "Program for Training Talents toward the 21st century", "The Chunhui Program", "Program of Academic Short-return for Scholars and Research Overseas", etc. (See: http://www.moe.edu.cn/english/international_2.htm).

Projects to Prepare for the Future: Sending Students Abroad

Sending students abroad is also an import part of international education cooperation and communication. From 1987 to 2005 China sent 930,000 students abroad to study in over 100 countries, and 25% of them have come back to China. In 2005, 89% of students going abroad did so at their own expense, while 7% were supported by Chinese public funding (Zhou, 2006). In 2006 the China Scholarship Council set up a project called "Building National key Universities through Sending Graduate Students Abroad" in collaboration with 49 key universities including Shanghai Jiao Tong University. According to this plan, between 2007 and 2011, the government will send 5,000 masters and Ph.D. students abroad every year and cover the tuition and living expenses of these students (China Scholarship Council, 2006). Students funded by this plan are being asked to promise to return on completion of their studies.

RESPONSE OF SJTU

Profile of SJTU

Shanghai Jiao Tong University (SJTU), founded in 1896, is one of the oldest universities in China. It is regularly ranked in the top seven by various ranking organizations in China. SJTU is strong in engineering, medicine and management fields, and many of the academic programmes are ranked as the national top three. It has 2,800 faculty members including 22 academics from the Chinese Academy of Sciences and Chinese Academy of Engineering. The total enrollments in SJTU are about 40,000, including 20,000 undergraduate students and 13,000 graduate students. There are currently about 2,000 foreign students studying at the university, including about 500 in undergraduate programmes and 100 in graduate programmes.

Located in one of the major international metropolitan areas, SJTU has been actively involved in international exchange and cooperation. It has established cooperative relationships with more than 100 universities abroad. As mentioned in earlier sections, it has conducted unique models of international collaboration such as the Joint Institute with University of Michigan, and overseas graduate schools.

SJTU Strategies

With its long-term goal of becoming a world-class university, SJTU is making special efforts in improving the quality of faculty, research and graduate education. Internationalization has become one of its main strategies for the next few years. Major practices and measures include:

In areas of education: establishing the Joint Institute with the University of Michigan, setting up more dual degree programmes and other degree programmes with leading international universities, increasing study abroad programmes and international internships, expanding bilingual teaching, starting

English-only programmes, launching summer schools and other short period programmes for students coming from international partner universities, etc.

In areas of research: conducting partnerships for each school with at least one international partner, building joint research centres with leading international universities and research institutes, setting up satellite research laboratories with major international corporations, participating in major international science projects, joint research projects and publications, etc.

In areas of faculty and management: recruiting deans and professors from leading international universities, increasing the percentage of faculty members with doctoral degrees from leading international universities, sending young scholars to leading international universities and research institutes, increasing short visits by and collaboration with world-class professors, International training of management staff, etc.

FINAL REMARKS

To face the challenges of globalization, both Chinese governments and top Chinese universities including the SJTU, have been paying special attention and taking special measures. Major progress has been made in areas of education and research. More has to be done in the future.

REFERENCES

Altbach, P.G. (2006). "Chinese Higher Education in an Open-Door Era". Available at http://www.bc.edu/bc_org/avp/soe/cihe/newsletter/Number45/p15_Altbach.htm

China Scholarship Council. (2006). Building National key Universities through Sending Graduate Students Abroad. Available at http://www.csc.edu.cn/

China Scholarship Council. (2007). Statistics of overseas students in China 2006. Available at http://www.csc.edu.cn/gb/readarticle/readarticle.asp?articleid=2560

Levin, J.K. (2001). "Public policy, community colleges, and the path to globalization", in *Higher Education*, 42 (2), p. 237.

Liu, N. C. (2007). "Flagship universities of China: differentiation, classification and world-class", in Altbach, P. & Balan, J. (eds), *World Class Worldwide: Transforming Research Universities in Asia and Latin America*, Johns Hopkins University Press, Baltimore.

Ministry of Education. (2003). Regulations of the People's Republic of China on Chinese-Foreign Cooperation in Running Schools. Available at http://www.moe.edu.cn/edoas/website18/info1273.htm

Ministry of Education. (2005). List of In-Operation Chinese-foreign Joint Education Programs Conferring Foreign and Hong Kong SAR Degrees (As of 30 June 2004). Available at www.jsj.edu.cn/mingdan/002.html

Ministry of Education. (2007). *National Education Development Statistical Bulletin 2006*. Available at http://www.moe.edu.cn/edoas/website18/info29052.htm

People's Daily Abroad Edition. (2007). New trends of Chinese universities inviting applications for a job. "Return from Foreign Countries and Changjiang Scholars". Available at http://news.sohu.com/20070517/n250063782.shtml

Zhou, M. S. (2006). Education input and output under the WTO framework and Chinese government education law and policy regulation. Available at: http://www.csc.edu.cn/gb/10th/forum/4/%B7%D6%C2%DB%CC%B3%B6%FE%A3%BA%D6%DC%C2%FA%C9%FA%BD%B2%B8%E5.doc

CHAPTER 11

Building Singapore's University Education System in a Globalized World: Issues, Policies and Challenges

Tony Tan Keng Yam

S ingapore is a small young nation with a relatively short history, becoming independent only in 1965. Over the last 42 years, Singapore has moved from third world to first world and built a modern economy with a per-capita income second in Asia only to that of Japan.

This paper will chart the role that education particularly university education has played in powering Singapore's economic growth.

1960s AND 1970s: ECONOMIC LEAP-FROGGING THROUGH EXPORT-ORIENTED INDUSTRIALIZATION

In the 1960s, Singapore faced the challenge of weak economic fundamentals. Labour participation was low, unemployment high and the labour force was poorly educated. In the region, political changes limited Singapore's access to the regional market.

The international environment, on the other hand, presented opportunities. The combination of threats and opportunities prompted a shift in Singapore's economic development strategy towards export-led industrialization. Going against conventional wisdom at that time, Singapore opened its economy to foreign investments and leveraged on Multi-National Companies (MNCs) to gain access to technologies, markets and management expertise.

To improve the investment climate, the Singapore Government laid down employment standards and built institutions to help manage labour-management relations. The Government also invested heavily in both physical infrastructure like transport and communications and soft infrastructure, particularly the necessary business and legal systems.

Together with monetary stability and fiscal prudence, Singapore's pro-business environment made it attractive for MNCs to invest in Singapore. The successive inflows of foreign capital enabled Singapore to quickly build up its manufacturing base, which doubled between 1965 and 1980. Over the same period, GDP growth averaged 10% per annum. Robust growth and sound economic fundamentals enabled the country to weather the oil crisis-induced slowdown in 1974, and transit into the next stage of economic development in relatively good shape.

In those early years, the Singapore Education Ministry focused on building a national education system which would provide mass education for all. Singapore increased the number of school places by building schools and recruiting teachers on a large scale. In its efforts to build social cohesion, Singapore also amalgamated different language stream schools, introduced bilingualism and instituted the singing of the Singapore National Anthem and the recitation of the National Pledge as daily rituals in schools. These remain key features of Singapore's education system today.

With the emphasis on primary and secondary school education and upgrading vocational and technical training institutes, Singapore had only one public university, the University of Singapore, and a Chinese Language university, Nanyang University, set up by the community, both of which merged to become the National University of Singapore (NUS) which celebrated its 100th anniversary in 2005. The emphasis at the university level in the 1960s and 70s was to rapidly expand enrolment in order to produce the professional manpower needed to staff a growing economy and to meet social needs. What was very important was to ensure that the rapid expansion of university enrolment did not result in lower educational standards.

1980s AND 1990s: INDUSTRIAL RESTRUCTURING AND UPGRADING

By the late 1970s, industrial restructuring had become necessary. Rapid economic growth created problems of labour shortage. Employers had little incentive to invest in worker upgrading as wages were kept cautiously low. Externally, Singapore faced increased competition from low-cost countries in the region.

In response, Singapore pursued the strategy of shifting from labour-intensive activities to more capital-driven and higher value-added industries. Fiscal incentives were introduced to encourage automation and mechanization, while efficient labour utilization and productivity enhancements were encouraged. Singapore's investment efforts also targeted manufacturing industries that were technology-intensive, such as computer parts, machinery, aerospace, petrochemicals, pharmaceuticals and biotechnology.

With Singapore's evolving economic structure, more skilled workers, technicians and university graduates were needed to fill the jobs available. Singapore therefore expanded its post-secondary and tertiary education sector to raise the standard of education and upgrade the skills of the people.

In 1981, the Nanyang Technological Institute (NTI) was set up with three engineering schools. NTI sought to train practice-oriented engineers for the burgeoning Singapore economy. Ten years later, NTI became Singapore's second public university, Nanyang Technological University (NTU), with the absorption of the National Institute of Education, which is Singapore's teacher training institute. Today, NTU has established an international reputation and nurtures tech-savvy, entrepreneurial leaders through a broad education in diverse disciplines.

The sharp pace of "catch-up" growth in the 70s and 80s meant that resource constraints and diminishing returns to investments were beginning to set in in the 90s. As a result, the cost-productivity advantage Singapore enjoyed over other countries began to narrow.

On the other hand, Singapore's indigenous technological capabilities were still relatively shallow compared with many developed economies and some newly industrialized economies. Government spending on R&D as a percentage of GDP was also below that of many developed countries.

The strategic focus during this phase of economic development was therefore to upgrade Singapore's capabilities and diversify the economy. Taking advantage of the regional boom in the early 90s, Singapore moved to develop an "external wing" for its economy. The rationale was that regionalization allowed Singapore to tap on the rapid growth of the regional economies and complement its linkages with the developed nations. It also provided an opportunity to strengthen MNC-linkages through co-investment in the region.

On the education front, Singapore sought to identify and develop the full spectrum of talents and abilities in its students, encouraging them to be responsive to globalization and technological change. To this end, the Government decided to introduce a diverse mix of institutions in Singapore offering an assortment of pedagogy, curricula as well as learning cultures.

In 1997, the Government mooted the idea of setting up a third university, the Singapore Management University (SMU), to provide more choices for Singapore parents and students. Located in the city, SMU was envisioned to be different from the two established institutions, NUS and NTU, as it would adopt an American-style broad-based education in contrast to NUS and

NTU's British-style system. Modelled after the Wharton School of the University of Pennsylvania, SMU would enjoy wide autonomy in its operations. SMU was an experiment in diversity which worked out well. SMU provided healthy competition to the more established business schools in NUS and NTU and also enhanced the diversity and quality of educational offerings for students in Singapore.

Since its inception, SMU has produced three graduating classes of students, all of whom were employed within six months after graduation. SMU graduates have been hired in a wide spectrum of professions, including finance, accounting, consulting and services sectors, and are well-regarded by industry. This is a testament to the quality of the new university.

SINGAPORE UNIVERSITIES — KEY CENTRES OF EXCELLENCE TO FOSTER AND ATTRACT TALENT

In Singapore, universities are viewed as key centres of excellence to foster local talent and to attract foreign talent to the country. Singapore's three universities have achieved much in a relatively short period of time. They are among the best universities in the region and have done well in providing quality education for undergraduates, producing the required graduate manpower to meet the needs of Singapore's economy, carrying out rigorous research and creating knowledge. In 1980, Singapore had only one university — the National University of Singapore (NUS) which educated 8,600 students every year. Today, Singapore has three publicly-funded universities — NUS, the Nanyang Technological University (NTU) and the Singapore Management University (SMU), with a combined student enrolment of over 40,000 students. The universities are well-regarded globally, and their graduates have contributed significantly to the growth and development of Singapore.

To ensure that Singapore's universities continue to improve and enhance their quality, especially in a fast-changing and increasingly competitive university landscape, the universities need to build up their own institutional characters and distinguish themselves from other universities. They need greater flexibility in order to chart their own strategic directions. SMU's successful experience demonstrated that NUS and NTU would similarly benefit from greater autonomy to differentiate themselves. Hence, to empower the universities to chart their own directions and build on their areas of strength, the Singapore Government decided to corporatize NUS and NTU, making them autonomous universities, similar to SMU, in 2006.

As autonomous universities, the three universities operate with greater autonomy, whereby their respective Boards of Trustees and university management are entrusted with the responsibility of managing the universities, under the general guidance of the Ministry of Education. Quality audits, conducted three-yearly by international panels of senior academics and experienced university administrators, ensure that the universities maintain high standards in their research and educational missions. By making the universities autonomous, Singapore hopes to foster a greater sense of ownership among the Boards of Trustees, senior management, faculty, students and alumni, who would now play a more active role in helping the universities achieve their missions.

In a fast-changing global university landscape, Singapore's publicly-funded universities need to respond to a dynamic environment. Competition for the best people — faculty, management and students — is becoming very intense, as people become more mobile and move to countries that offer them better opportunities. Singapore's universities need to attract the best in order to stay ahead of their competitors, and provide Singaporeans with a quality university education. The establishment of the International Academic Advisory Panel (IAAP) in 1997 was a major step in helping Singapore to upgrade its universities. The IAAP, which includes senior businessmen and eminent academics from top universities in the world, meets biennially to review Singapore's university sector and provides advice and guidance to the Government on what measures are needed to assist Singapore universities in their quest for excellence.

BRINGING THE WORLD TO SINGAPORE

The progress that Singapore has made in its university sector is a result of the strategy of keeping Singapore's society and economy open, flexible and adaptable. Singapore's success hinges on developing and attracting able and talented people. The Government thus continues to invest heavily in education to ensure that every Singaporean is equipped with the necessary skills and know-how for the future. Singapore has also welcomed global talent to augment its indigenous talent pool. Singapore's openness to global talent is its key competitive advantage. In this sense, the Government seeks to bring the world to Singapore.

CREATING A DIVERSE UNIVERSITY SECTOR

To be at the forefront of the latest developments, Singapore needs to create a diverse, differentiated and competitive university sector that will support its economic growth and social development. A vibrant university sector will not only attract and retain top talent, it will also help to create jobs and wealth.

Singapore's university sector has therefore evolved into a tiered system. The three Autonomous Universities form the bedrock of the sector, and meet key national objectives. Forming another tier in the system are world-class private educational institutions. Bringing the best institutions that the world has to offer to Singapore would enhance the educational opportunities for our students and provide opportunities for Singaporeans to establish valuable networks.

One of the first players to set up a campus in Singapore was INSEAD. In 1997, INSEAD considered venturing into Asia, and explored 12 locations around the Asia Pacific, before deciding to set up a branch campus in Singapore. Today, INSEAD's branch campus in Singapore has done very well, attracting close to 400 MBA students from over 70 countries. Many students from Europe consciously chose to study in the Singapore campus, rather than INSEAD's main Paris campus, as they want to develop the Asian perspective provided at the Singapore campus.

Speciality institutions such as the DigiPen Institute of Technology, Culinary Institute of America and New Zealand's Southseas Film and Television School have also been established in Singapore. These speciality institutions allow students with a keen interest in niche disciplines to learn about the latest developments from the best people in these fields.

The response from Singaporean local and foreign students to these new players has been enthusiastic. In fact, Singapore's foreign student intake has seen a sharp increase over three years, from less than 50,000 international students in 2002 to 80,000 international students this year. With a diverse mix of institutions in Singapore offering an assortment of pedagogy, curricula as well as university culture, Singapore is confident that the country can distinguish itself as a premier education hub.

DEVELOPING CITIZENS WITH A GLOBAL OUTLOOK

The corporatization of Singapore's universities was intended to allow them more flexibility to respond to the challenges of the global economy. It is, however, just as important for Singapore to develop its students to become global citizens, with a global outlook and equipped with the skills, knowledge and motivation needed to operate in an increasingly interconnected world.

Today, students in the three autonomous universities already have the chance to interact with over 9,000 foreign students on-campus. The enrolment of foreign students in Singapore universities comprises 20% at the undergraduate level and higher at the postgraduate level. These foreign students hail from our close neighbours such as Malaysia and Indonesia, China, India and other parts of Asia, as well as Europe and US. The presence of foreign students in Singapore's universities enriches the learning experience for our own students, and gives them a taste of different cultures all in the same classroom. This adds an important element of global orientation to their university experience.

In this aspect, Singapore's universities are doing more. Students can now look forward to a wide range of educational opportunities overseas through student semester exchange programmes and joint programmes with top overseas universities. To date, our universities have student exchange agreements with over 200 overseas partners ranging from Asia to Europe to the US. These overseas stints expose our students to different education systems, ways of life and cultures. Currently, up to 40% of each cohort of students in the universities experience some form of overseas exposure during their studies. Going forward, the universities are targeting to send half of each cohort overseas.

At the institution level, Singapore's universities have also forged global partnerships with overseas universities in research and teaching, as well as participating in global university networks. Such global networking aims to expand educational and other forms of cooperation among the member countries, promoting dialogue among members on the latest education issues so that Singapore can become an effective player in the global knowledge economy. It is through these meetings that universities come together and agree to collaborate on joint/dual degree arrangements, as well as student and faculty exchanges.

NUS has been very active on this front, and is part of global university alliances such as the International Alliance of Research Universities and the Association of the Pacific Rim Universities. In fact, NUS was elected to lead the 36-member Association of the Pacific Rim Universities for two terms, an endorsement of NUS's international standing and capabilities.

2000 AND BEYOND: BUILDING A KNOWLEDGE-BASED ECONOMY

In the 21st century, the global economic landscape is changing dramatically with the rise of China and India. China has a population of 1.3 billion and its economy is growing strongly at 8 to 10% a year. India has a population of 1.1 billion and is the second fastest growing Asian economy, at 6 to 8% a year. As the investment environment and workforce quality in these countries improve, China and India will offer tremendous business opportunities for global investors.

However, with internationalization and the opening up of our neighbouring economies, there will be increased competition for jobs and investments. As Singapore's economy matures, rapidly rising costs will further erode Singapore's attractiveness as an industrial and business centre. Singapore must find sustainable ways to differentiate itself, not just based on cost and efficiency.

In a globalized knowledge economy, talent will be the key to economic success. Talent will provide the intellectual and innovation capacity to sustain the technological edge and competitive advantage of a country. Indeed, investments and economic growth will follow talent. This will be the economic paradigm of the 21st century.

PUSHING THE BOUNDARIES

To bring Singapore universities to the next level, the Government has committed to provide more resources for Research and Development at the universities. Singapore universities will be able to leverage on the additional resources to enhance their research endeavours, as well as boost the overall quality of educational experience for their students.

A recent initiative by the Ministry of Education and the National Research Foundation (NRF) is to establish a small number of world-class Research Centres of Excellence (RCE) at the universities. The RCEs will be headed by eminent scientific leaders and will conduct investigator-led research with a global impact. NUS has been selected to set up the first RCE on Quantum Information and Science Technology later this year.

To succeed in the knowledge economy, Singapore needs to be creative and entrepreneurial, ready to take risks and seize opportunities. Singapore can no longer fall back on tried and tested strategies. Singapore needs to fundamentally rethink its strategies to tackle the challenges ahead. This would involve venturing into uncharted territory. Breaking new ground, the NRF is undertaking a bold initiative to work with selected top research universities around the world to develop a campus which will house world-class research centres in Singapore. This will be known as the Campus for Research Excellence and Technological Enterprise or CREATE.

CREATE is envisioned to be an unprecedented multinational, multidisciplinary research enterprise, strategically located in Singapore, the nexus of East and West. It will be a complex of several research centres from world-class research universities, pursuing research programmes in areas that are aligned to Singapore's strategic interests.

CREATE will be a talent magnet and innovation hub, and will serve as the Asia research campus of institutions that until now have focused their research in their home countries. Many US and European universities are eager to establish a presence in Asia because of the keen awareness of the rise of Asia and the increasing shift of global dominance towards Asia. CREATE presents them with a unique opportunity to start in Singapore.

The Massachusetts Institute of Technology (MIT) will be establishing the first research centre within CREATE to be called the Singapore-MIT Alliance for Research and Technology (SMART) Centre. When fully established, it is anticipated that the centre will house 5-6 research groups. Over 400 faculty, post-docs, students and other technical staff from Singapore, MIT and other overseas institutions are expected to be involved in the centre. The first research group within the centre, which will focus on Infectious Diseases, will start operations in temporary premises in NUS on 1 July 2007.

NRF is also in discussion with the Swiss Federal Institute of Technology (ETH) and the Technion — Israel Institute of Technology for them to establish similar research presence in CREATE.

Other than research centres, CREATE will also house corporate labs, which would contribute their knowledge-creation capability and create more research career opportunities in Singapore. Corporate labs generate cutting-edge knowledge for products and services which do not even exist today. The presence of corporate labs in CREATE would allow them to interact with the research centres, and their industry-oriented research would add to the vibrancy of research activities in CREATE.

For CREATE to succeed, there should be intensive collaborations between CREATE and the Singapore-based universities, polytechnics, laboratories and research institutes. CREATE could work with NUS and NTU to jointly recruit graduate students who would be enrolled in the universities' PhD courses, but do their research at CREATE. These students will be given the rare opportunity of being under the supervision of senior faculty of world-class research universities linked to CREATE.

Panels and networks comprising visiting committees and entrepreneurs could also interact with the researchers in CREATE to encourage innovative technology applications and promote entrepreneurship and services to the business community and wider society. Such interactions would drive all parties to strive for higher standards of research performance, and the synergies created from these collaborations would allow CREATE and our universities to reach greater heights of excellence.

NURTURING THE SPIRIT OF ENTREPRENEURSHIP AND SOCIAL RESPONSIBILITY

Apart from technical knowledge and exposure to different cultures, Singaporeans also need the right mindset to thrive in an environment of rapid and unpredictable change. In particular, Singapore needs to nurture the spirit of entrepreneurship and creativity and a sense of social responsibility in our young.

Today, Singapore's universities organize entrepreneurship programmes, workshops and seminars on a regular basis to educate aspiring entrepreneurs. Such events bring together working professionals and members of the university community, as well as the public, for networking opportunities, and sharing of knowledge and experience. Seed funding and venture support are also available to help budding entrepreneurs among the university community to realize their aspirations.

NUS has also established five Overseas Colleges in global entrepreneurial hubs such as Silicon Valley, Shanghai and Bangalore, where students are immersed in a dynamic environment, engaging in full-time internships with start-ups and taking entrepreneurship courses part-time at the partner universities. The Overseas College initiative is bearing fruit, and we have seen that students are increasingly active in establishing their own start-ups.

In addition, our universities have partnered industry and the wider community on collaborations which seek to achieve strategic national and social objectives. For example, NUS is collaborating with the Public Utilities Board and Delft Hydraulics to establish a Centre of Excellence for water knowledge. This Centre will focus on multi-institutional and interdisciplinary research, information exchange and technology transfer related to water management, hydraulic engineering and urban water cycles. The outcomes of the Centre's research would be of strategic importance to Singapore.

BALANCING THE ROLES OF TEACHING AND RESEARCH

As Singapore's national universities evolve into research-intensive universities, their research activities will increasingly be given higher priority as this would generate additional funding for the universities. Unlike teaching, research is also more measurable and is increasingly used in university rankings.

When the IAAP met in Singapore early this year, it was noteworthy that the Panel stressed repeatedly that it was imperative for universities to continue to maintain excellence in teaching, even as they aspire towards research excellence. The IAAP strongly affirmed teaching and research excellence to be the twin pillars for the success of universities. That said, all research-intensive universities face the struggle to maintain undergraduate teaching excellence. The universities need to tackle issues like how faculty allocate time between teaching and research, and how to create an environment where undergraduate education continues to be highly valued.

CONCLUSION

In summary, Singapore's university sector has made tremendous progress in the past 25 years. Singapore universities today are no longer ivory towers of pure academic pursuits. They exist in a complex societal and economic ecosystem, and interact with many parties — research institutes, businesses, government agencies and the wider community. These interactions are multi-faceted, spanning education, economic, social and cultural dimensions. The new knowledge that they create has practical implications on the economic and social development of Singapore.

As Singapore moves forward, the country needs to continue to nurture its own talent as well as attract the top brains from overseas to locate, work, live and contribute to the country. International talent will add diversity and intellectual capacity to our learning environment, and at the same time spur Singapore's own home-grown talent on to greater heights. The intellectual interactions among the various stakeholders would be of mutual benefit to all involved. These efforts will help push Singapore towards the next level of international competitiveness.

Throughout Singapore's short history, the nation's university education system has evolved to meet societal needs and to support the country's economic progress. Singapore is a small country and people are its only resource. Continued investment in people is the only way Singapore can succeed in a globalized world. In the next phase of development towards building a knowledge-based economy, Singapore needs to develop a workforce that can respond dynamically to the rapidly changing needs of the economy. Learning will become a lifelong process. Singaporeans will engage in skills and knowledge upgrading not only through full-time courses but also through other means, including short courses and part-time education programmes which may lead to formal qualifications.

With the rising aspirations of parents and students, demand for access to university level education will increase. There will also be a need for more graduates to staff an increasingly complex economy. It is therefore timely for Singapore to consider increasing the number of university places. One possibility, as recommended by the IAAP at its meeting earlier this year, is to establish a high quality liberal arts college which would complement, but provide a different education from NUS, NTU and SMU.

Building Singapore's university education system is an ongoing work-in-progress. Only by constantly re-examining and re-inventing the university education system can Singapore's universities not only achieve higher peaks of excellence in teaching and research, but also address the larger, fundamental role that universities play in today's society.

CHAPTER 12

Globalization of Research Universities in Korea

Nam Pyo Suh

INTRODUCTION

An important consequence of economic globalization is expected to be that only a few leading universities will dominate the world of higher education, just as a few companies are dominating different industrial sectors worldwide. Globalization has thus become a major goal for most research universities in Korea. It is driven by a number of other factors as well, including the industrial demand for graduates who can work globally, the need for global collaboration in knowledge generation and technology innovation, and the search for talents and technologies that are no longer bound by national boundary. Korean research universities also must globalize their educational and research programmes to be competitive, viable and effective. There are many different versions of globalization, but the common elements are cooperation among universities and industrial firms in other countries, instruction in English, exchange of students, recruiting of foreign students, and hiring of international instructional staff. There are many challenges in achieving the goal of the globalization of Korean universities. These universities, like their counterparts in other non-English speaking countries with monolithic cultures and people, face a set of structural problems. To overcome these challenges, the Korea Advanced Institute of Science and Technology (KAIST) has established strategies and policies which will be reviewed in this paper.

Brief History of Modern Korea

To understand the globalization of higher education in Korea, it is first necessary to understand the modern history of Korea. During the last four decades, both higher education and the economy of Korea have grown exponentially. Economically, before 1960, Korea was not industrialized, having gone through 35 years of Japanese colonization, followed by the Korean War from 1950 to 1953.

Industrialization of Korea began in the early-1960s. The initial phase started in low-value add, labour-intensive industrial sectors such as apparel, textile and leather goods, following the typical process of industrialization of developing nations in the latter half of the 20th century. After having established labour-intensive industries in the 1960s, Korea began the process of transforming its industry from that of labour-intensive industries to higher value add, capital-intensive industries in the 1970s. It made significant investments in heavy industries such as shipbuilding, steel, machinery and automobiles. Then, beginning in the mid-1980s and 1990s, Korea began to invest in technology-intensive businesses such as semiconductors, LCDs and telecommunications. Today, Korea is investing in R&D that may lay the foundation for knowledge-intensive industries.

During the past four decades, Korean industries have performed well. Korea is now the first among industrialized nations in shipbuilding, DRAMS, and LCD technologies, and is in the top five or six in IT-related business, steel-making, and automobile production. Korea's IT and Internet infrastructure is considered to be one of the most advanced in the world. Korean exports in 2006 exceeded $300 billion, which was larger than the exports of all 53 African nations combined, and about equal to that of all Latin American nations combined, excluding Mexico. Now many Korean industrial firms, like their counterparts in the US and Europe, have begun the inevitable process of moving some of their production of automobiles, steel-making, and consumer electronics to lower-labour cost countries with large markets.

Korean industrialization has been possible because Korean society, which has its cultural roots in the teachings of Confucius, has always put a high premium on education. Korea's education system has always been highly competitive, with better students going to a few highly selective schools, which is the case even as Korea has vastly expanded its educational system.

During the past four decades, higher education in Korea has grown both in quantity and quality, starting from a handful of undergraduate institutions at the end of the Second World War. Korea began the expansion of its university system in the 1950s, even before there were industrial jobs available, by establishing both public and private universities. By the 1970s, in response to the high industrial demand for education, Korea accelerated the expansion by creating many new private and national universities with primary emphasis on undergraduate education. Since then, Korea has expanded its graduate education because of the growing industrial demand for highly educated personnel, patented technologies and technology innovation.

Now, with the entry of Korean industries into the knowledge-intensive businesses, the leading industrial firms in Korea are searching for the most talented scientists and engineers worldwide — irrespective of their nationality. The challenge for Korean universities is to respond to the demand for highly educated personnel, to meet the aspirations of the Korean people for better education, to lead in the generation of basic knowledge and technologies, and to be able to compete for talent and financial resources with the leading universities worldwide.

Korea's Educational infrastructure

To understand the role of Korea's research universities, it would be useful to understand the overall educational infrastructure and the investment made in education in Korea. There are 360 higher educational institutions in Korea, including 26 national universities and 173 colleges and private universities. Most of the 26 national universities and many leading private universities in Korea have graduate schools offering masters and doctorate degrees. However, a mere five or so graduate schools dominate graduate education.

In 2004, there were 2,734,238 students in these colleges and universities, up from 179,877 in 1970. In 2004, more than 81% of high school graduates in Korea went to colleges and universities, which is a substantial increase from 33.2% in 1990. Because the entrance to college is highly competitive, parents of K-12 students spend a large portion of their income — estimated as high as 30% — on private education and tutoring in the evenings after regular school hours.

The number of students attending Korean universities is likely to decline in future years since the birth rate in Korea is low. A fairly large number of parents send their children abroad for education in other countries, such as the US, where the competition for entrance to better universities is less severe than in Korea. Therefore, some universities and colleges also will face a serious problem due to the lack of students.

The Ministry of Education micromanages all schools — from elementary education through college education, and research universities — except KAIST. The government sets the policy on the entrance examination to colleges, the number of faculty positions, etc. This uniform educational policy has created a costly and inefficient educational system which has been controversial and criticized by nearly all, and yet it still continues.

KAIST AND OTHER RESEARCH UNIVERSITIES IN KOREA

By 1970, it had become apparent that, with rapid industrialization, Korea would need scientific and technological workers with advanced science and engineering education. Until then, most Koreans who were interested in graduate education went to the United States and Europe — and many stayed where they emigrated. Thus, in 1971, the Korea Advanced Institute of Science and Technology (KAIST), the first university in Korea for graduate education in science and engineering, was established under a special law. The establishment of KAIST marked the beginning of a new era for research universities in Korea.

KAIST is the only university in Korea that can set its own system because it is not controlled by the Ministry of Education. Rather, KAIST is controlled by a board of trustees and receives its basic funding from the Ministry of Science and Technology (MOST) of Korea. In its early days, KAIST students were granted many special privileges: deferment of mandatory military service; free education, including meals, lodging and even spending money; and up-to-date research facilities. Professors were recruited from overseas — mainly expatriates from the US — at two to three times the then prevailing professorial salary in Korea. Some of these special privileges are still in place, except the faculty salary, which is now in parity with other universities.

The establishment of KAIST has had a profound effect on other universities. The creation of KAIST helped these other institutions by setting a new standard for universities, including the development of established graduate programmes, a more competitive compensation system and the creation of funds for research support.

Current Status of KAIST

KAIST has been rated the best university in Korea. The quality of KAIST students is exceptionally high. KAIST accepts 70% of its freshmen from 19 special science high schools and a school for gifted students, based on their high school grades and interviews, without requiring a special examination. Each one of these science high schools is highly competitive, accepting about 100 students out of a potential pool of 100,000 eligible students. Out of the 1,800 graduates produced by these science high schools every year, KAIST accepts only about 700 students a year, although most of the applicants from these science high schools would be equally good students.

KAIST has 3,350 undergraduate students and 4,465 graduate students. This year's freshmen class consists of 7% foreign students. KAIST's goal is to increase the number of undergraduate students to 4,000.

There are 686 faculty members (424 tenure-track professors) and about an equal number of staff members. A significant proportion of KAIST professors were educated primarily in the US and some in Europe. There are 91 faculty members who are foreign nationals, of whom 34 are foreign nationals (mostly Korean-Americans) born in Korea.

KAIST has produced 32,941 graduates — 8,453 BS, 17,762 MS, and 6,726 PhDs — in 36 years. It has been the major supplier of PhDs to Korean industry and universities. Twenty-five per cent of PhDs at Samsung Electronics, the world's largest manufacturer of DRAMs, and about 10% of all professors in Korea are KAIST graduates. Some KAIST graduates are also now becoming professors in other countries.

The goal of KAIST is to become one of the best universities in the world. To achieve this goal, KAIST has recently recommitted itself to providing the best undergraduate and graduate education, improving the effectiveness of its research investment and empowering its faculty. KAIST has instituted a multi-pronged approach to globalization: instruction in English, enrolment of foreign students, recruitment and appointment of international faculty, faculty and student exchange programmes, participation in and organization of international conferences, creation of dual and joint degree programmes with universities in other countries, and research collaboration across the globe.

KAIST's Emphasis on Research at the Two Ends of the Research Spectrum

In research, KAIST is a global university. The KAIST faculty has been active in international conferences, collaborating with many researchers across the globe. They also have published extensively in international journals and obtained many patents in a number of countries. The annual publication rate of our faculty is around five papers per faculty, which is on par with the leading universities in the US. Many KAIST professors are the recipients of international awards in various engineering and scientific fields, especially in semiconductors, IT, composite manufacturing, biology, materials and engineering.

Notwithstanding these achievements, KAIST also has implemented a couple of policy changes to strengthen the effectiveness of its research. First, the contributions of its faculty are assessed based on the impact made by their research, not by the number of papers published. Faculty members are strongly encouraged to work at the two ends of the research spectrum where the impact is greatest: basic research and technology innovation. (Shown in Figure 1.)

Figure 1: Research Spectrum vs. the Research Effort spent by Researchers, and Research Spectrum vs. the impact made by Research

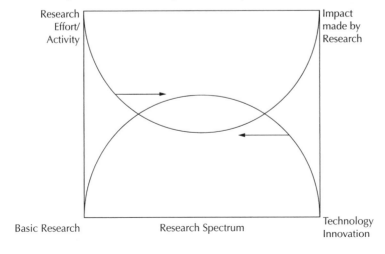

Second, we have created research organizations, the KAIST Institutes, in seven areas to promote research at the narrowly focused intersection of different disciplines, where faculty and students from various departments work together. New faculty positions are allocated to the Institutes, and every department can recruit faculty members who can participate in these institutes. There is no formal allocation of faculty positions to the departments. The research institute and the department must agree on faculty candidates. The faculty member belongs to the department that hired the professor to do teaching, but is free to do research outside the department. However, when there is an exceptionally gifted faculty candidate, the department is allowed to hire the person at any time regardless of the candidate's field of specialization.

GLOBALIZATION OF KOREAN UNIVERSITIES: PROS AND CONS

The globalization of universities in Korea has been driven by government and industry, as well as by the universities themselves. To remain competitive in the global economy, Korean government leaders understand that Korean universities must have a world view. Large Korean industrial firms that conduct business in many countries require employees who not only have proficiency in English, but also have skills that match their competition. To remain academically competitive in an increasingly flat world, universities know that they must prepare their students for global jobs.

While these are valid concerns on globalization, the proponents of globalization believe that its benefits far outweigh its disadvantages. In the global economy, a few leading universities will dominate research and education, just as a few leading industrial firms have consolidated their positions in their industries. They will attract the best brains from all corners of the world, as well as financial support for research. Students and faculty in these institutions will have competitive advantages, which will enable them to amplify and leverage their research capabilities. Unless a university can compete on a global scale, it may not provide the education and research opportunities their best students deserve.

GLOBALIZATION AT KAIST

KAIST is implementing its globalization plan with the support of the Korean government, which is providing $100 million over five years. The KAIST's programme for globalization is as follows.

Undergraduate Programme

KAIST has taken several steps to globalize its undergraduate programme. First, all freshmen courses are taught in English. To support this ambitious practice, KAIST has strengthened the language-learning centre where students can hone their English language skills and has set up an English cafe where only English is spoken. In addition, some of KAIST's best professors who are fluent in English are teaching freshmen classes.

Second, 5.5% of the students in the freshmen class of 2007 are international students, coming from nations in South-east Asia, Central Asia and Eastern Europe. To accommodate students and faculty from other countries, KAIST will be strengthening its healthcare system to make it easier for all students, faculty and staff to receive medical services on campus. In addition, KAIST is planning to build a new International Student Center, funded by a local church, and a new apartment building to improve the accommodation for international faculty.

Third, KAIST is in the process of creating a dual degree programme with universities in the US, Europe and Asia in order to generate graduates who can work with and in other countries. Under the programme, participating students at KAIST and its counterpart university will earn two B.S. degrees after four years, splitting their time equally between the two institutions.

To teach the synthesis and design process to all students, a design subject is required of all freshmen, just like mathematics, physics, chemistry and biology. This undergraduate programme, which emphasizes both analysis and design, is unique. The goal is to impart to the student the ability to think and reason in the two opposite domains of synthesis and analysis with equal facility.

Graduate Programme

KAIST has a large number of research collaborations with many universities in the US, Europe, Japan and China. For example, the KAIST Physics Department has research collaboration with the Cavendish Laboratory of Cambridge University. The KAIST business school also has established a dual masters degree programme for business and law with the law school of Northwestern University in the US.

Research

KAIST has established research institutes — KAIST Institutes — in such areas as biology, IT, entertainment, design of complex systems, energy, nanoscience and technology, and mega-city. These research institutes will conduct research at the intersection between disciplines. For example, in the KAIST Institute for the BioCentury, professors and students from several departments such as biology, chemical engineering, mechanical engineering, physics and chemistry, will work together on joint projects. As part of this research effort, they also will collaborate with industrial firms and universities both in and outside Korea. KAIST is currently seeking special research collaborations with leading global industrial firms.

Faculty

KAIST is actively recruiting international faculty members with the goal of eventually having 100 non-Korean faculty members out of 700 tenure-track faculty members in four years.

We also have appointed many faculty members who are teaching at foreign universities as adjunct professors who spend a significant amount of their time at KAIST and KAIST-affiliated organizations such as the Korea Institute for Advanced Studies.

External Advisory Council

Each unit of KAIST has an advisory group called the External Advisory Council (EAC). They review academic programmes and research projects of academic departments and research institutes. One third of the EAC members — about five — come from other countries, and they serve as ambassadors and advisors for KAIST.

CHALLENGES THAT MUST BE OVERCOME FOR GLOBALIZATION

Globalization is a challenge in Korea for a number of key reasons, including language, culture and financial resources. These challenges must be addressed for Korean universities to successfully compete against the world's best academic institutions.

Linguistic barrier

KAIST's freshmen class is now instructed in English. However, the linguistic barrier to learning will be present for some time. The Korean language linguistically belongs to the Ural Altai Language group (spoken by Mongolians, Turks, Hungarians and Finns), which is distinctly different from English in grammar, structure, etc. Although English is now being taught from the elementary school level, many Korean students coming in as freshmen at KAIST are not proficient in English. KAIST needs to increase the number of international students and faculty to help convert the campus into a bilingual campus. KAIST plans to accept about 10% of its undergraduates and a slightly larger number of graduate students from overseas. This year's freshmen class consists of about 6% international students.

Cultural constraints

There are many cultural constraints in the globalization of the higher educational system in Korea — from eating etiquettes, interpersonal relationships and cultural values. Korea has been a country with virtually one nationality and one race. KAIST must teach its students the social and cultural norms in other countries, as well as how to respect them by learning how to adopt culturally sensitive behaviour. The peoples of all nations must adjust their social norms and accept others to be able to work across cultures in the global economy.

Financial resources

Research universities need financial resources. For public universities, government support is the primary source of funding. At KAIST, the rate of progress in achieving its goals will be gated by government funding of its programmes.

The Korean government is aware of the importance of the globalization of research universities. The Ministry of Education started the BK21 Program (Brain Korea in the 21st century) eight years ago to fund graduate fellowships and research. These grants can be used to finance global collaboration. Other ministries also fund research at universities in such areas as telecommunications, defence, construction, environment, culture and entertainment; some of this funding provides for global collaboration.

Industrial support of academic research at research universities also promotes industrial collaboration across national boundaries. Currently, industrial support is significantly less than government-funded research.

Foreign faculty

One of the major goals of KAIST and other universities is to recruit outstanding foreign faculty. They bring a new world view into Korean education and offer unique skills and talents in instruction and research. Although some universities have done better, most Korean universities have difficulty hiring full-time foreign faculty. KAIST has been able to hire Korean-American faculty members and some American and European faculty members, but the number of faculty members is short of its goal of having at least 10% foreign faculty in five years.

Foreign students

The number of foreign students is increasing in Korean universities, but still the number falls far short of the target. Like international faculty, these students will bring new ideas to Korean education and their inclusion will be a signal that universities are offering the highest quality education the world can offer. It is going to take an aggressive effort to recruit students from overseas, especially from the US and Europe.

PROSPECT OF GLOBALIZATION AT KAIST

Since KAIST's goal is to become one of the world's premier universities in science and technology, globalization is just a matter of time. With further growth of the Korean economy and the globalization of Korean companies, there will be further incentives for Korean students to prepare to work in and outside Korea and, conversely, for international students to study in Korea. Therefore, efforts made by KAIST for globalization will continue to gather momentum in the future, although it may not reach the level of globalization that Singaporean universities have attained.

Globalization of KAIST and other higher educational institutions does not mean that these institutions will abandon their basic Korean values and pride. On the contrary, as Korean universities globalize, it is Korean culture that will make them truly unique and special, and Korean culture can be shared with a wider international audience.

CONCLUSION

The globalization of higher education worldwide is driven primarily by economic necessity. Economic advances cannot be achieved by staying insular; countries must share knowledge and collaborate in research to produce workers who can work, lead and innovate.

The globalization of higher education is inevitable from a historical point of view. In the 21st century, knowledge can diffuse faster in the era of information technology, people can travel almost anywhere in the world in 24 hours, and synergy takes place when information is exchanged on a global scale. Most of all, the world needs people who can facilitate this process of globalization, which is the role of higher education in all countries.

In Korea, most research universities have begun the process of globalization with varying degrees of success. This process will accelerate and grow both in scope and substance during the coming decade, as changes demonstrate its positive impact on Korea's development in all areas.

KAIST has made significant changes to become a global university. We have a new undergraduate curriculum, new advanced research institutes, more international students and faculty, exchange of students with universities in other countries, and significant international collaborations in education and research. These changes should accelerate KAIST's goal of becoming one of the best universities in the world.

CHAPTER 13

Science and Technology in Brazil[1]

Carlos H. Brito Cruz

INTRODUCTION

Scientists in Brazil published 16,950 scientific articles in indexed journals in 2005. The country is the 17th-largest producer of science in the world. Nine out of ten of these articles were generated in public university laboratories. Scientists and engineers in business sector R&D activities created several cases of world-class competitive innovation. These include oil self-sufficiency, the most efficient ethanol in the world, commuter jet planes, the most productive soybean production, a national system for electronic elections that can count more than 100 million votes in hundreds of candidates by midnight on election day and the best flex-fuel cars. Still, the Brazilian business sector registered only 283 patents at the USPTO in 2005. While Brazil invests 1% of its GNP in R&D, most of the scientists in Brazil — 75% of them — work in academic institutions. Although business-sector leaders have recently recognized the importance of creating knowledge to warrant not only some degree of competitiveness, but even for being followers in the global technology race, only in the last eight years have effective policies for fostering industrial and service sector R&D been put into operation.

This paper describes some characteristics of the Brazilian Innovation System in terms of its institutions — universities, government laboratories, institutes and funding agencies and business sector R&D facilities.

THE BRAZILIAN INVESTMENT IN R&D

Brazil has been investing around 1% of its GNP in R&D for the last five years (MCT, 2007), roughly 60% of it being invested by the public sector, and 40%

---

1 This article was prepared from previous reports on the subject by the author.

from the private sector. At a level of 1% GNP invested in R&D, while Brazil exceeds Latin American standards (Figure 1), it lags well behind the index practised by OECD countries (Figure 2). The average level for R&D investment for the 17 OECD countries is at 2.24% of the GNP, a percentage that has been steady for the past decade.

Figure 2: R&D investment by Latin American countries, measured as a percentage of their GDP's. Data is for 2004 or most recent year

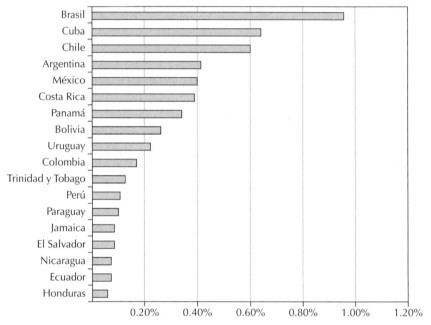

Source: http://www.ricyt.org/indicadores/comparativos/05.xls on 25 Feb 2006.

In absolute value invested in R&D, Brazil's 13 billion PPP dollars compares to the investment practiced by Spain (9 billion PPP dollars) or Italy (17 billion PPP dollars).

An important feature of the Brazilian investment is that, as happens in most developing countries, most of the burden (60%) is carried by the public sector.

THE INSTITUTIONS AND THEIR DEMOGRAPHY

The funding data presented in Section 2 reflects the fact that most of the R&D activities in Brazil are carried out in academic institutions. The demographics of the R&D institutions and companies in Brazil is consistent with this observation.

Researchers in Brazil work mostly in full-time academic positions, 74% of them in universities and another 10% in research institutes. Only 16% of the

Figure 3: A comparison of the Brazilian investment in R&D (in 2004) with that of OECD countries (2003 or most recent year)

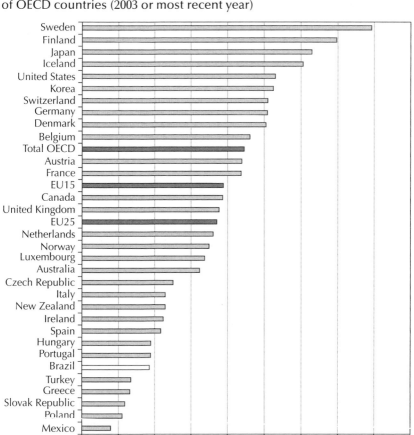

R&D investment (% of GNP)

Source: Brazil: http://www.ricyt.org/indicadores/comparativos/05.xls on 25 Feb 2006; OECD countries: S&T & Industry Outlook 2005 (OECD, 2005), Table A.2.1.

researchers work in business sector R&D, which is consistent with the smaller portion of private R&D expenditures, as compared to the public one. The small number of private sector scientists has a strong effect on Brazil's industry deficiency to generate patents. It is also one of the main restrictions to the development of stronger university-industry scientific linkages.

International comparisons underline the weakness of business-sector R&D in Brazil as compared to OECD countries: in Korea and the US, close to 80% of the nation's scientists work for the business sector, and in Australia or Spain this percentage is close to 60%, almost twice as much as that observed in Brazil.

Table 1: Number of scientists in R&D positions in universities (year 2002), research institutes (year 2002) and business sector (year 2003), in Brazil

Institution	Quantity	%
Full-time university faculty (1)	90.631	73%
– Federal universities	43.494	
– State universities	25.299	
– Private universities	21.838	
Researchers in public R&D institutes (2)	9.422	8%
Researchers in private R&D institutes (3)	2.500	2%
Researchers in business sector R&D (4)	21.795	18%
Total	124.348	100%

Sources:
(1) C.H. Brito Cruz, "A universidade, a empresa e a pesquisa", in "Brasil em Desenvolvimento" (UFRJ, 2004).
(2) Fapesp, "Indicadores de C&T&I em SP e no Brasil", Tabela 4.12 (Fapesp, 2004). Available at http://www.fapesp.br/materia.php?data[id_materia]=2060.
(3) http://www.cgee.org.br/cncti3/Documentos/Seminariosartigos/Geracaoriqueza/DrMarcel%20Bergerman.pdf
(4) IBGE, PINTEC 2003, Tab. 1.1.12.

THE BRAZILIAN UNIVERSITY SYSTEM

Most of the higher education enrolment in Brazil is composed of students attending university type (4 years or longer) courses. Institutions are federal, state or privately owned and managed.

As of 2005 there were 4,453,156 students enrolled in undergraduate courses in Brazil. This translates to a gross enrolment rate of 19% of the age cohort (between 18 and 24 years old) and a net enrolment rate slightly above 12%.

73% of the enrolment is in private higher education institutions, which have very little research and courses of limited quality, with a few exceptions of course.

There are 2,165 higher education institutions, 231 of them public. These institutions graduated 717,858 students in 2005, out of which 36,918 (5%) are engineers and 56,436 (8%) are in science, mathematics and computer science. The distribution of graduates among the fields of knowledge is shown in Figure 3, in comparison to the proportions in some OECD countries.

There are 176 universities, 90 of which are public. Most of the scientific research is carried in these public universities, although with a heterogeneous distribution — six universities respond for 60% of the scientific papers that originate from Brazil. Universities are a recent institution in Brazil: the first Brazilian university was the University of São Paulo (USP), a state university, created in 1934.

Figure 4: Percentage of graduates classified by fields of knowledge

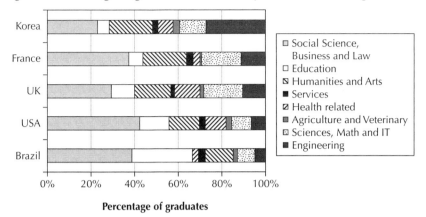

Percentage of graduates

The public university system has been the basis for a successful policy which started in the early 1950s for the development of a system of graduate courses associated with research universities. Two federal agencies were created in 1951 to foster research and graduate studies: the Brazilian National Research Council (CNPq in the Portuguese language abbreviation) and the Coordination for the Training of Higher Education Faculty (CAPES). These were joined by the State of São Paulo Research Foundation in 1962 and the federally owned Fund for Research Projects (FINEP) in 1967. These four organizations are the main funding agencies for research in Brazil.

While Brazil has been able to increase the number of doctorates granted every year, reaching close to 10,000 doctorates concluded in 2006, the country still faces a shortage of higher education graduates, especially in engineering.

At the undergraduate level, there is an enormous challenge: in 2004 only 12% of the youth at age 18 to 24 years old were enrolled in higher education courses. This percentage must be tripled so that Brazil reaches a level on a par with the low end of OECD countries. The country's strategy so far, based on the expansion of private institutions offering 4-5 year courses together with an expansion in the enrolment at public universities which also offer 4-5 year courses, was not successful enough to dramatically raise the enrolment rate.

SCIENCE, TECHNOLOGY AND INNOVATION OUTPUTS

Scientific publications

The number of scientific publications originated in Brazil has been growing steadily for the past 26 years (Figure 4), reaching a number of 12,627 in 2003 and 16,950 in 2005. The growth rate has been larger than that of the world total number of publications, so that there was also an increase in the percentage of theses articles that were originated in Brazil, climbing from 0.4% in 1981 to 1.6% of the world total in 2003. This growth in the number of scientific publications is closely related to the growth in the number of Ph.D.s graduated yearly, which, due to a steady policy, which now lasts for 50+ years, regarding graduate education, expanded from 554 in 1981 to 8,094 in 2003.

Figure 5: Evolution of the number of scientific articles originated in Brazil (bars) and its percentage over the world total (circles)

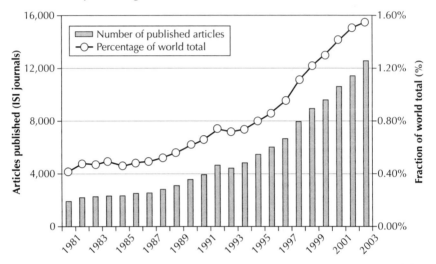

Source: National Science Indicators, Institute for Scientific Information, Philadelphia.

Figure 6: Number of doctorates granted yearly in Brazil

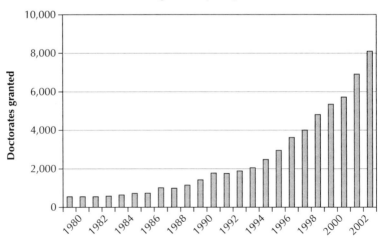

Source: CAPES, Plano Nacional de Pós-graduação, 2005.

The impact of articles originated in Brazil has grown, from 1.056 citations per article, for those published in 1981, to 1.862 citations per article, for those published in 1998 (Leta & Brito Cruz, 2003). For all fields the presence in terms of the fraction of world publications has grown in the same period, and the fields at which the scientific articles originating from Brazil have the largest presence are Agronomy and Veterinary (3.07% of world total publications), Physics (2.04%), Astronomy and Space Science (1.89%), Microbiology (1.89%) and Plant and Animal Sciences (1.87%).

Data from 2000 shows that 50% of the publications were in the field of Life Sciences, 33% in the Physical Sciences, 13% in Engineering, Technology and Mathematics, and 3% in Social and Behavioral Sciences. This is a distribution similar to the average for OECD countries (OECD, 2003). The participation of Engineering, Technology and Mathematics has been growing steadily, from a fraction of 10% in 1991.

The existence of a growing scientific community has allowed for the development of special research programmes that require a large number of researchers; a good example was the Genome Project, organized in São Paulo, which sequenced for the first time the DNA of a phytopatogenic bacterium, the Xylella Fastidiosa. This Program, organized in partnership with the Citrus Producer Association (Fundecitrus), generated advanced science, while at the same time contributing knowledge that allowed the researchers at Fundecitrus to devise ways to control a disease of the orange trees (citrus variegated clorosis, CVC) and generating at least two spin-off companies in the field of genomics and bioinformatics (Simpson, 2000).

Another example is the Biota Research Program, one of the largest biodiversity research efforts in the world, which groups more than 500 doctoral level scientists to study and map the biodiversity in the State of São Paulo. Since 1999 BIOTA, a "Virtual Institute for Biodiversity", has been studying the biodiversity in the state of São Paulo, Brazil. The mission of the institute is to inventory and characterize the biodiversity of the State of São Paulo, and define the mechanisms for its conservation and sustainable use. In six years, with an annual budget of approximately US$2,500,000, the Biota/Fapesp Program supported 75 major research projects — which trained successfully 150 MSc and 90 PhD students, produced and stored information about approximately 10,000 species and managed to link and make available data from 35 major biological collections. This effort is summarized in 464 articles published, in 161 scientific journals. Furthermore, the programme has published, so far, 16 books and two atlases.

The articles published in ISI journals do not tell the whole story about Brazilian scientific production. For developing countries, many times a relevant part of the generated knowledge is published in local journals, some of which have international circulation. In order to enhance the visibility of Brazilian science production Fapesp and the Latin American and Caribbean Center on Health Sciences Information organized since 1999 an open access web portal, Scielo (Alonso, 2002) (Scientific Electronic Library Online — www.sci-elo.org). Scielo offers access to 148 peer reviewed journals and has mirrors in Chile, Uruguay, Venezuela and Cuba.

Table 2: Number of journals, articles published per year and number of downloads from the Scientific Electronic Library Online, Scielo

	Journals	Articles, by year	Downloads, by year
1996	0	2,707	
1997	9	1,738	
1998	25	2,723	4,896
1999	35	3,646	67,725
2000	54	4,629	392,576
2001	66	5,570	1,070,988
2002	96	6,929	1,982,009
2003	115	8,101	4,071,871
2004	131	9,122	12,607,965
2005	148	10,048	27,921,378

Source: Scielo management.

Patents — industrial and academic

In 2004 there were 106 utility patents originated in Brazil issued by the United States Patents and Trademark Office (USPTO). This is a dismal quantity, considering the size of Brazilian economy and its scientific infrastructure described above, and although it compares well with the patenting activity of Brazil's Latin American neighbours, it is dwarfed by the numbers from Korea, Australia or Spain (Figure 6).

The number of scientists working in the business sector affects directly the number of patents that originate in the country. Other factors, such as the dominant industry sectors and export coefficients, affect the number of patents too.

Academic patenting has been gaining momentum in Brazil, especially since the examples of some institutions, such as the State University of Campinas (Unicamp) and Federal University of Minas Gerais (UFMG), gained country-wide visibility. Unicamp has had a strong patenting effort going on for more than two decades, and is the Brazilian academic institution which bears the largest patent stock, being the largest patent holder in Brazil for the period

Figure 7: Number of USPTO patents registered in 2004 by South Korea, Australia, Spain, Brazil, Mexico, Argentina and Chile

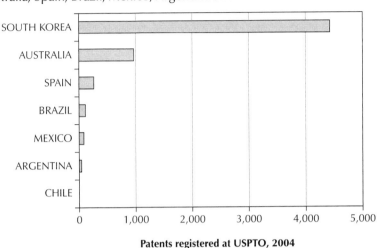

Patents registered at USPTO, 2004

Source: USPTO, at http://www.uspto.gov/web/offices/ac/ido/oeip/taf/cst_utlh.htm, on 26 February, 2006.

1999-2003 (Figure 7). The university created, in 2002, a Unicamp Agency for Innovation, a Technology Transfer Office, which demonstrated a strong licensing effort generating revenues from its intellectual property. Most of the licences were exclusive, since the licensee takes part in the development of the IP through a cooperative R&D agreement.

The Unicamp Agency for Innovation, Inova, was created in 2003, with the mission of fostering university industry linkages through cooperative R&D, consulting and intellectual property licensing. With a staff of 49, the Agency has licensed 40 patents and three non-proprietary technologies in 21 contracts. Prior to Inova's foundation the university had as few as eight licensed patents.

In 2004-2005, 87 cooperative R&D contracts with private companies dealt by Inova increased by 60% university revenues from this source. Patents applied at the Brazilian Instituto Nacional de Propriedade Industrial (INPI) in 2005 were 66, a one-third rise from 50 in 2004, making 2005 the best year for IP generation in Unicamp's 39-year existence. Licensing contracts include mainly pharmaceuticals and phytotherapeutic agents, food processing and nanotechnology-incorporated products. The first licensed technology (May 2004) originated Aglycon Soy, a soy-derived phytotherapeutic agent for menopausal women, which reached the market in 2007. Inova executives estimate the product will generate R$12 million per year royalties from 2008 on.

The BiphorTM licensing-contract, with Bunge Alimentos, has been Inova's most significant achievement when IP issues are involved. It is a nanotechnology-based, environmental-friendly new white pigment for paint, coatings and allied products, jointly developed by Bunge Alimentos and Unicamp's Chemistry Institute. According to Bunge, its white pigment will have a 10% world market-share by 2010. Expectations confirmed, royalty payments to Unicamp can reach US$45 million over the next decade.

Inova also works closely with the 100 companies that spun-off from Unicamp in the last 20 years, coordinating the studies for the implementation of a Technology Park in a 7 million sq. meters area adjoining the University.

Figure 8: Main patent originators in Brazil, in the perios 1999-2003, for patents registered at the Brazilian Patent Office (INPI)

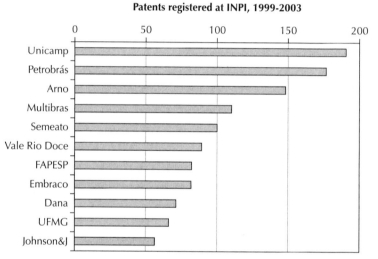

Source: FONTE: Pedidos de Patente BR publicados, BANCO DE DADOS EPOQUE

The fact that three academic institutions (Unicamp, Fapesp, the State of São Paulo Foundation for the Support of Research and UFMG, the Federal University of Minas Gerais) appear among the 10 largest patent generators in Brazil seems to indicate two things: first, that the academic institutions embraced the idea of protecting their intellectual property and looking for opportunities to generate businesses with it; and, second, that industry efforts to generate intellectual property are still weak since it is rare to find, among industrialized economies, situations in which academic institutions generate more patents than industry.

Universities must bear in mind that very few research universities have been, so far, able to make more money out of licensing than they spend doing it (Mowery, 1999). The actual motivation for a university to license its IP should be to fulfil its mandate to diffuse knowledge through society and to create opportunities for its students. An exclusive focusing on financial results has undone many efforts in technology transfer and licensing in Brazilian universities and even R&D public agencies, as it might have done worldwide. There is still a lot to be learned in Brazil about the benefits to society of generating new businesses through excellent higher education, an activity at which Brazil has already obtained some important successes, as for example, the case of the Aeronautics Technology Institute, one of the best engineering schools, which gave rise to Embraer.

Products and success cases in business-sector innovation

Brazil has some very successful cases of knowledge-based innovation. The agribusiness sector, benefiting from the public R&D investments at Embrapa and other organizations in the National System of Agricultural R&D, obtained outstanding results in both production and productivity. Soybeans, oranges, coffee are important items in the export balance due, in good part, to years of continuous R&D.

Energy from ethanol is another demonstration of the country's capability to generate and use knowledge to generate opportunities. The "Proalcool" (Alcohol Program), devised in the 70s, is the world's largest operation for the use of ethanol as fuel for automobiles. In 2005, 50% of the automobiles sold in Brazil were of the flex-fuel type, while in January 2006 this percentage went up to 74%. On top of that, the country adds 25% of ethanol to the gasoline to reduce emissions and also import costs. In 2005 Brazil was the largest ethanol producer in the world — at 15.4 billion litres — at a cost of US$0.19 per gallon, less than half of the world average of US$0.40. Industry, government institutes and universities R&D developed better sugarcane and more efficient planting and harvesting methods, together with developments in the ethanol refineries and their associated costs.

Jet aircraft is another case for which Brazil has used and produced knowledge to obtain a very competitive product and develop the 4th-largest aircraft manufacturer in the world. Following the 50-seat ERJ-145, Embraer has developed the 90-seat ERJ–190, of which the first unities have been flying commercially since the beginning of 2006.

In all these cases the main asset has been well educated human resources, formed in higher education institutions built to conform to the best world academic standards. Besides the human resources, all the cases have, at some point, depended on government policies for using its purchasing power to stimulate the technology development. Finally, a successful public-private partnership got the ideas to the market.

The challenge that the country has not yet overcome is that of diffusing the practice and the value of innovation through all sectors of industry. Years of a closed market and economical instability took their toll on the adoption of an innovative attitude in the business sector. With both government and industry leaders' attention directed to technology innovation, momentum has been building to develop this important area.

CONCLUSION

Brazil has developed a competitive academic science base, and the country must address important challenges to increase its industrial R&D sector. Important challenges exist for academia too.

In the academic sector, while the number of scientific articles and the number of doctorates granted yearly have been climbing, the country must find sensible ways to foster the development of the homogeneity of the academic base, both in regional and in terms of fields of knowledge perspective. Engineering and Computer Science stand as two fields in which an effort is required to form more graduates and doctorates and to increase the international insertion. However, the advancement of knowledge in Brazil might benefit from a more balanced government approach between directed and unfettered research. Recently there is a seemingly excessive tendency to direct the calls for projects to specific objectives, hurting curiosity-driven research which is the base of a strong academic system.

Industrial R&D suffers from a lack of government support, a situation which has been changing markedly for the last eight years. Recent measures such as the Law for Innovation and its consequences, as the refurbishing of the Tax Incentive legislation and the introduction of a subvention policy are expected to have an important effect in fostering industrial R&D. These measures are in the framework of the National Industrial, Technology and Exports Policy (PITCE in the Portuguese acronym), which also established areas of focus for the government actions.

The public portion of the R&D investment amounts to 0.56% of Brazil's GNP. This percentage is below the average OCED country by 0.12 percentage points, or 18%. In absolute values, raising the fraction of public R&D investment to the level of the average observed for OECD countries amounts to an additional 1.7 billion PPP dollars or R$2 billion (Reais from 2004) in additional money from public sources.

On the side of private R&D investment, it is clear that, when compared with the values practiced by developed countries, that is where the largest gap occurs. The private sector R&D investment in Brazil is close to 0.37% of the GNP, while the OECD average is 1.38% of the GNP, or 3.7 times higher. In absolute values this translates into the Herculean challenge of raising the private R&D investment to 13 billion PPP dollars, from the 3.8 billion PPP dollars practiced in 2000. This will require policy instruments much more effective than the ones used so far to this end.

A final note is in order here, addressing the question, frequently raised in many political circles in Brazil: "Why should the taxpayer money pay for R&D?" As a tentative answer, I would say that there are at least two equally relevant reasons for this.

One is that contributing to the universal pool of knowledge makes Brazilians more capable of leading and creating its own destiny. Like any human being, Brazilians are visited by the fundamental questions that we all ask ourselves: how did the universe begins, how does it work, why is that society behaves the way it does, what drives human beings towards good or evil, understanding the classics or studying literature. Studying these and countless other questions improves the human being and this alone would be reason enough to use taxpayer money to discover science-based answers, even partial ones, to the fundamental questions and to improve our knowledge of the universe and of mankind. Making Brazilians, and mankind, wiser through good and sound science is a beautiful and worthy endeavour, which certainly justifies public investment in science by itself. This is much more the job of Universities, the best ones, than the job of industry or the private sector.

The other reason, which seems to be far more popular nowadays, is that more knowledge, obtained according to the rules of the scientific method, makes society richer. This is a utilitarian view, and it has a strong appeal, especially since the Atomic Bomb, The Genome and the Internet. In this view, which I believe is complementary to the preceding one, but not (mostly) antagonistic to it, science is seen as a productive force, as it has been since the early steps of mankind. This line of reasoning depends strongly on industry and other enterprises, and, if successfully trailed, translates into making Brazilians richer.

The big challenge is to couple these two reasons, seeking to obtain the most and the best from the two worlds; to create the conditions in which Universities and the Private Sector might, through good and sound research as Francis Bacon once wrote, make the country a better place and a full member in the concert of Nations. I believe this can be done, but I also know that accomplishing it requires a lot of study, thinking and tolerance from all of the parties involved.

REFERENCES

Alonso, Wladimir J. & Fernández-Juricic, Esteban (2002). "Regional network raises profile of local journals". *Nature* (online), 415 (2002). Available at: http://www.nature.com/login/scidev_login.taf?ref=/nature/journal/v415/n6871/full/415471c_fs.html.

Leta, J. & Brito Cruz, C.H. (2003). "A produção científica brasileira", in *Indicadores de ciência e Tecnologia no Brasil*, Org. E.B.Viotti e M.M.Macedo, Ed. Unicamp, Campinas, pp. 121-168.

MCT, Ministry for Science and Technology of Brazil (2003). "National Science technology and Innovation Indicators", data obtained on 25 February 2006; at http://www.ricyt.edu.ar/indicadores/PorPais/BR.xls.

Mowery, D.C., Nelson, R.R., Sampat, B.N. & Ziedonis, A.A. (1999). "The Effects of the Bayh-Dole Act on U.S. Research and Technology Transfer", in *Industrializing Knowledge: University-Industry Linkages in Japan and the United States*, Branscomb, Lewis M., Kodama, Fumio & Florida, Richard (Eds). Harvard University Press.

OECD. (2003). "Science and Technology and Industry Scoreboard, 2003", OECD, p. 73.

Simpson, A. *et al.* (2000). "The genome sequence of the plant pathogen Xylella fastidiosa", *Nature*, v. 406, pp. 151-157.

PART IV

• • • • • • • • • • • • •

Shifting Paradigms for Global Competition and Cooperation

CHAPTER 14

Global Success: Real World Research 'Meets' Global Practitioners

Peter Lorange

INTRODUCTION

In this chapter we will first discuss the intensified global competition that seems to be evident between academic institutions. We will then point out two dimensions that might enhance stronger academic value creation in this emerging context. The first is more emphasis on realistic research — "real world" relevance in research. The second is bringing a balanced cross-section of leading learning partners into the classroom — "the global meeting place" — to become exposed to the tentative research results. Note that we use the term "learning partner" to signal the two-way learning that goes on when "real world, real learning" meets the global meeting place. The words "student" or "participant" perhaps indicate more of a unidirectional communication *from* the professor, and we do not agree with this. Likewise, the word "client" suggests a one-way relationship.

We shall then discuss several resulting implementation issues. The first is that, although a lot of research tends to be rather abstract, many business practitioners would prefer more "realistic" approaches. In addition, many learning settings are local — or at best regional — rather than global environments, which are increasingly in demand today. There might thus be a "disconnect", in that the research does not meet the needs of the learners.

A second implementation issue, related to the first, might have to do with the typical values set within academic institutions, which often give preference to more axiomatic, more narrowly focused research and teaching. This is in contrast to a more eclectic approach in both areas that might now be more effective.

A third implementation issue might have to do with the lack of "entrepreneurs" in academic research and teaching. These individuals take the initiative, are willing to run some risks and see new opportunities before they are obvious to everyone else.

The third part of the chapter deals with the need for cooperation to achieve global success and to make modern academic value creation more effective. A more networked approach — not so much conventional hierarchy — is essential to achieve this. Three areas of cooperation are highlighted: First, with other academic institutions — but how can this be done without becoming bogged down in excessive bureaucracy? Second, by having research centres in different geographic regions — but how can this be achieved without fragmenting one's faculty? Third, with leading corporations worldwide — but how can an action-oriented focus be maintained here?

We thus see that a number of key managerial issues in terms of the way an academic institution is run might have a central bearing on whether it achieves global success or not. In the final part of this chapter we shall discuss two such issues: (1) allocation of sufficient resources to the international dimension, and (2) adoption of a minimalist operational mode. Both are essential in order to achieve a global reach and to foster a non-bureaucratic managerial approach to keep things simple and maintain momentum. For further elaboration on several of these issues see Lorange (2008).

GLOBAL COMPETITION

Global competition among academic institutions seems to be intensifying on all fronts — when it comes to attracting both faculty and students, ensuring global research and marketing the offering. Still, many academic institutions remain for the most part rather local, serving local markets or, at most, regional ones. There are relatively few truly global academic institutions. At the university level, outstanding global institutions would include Harvard, MIT, Stanford, Chicago, Oxford, Cambridge and so on. At the business school level, there are INSEAD, London Business School, IMD and a few others.

In spite of the relatively small number of truly global academic institutions, there appears to be a clear trend toward a more global focus. It seems that global success is increasingly likely to be a determinant for strong academic value creation. Winning academic institutions thus probably need to make themselves more attractive to other globally minded stakeholders — learning partners with a global point of view, internationally oriented faculty members, corporations with an international focus and the like. How, then, can an academic institution become more effective as an attractive international academic value creator?

THE KEY ROLE OF RESEARCH AND LEARNING PARTNERSHIP

First of all, it seems vital that research should be at the forefront — but it must be research that the global community finds relevant. This might give rise to a call for a different type of research. It would complement the perhaps more widespread classical research, with its typically strong focus on axiomatically based themes, characterized by hypothesis testing and often carried out within rather narrow academic departments. Today, by contrast, more cross-functional, more eclectic research might be called for in order to tackle some of the key issues that are emerging on the international scene. This would require world-class faculty who might be able to work interactively with other top faculty on eclectic projects. There would probably be greater emphasis on a more international, often practical, outlook — perhaps shaping itself along the lines of what Joel Mokyr (2002) describes as *propositional* knowledge, focused on understanding and developing basic laws and models. Speedy transfer of this "work-in-progress" propositional research — not necessarily fully complete, but offering good ideas for further debate — into academic teaching programmes would appear to be key too.

It would be equally important to make sure that the academic auditorium is filled with learning partners who are *both* advanced — in terms of education and work experience — *and* from many parts of the world. This would constitute a global network of learners, able to bring to the table their *prescriptive* knowledge — which, according to Mokyr, is gained through experiencing, understanding and developing techniques to manage specific situations — thus complementing the propositional knowledge coming from the research. Two things appear key here: A focus on cross-cultural insights, and on discussing dilemmas rather than trying to come up with definitive "right" or "wrong" answers.

Perhaps, therefore, one can think of academic value creation as "real world, real learning" — from strong research — coming together with "the global meeting place" — achieved through a balanced global audience in the auditorium. In other words, cutting-edge research meets practical insights or, as Mokyr (2002) puts it, propositional knowledge meets prescriptive knowledge. All stakeholders in the process would learn — professors as well as learning partners. It would be a case of "lead *and* be led". And the likelihood of being able to address global issues of central concern meaningfully would indeed be higher.

SOME IMPLEMENTATION CHALLENGES

The process outlined above for modern international value creation — as set out by Mokyr and others — may have a strong general appeal as a way of pursuing global success. In practice, however, there can be real implementation barriers. Let us discuss three here.

First, as already indicated, because much research until now has often been rather axiomatic and discipline-based in nature, this may not necessarily lend itself to broader debate around more global issues. The propositional knowledge coming out of this research may not be of sufficient interest for international learning partners. In order to make this process of propositional knowledge *meeting* prescriptive knowledge work realistically, there would probably need to be some sort of minimum relevance requirement along an international dimension.

Second, since many academics have their career, remuneration and peer group feedback linked to rather narrow axiomatic realities, this could breed conservatism. Thus, in order to research more global phenomena, we would call for a "new" academic value creation process. It would typically be more cross-disciplinary, less silo-oriented and with tentative propositional research results being presented sooner. We can of course expect resistance from many classic academic sources in this regard.

The third implementation challenge has to do with identifying "academic entrepreneurs" to play a more prominent role within leading academic institutions. Such people would be good at three things:

- *Seeing new opportunities* before they are obvious to everyone else — perhaps global issues would be a particularly interesting focus here.
- **Networking with other academics** and other qualified people to develop a team of researchers who might effectively be able to study an emerging global issue that requires additional research and lead to better understanding.
- *Inspiring others* to work together in a networked setting. He/she would be a good leader in a charismatic sense, not by virtue of his/her formal position.

Overall, to improve the chances of global success, it is important to have academics with a more open attitude to critical research issues related to the international scene. They need to be willing to take risks, in terms of learning through "failure" — for example by publishing initial research outcomes quickly to stimulate debate in the classroom. This in turn can feed back into the research.

THE NEED FOR COOPERATION — IN NETWORKS, NOT HIERARCHICALLY

Although it sounds appealing in theory, it might, in practice, be difficult to have propositional knowledge meet prescriptive knowledge in such a way that academic value creation flourishes. The organizational models of formal academic institutions may typically be rather hierarchical, even "closed", and would not necessarily be well suited to pursuing global pre-eminence. A more networked approach might be better, to ensure more eclecticism, more flexible academic career management and more internationalism. Initiatives that require cooperation are more likely to make global success a reality. I shall point out three areas of possible cooperation.

An obvious one would be to cooperate with other academic institutions that have complementary competences to offer. Access to other knowledge and resources worldwide could have an effect that is greater than the sum of its parts. Thus, both the propositional base — from joint research — and the prescriptive base — from pooled learning partners — might be strengthened.

A second area of collaboration might be in establishing research centres in key sites around the world, thus also providing a more "local focus" for a global institution. This type of research — and thus the propositional knowledge — might be more realistic, as a result of being "closer to the action." At IMD, for instance, we have created two such research centres in Shanghai and Mumbai. However, the faculty remain united in one location — in this case Lausanne — and only visit the research centres for shorter intervals of time. Keeping the faculty together, as one eclectic resource, seems important not only for research but also for enhancing global success. Off-campus research centres should not lead to faculty fragmentation, i.e. to *less* global effectiveness.

In my opinion, the establishment of campuses around the world does not necessarily achieve an international focus. On the contrary, it might lead to a *less* global meeting place, as local or regional audiences are drawn to the satellite campuses closest to them instead of travelling further afield to benefit from — and contribute to — a more complex learning environment. A single *global meeting place* — one location in the world — would probably be more effective for creating the propositional-meets-prescriptive interface in academic value creation.

A third area of cooperation might be with leading companies worldwide. This might benefit the research side by providing access to better propositional knowledge from a broad spectrum of top international players. And it might lead to more skilled and experienced executives coming from all over the world — a stronger prescriptive base. At IMD, for instance, we have cooperations with 183 corporations from 22 nations, ranging from Switzerland (37) and the United Kingdom (21) to Austria (1), Greece (1) and Kuwait (1). Global success criteria might be better articulated by leading practitioners than by anyone else, given the feel for these issues that this group of stakeholders would have.

KEY MANAGERIAL ISSUES TO ENHANCE GLOBAL SUCCESS

When it comes to implementation and cooperation, as discussed above, managerial issues are often what make the real difference. Ultimately, the goal of global success is more likely to be attained if sound managerial practices are in place. Let us highlight two:

First, achieving a realistic global focus would require extra resources in order to attract faculty members from diverse backgrounds worldwide, overcome cultural and language barriers, and counteract formal research training biases. Also, attracting participants from all over the world usually requires heavy marketing. The bottom line is that creating a global meeting place — to foster the generation of realistic prescriptive knowledge inputs — is typically a challenging task that calls for plenty of resources.

The academic leadership must be willing to commit to pumping resources into global projects that might emerge as promising. This typically calls for some sort of "strategic budget", which can be tapped into when needed, and not only when the annual budget cycle dictates.

Second, administrative necessity calls for an action-oriented, non-bureaucratic and pragmatic way of managing. Global projects are typically be complicated enough as they are. To maintain *speed* and drive, a minimalist management approach is recommended. Too often, academic institutions end up applying rather bureaucratic procedures for managing international cooperation, which could — paradoxically — reduce the chances of global success.

CONCLUSION

We have noted that competition between academic institutions seems to be becoming increasingly global, and that sustainable success probably lies more in fostering effective academic value creation in a global context.

With this as a starting point, we prescribed an approach to academic value creation inspired by the thinking of Joel Mokyr. He prescribes that propositional knowledge from research should "meet" prescriptive knowledge from a well-balanced participant group. We would add that this could take place in a global meeting place. It is this dialogue between the two types of knowledge that, above all, might symbolize effective academic value creation in the modern context for tackling key issues of global concern.

We do, however, realize that it can be difficult to make this happen in practice, particularly because of several implementational challenges. One such implementation problem would be that many academics do not necessarily focus on practical, eclectic research. Rather they might still be attracted to more classic axiomatic — perhaps more narrowly defined — research. A second implementational issue might have to do with the more conservative bent of traditional academics, who are perhaps more reluctant to diverge from the "accepted" career path often governed by silos, peer review and classical publishing. Third, having enough "academic entrepreneurs" would be key for tackling global research issues, since this typically requires more eclecticism and willingness to take risks.

We also advocated a strong emphasis on networking — with three areas of networked cooperation — for tackling the key global issues, to make the propositional-meets-prescriptive academic value creation process more workable. The first area has to do with cooperating with academic institutions from other parts of the world, thus achieving more complementarity, but without becoming bogged down in bureaucracy. The second might be to establish research centres to foster research activities around the world, to enhance the "local focus" within a "global context" for more propositional complementarity. But this must not be done in a way that would fragment the faculty team — it must be *one* team able to tackle the globalization diversity issues. Third, cooperation with leading corporations worldwide might be another way to enhance the global academic value creating process. But action orientation and speed must be part of such cooperation, which is *not* that easy for academic institutions to achieve. All in all, networked cooperation potentially offers many opportunities that might enhance one's global focus, complementing the more traditional, academic value creation.

Finally, we pointed out that two managerial issues, i.e. approaches to the leadership of academic institutions, might prove quite decisive in whether global success is achieved or not. First, there is a clear need to allocate the necessary resources to strive to achieve a more realistic global research agenda and better global understanding. This would call for an ad hoc "strategic budget" for academic leaders to draw on in the middle of a budget cycle. Second, we highlighted the importance of minimalist simplicity in all management routines. This is in contrast with what we often find in academia, which can be rather bureaucratic and slow moving at times. Simplicity, speed, no bureaucracy and pragmatism would be called for. Global success through real world research "meeting" global practitioners might be an achievable goal, after all.

REFERENCES

Lorange, Peter. (2008). *Thought Leadership Meets Business: How Business Schools Can Become More Successful*. Cambridge University Press, Cambridge.
Mokyr, Joel. (2002). *The Gifts of Athena*. Princeton University Press, Princeton, NJ.

CHAPTER 15

Universities as Content Providers

Dennis Tsichritzis

INTRODUCTION

The main mission of the University was and still is Education. Naturally, Universities are also involved in many other activities like Research, Innovation, Incubation of small companies, services, etc. Education is, however, the main goal. To achieve this goal, Universities daily produce and disseminate content using different instruments. By content we mean any form of encoding of knowledge. The instruments for encapsulating contents range from the traditional to the very modern. To name just a few, Universities produce and deliver:

- Lectures.
- Seminars.
- Lab experiences.
- Publications and Books, and.
- Educational material in electronic form.

Up to now, Universities as content-providers have been rather conservative. The following are some self-imposed restrictions in their educational activity.

- They package their content in a strict format in courses and programmes.
- They deliver their content at a fixed rate and fixed schedule.
- They mostly insist on face-to-face communication.
- They do not archive or reuse what they produce except as a script in lecture notes.
- They mainly serve their local needs.

175

- They do not put any great value on their content.
- Professors are not evaluated on their content production capabilities except for new knowledge.
- Universities import very little content from elsewhere.

In the last few years we have seen an increased awareness of the value of content and many prestige universities produce lectures and courses and distribute them widely via the Internet. In this volume you will find many examples of such Open Courseware. However, for many Universities content production still means shooting videos of on-going educational activities as they happen. Some Universities do it professionally, but many can only afford amateur equipment and procedures. The costs remain high and the quality is not uniform. Moreover, there is no business plan for recuperating the costs, or creating wealth for the University. The Universities produce content for the same reasons as publications or books. The main purpose is to increase their fame and to make their courses and programmes remotely accessible to a wide audience.

CONTENT-PROVIDERS

Content-providers, on the other hand, are in the midst of a revolution. There are many technologies which converge and provide the platform for this revolution. Hand-held devices like the Nokia 95 or the I-Phone provide universal access and top functionality combined with sleek user interfaces. Broadband communications, tools like Joost and Bittorent and video streaming protocols enable delivery all over the world. Services like Youtube and Flickr provide repositories. Finally, users are accustomed to content services for pictures and videos of high quality and global reach.

We will pass in review the different content sectors and sketch what is happening.

- News from print form and TV is moving in the direction of Blogs for text, Microblogs for pictures and postcards and Vlogs for video cuts.
- Television programmes are becoming available in personalized form and at chosen slots.
- Music is delivered through I-tunes and similar services.
- Encyclopedias are being increasingly replaced by dynamic Wikipedias.
- Radio is going the direction of Satellite and Software Defined Radio.
- A host of location based services are offered on the basis of Google Earth and Google Map.
- Manuals and how-to-do material are offered by Howstuffworks.com and similar services.
- Training and Company news videos are becoming affordable and widely used.

Most of these services are successful because they operate in a different way.

- There is no clear distinction between content producers and content consumers. There is a community of users that operate as producers and consumers interchangeably.
- The services have global reach and aim at volume usage.
- The services are based on innovative business models for creating value and revenue.

When all of this is happening in the Media world, the Universities' efforts look pale in comparison. In a few years the children who at an early age are accustomed to Media services (the Google generation) will reach Universities. Will the Universities be ready for them? Every student can capture in video clips everything that is being said and disseminate it instantly. Every student can compare on-line and real time the lecture of his professor with clips of the best authorities on the subject. Will our system of courses, programmes, professors, lectures, etc. be able to cope? How are we going to retain authority and capture the imagination of such students?

We will pass in review our traditional instruments for education and discuss some necessary changes.

LECTURES AND SEMINARS

The purpose of a lecture is to package and deliver knowledge. There are at least four aspects in a lecture which are supposed to make it interesting and worth attending:

- To motivate and entertain.
- To inform.
- To compare and analyse, and.
- To excite the intellect.

Most lectures, however, end up being purely informative. The unavoidable repetition and routine, coupled with the pressures of scholarly success in Research, eventually take their toll. However, exactly this aspect — "to inform" — loses its meaning when everything is widely available and in excellent quality. Students want to be motivated, excited and entertained. They need careful analysis between theories, facts, opinions, conflicting hypotheses, etc. For all this, they have to interact in groups, to participate in communities, to exchange ideas. The lecturer is no longer the sole reference or the content-provider. The lecturer is an important participant, he is a coach, an animator, but very far from the sole authority he is now. In addition, he loses the strict and undisputed monopoly of ideas and interpretations.

The concept of a large lecture hall loses also its meaning. An electronic forum can expand arbitrarily and only the exchange dynamics limit its expansion. When people need to react face to face they can do it in small rooms, in coffee shops, alcoves or sitting on a bench under a tree. In addition, students will be able to interact in mobile form and from remote locations. Social skills and leadership will be redefined over the Internet.

COURSES AND PROGRAMMES

Lectures and courses are serial. That is, they cover a subject as a series of ideas. This situation arises mainly from the media communication genre. Spoken word in an ex cathedra lecture is serial and written material in books and papers in serial. People, however, do not think serial. Neither do computer systems today organize information serially. If people organize in their minds the ideas in a semantic network and all associated material is stored and retrieved from a semantic web, then the course itself does not have to be serial. Some loose ordering is necessary in order to provide discipline of exploration and keep in step a community of learning. This is more a complex path through the web according to interest and goal and has the sole purpose to organize time and focus the discussion.

In addition, the steps can be shortened and extended depending on progress and not according to a particular schedule. The strict and inflexible schedule coming from lecture hall availability and participants' timetables is no longer relevant. Neither are exams and grades relevant. The system itself can keep track of progress and the professor as a coach can judge maturity. Some sort of level indication is perhaps necessary, but more for formal reasons. We need to establish in a concise form the level of knowledge in a subject.

If courses are loosely organized internally, so are programmes. Prerequisites of subjects still have some meaning. Knowledge of different subjects has many levels and sometimes tools from one discipline are used in another. This gives rise to a partial ordering of subjects, each organized as a discussion course. One can enter at the bottom without prerequisites and reach one or more particular tops associated with subject domains. A sufficient number of these subject domains represent a discipline. Degrees can still be specialized by insisting on a number, or core, of necessary disciplines. There is, however, the flexibility of having an unorthodox basket of disciplines which can provide a good basis for a career. If somebody wants to be chef in a restaurant he needs chemistry, agriculture, art, management, public relations and business administration. All these exist today in a University, but there is no easy way to package them or a corresponding degree. Neither can Universities dynamically restructure to serve all potential needs.

PROFESSORS AND STUDENTS

In a University today there is a strict separation of people who know (the professors) and people who are there to learn (the students). Moreover, once a person achieved a rank (as professor) he keeps it for life. In addition, a lower rank (a student) has no right or means to disseminate his knowledge. Such strict separation of producers and consumers is no longer relevant for other content-providers. Why should it remain relevant for Universities? Learning communities in the future will evolve where producers and consumers intermix and change roles. A person can obtain and share his knowledge with other persons who are his peers, or follow students. In a similar manner as in today's graduate schools a student can be more of an expert than his professors in a narrow field. In addition, by sheer inquisitive persistence he can obtain some inside knowledge on a subject which may be unknown or ignored by his peers.

In such an environment, there is still a need for guidance and authority. In every discussion forum we need persons who play a special "mentor" role. They have a plan, a guide, some "must cover" material and an enthusiasm for the subject. They monitor and channel the discussion in particular directions. They also keep track of progress, with help from the system and decide on levels of knowledge for the participants. A person can be a "mentor", and at the same time a simple participant in a different forum. The best in a discussion forum can obtain some sort of licence to be a "mentor" and organize similar subjects for others.

There is still a need for professors. A professor is a person who has achieved undisputed authority because of his knowledge, communication skills and reputation. He is some sort of "guru" or "evangelist" on a subject. He intervenes to settle difficult issues, elevates the discussion level and provides necessary depth. He should be in constant pursuit of innovative ideas, and his communications in terms of Blogs and Vlogs should be treasured.

Needless to say a University does not need too many of these "gurus" as professors. Nor is it easy for a person to achieve such status. A person can only reach the rank by international, global acclaim and retain it only for as long as he is in a position to command it. It is not a matter of progressing through ranks and eventually keeping it for life. On the contrary, there will be very few persons who can keep the pace for long and dispense the energy needed.

EDUCATIONAL MATERIAL

Books and papers are the main repositories of knowledge today. Even in electronic form organized in digital libraries, they will represent only a small portion of the incoming avalanche of knowledge's progress. They will be used mainly as historical references and less as portraying what is currently known. The change of paradigm occurs for a very simple reason. It takes two simple actions to take a photo, point and click. Taking a video clip is slightly more complicated. Comparing that effort with just typing a paper, it is rather obvious what will happen. People will increasingly talk to a camera and organize other similar material to explain their ideas. There are already software systems (like Ricoh MP Meister) extensively used for training people or explaining subjects. In a similar way we will see specialized web services which will archive and provide these "educlips" (educational clips). The photo web services like Flickr and video services like Youtube will spawn specialized sections for educational subjects and courses.

A person will be judged by the amount of "educlip" footage that he is producing and its success — similar to the way by which papers and citations are used today to judge the amount and quality of intellectual output. A University as a site of learning communities will be judged accordingly. Copyright issues need to be sufficiently relaxed to enable free exchange and global reach. The volume of usage will be far more important than any amount of revenue obtained through strict control. As the content providers are finding "free is the new paid".

CONCLUDING REMARKS

There are two critical issues for the evolution of such a scenario of learning environment. First, will it scale? Second, will the Universities be able to play an important role?

The first question of scaling is rather easy to answer. This open, free learning environment will scale better than the traditional model. Trying to serve thousands of students according to traditional models has practically drowned the Universities. Many services from Google to Wikipedia have shown that they can scale much better than traditional methods. Peer to Peer protocols for video communication give good solutions for video streaming so there are no insurmountable technical problems. The rest is a subject of organization. Dealing with many fora at the same time is difficult, but not unrealistic, since the availability of mentors increases in parallel with the presence of the students.

The second question — the Universities' role — is much more difficult to answer. Universities can play a role in the emerging educational service sector only if they significantly change their existing structures and regulations. It is almost unrealistic to expect such a huge change of culture to occur without major changes in Governance and Management procedures. Just to separate the existing professors into "Gurus" and "Mentors" will be very difficult. Especially, since only the "Gurus" have special status and that only temporarily. Needless to say that in such an environment, tenure has no meaning.

We expect service companies to be able to position themselves in that environment very fast. Already we see companies organizing learning communities (like Sun's GLEC). By learning communities we do not mean "Corporate Universities" which is an attempt by some companies to start traditional style Universities. We mean services linking consumers and producers of knowledge and expertise. Companies like Google or Yahoo that already have the knowledge repositories are in a privileged position. All they need to do is to have some "Gurus" (easy, with the amount of money they command) and organize the learning communities. They can do it on their own or in partnership with prestige Universities for brand name and degree recognition.

Most Universities are in a much more difficult position to make their presence felt. They cannot organize learning communities on a grand scale as a service themselves. They lack the means and the expertise. They may not be in demand as partners if they do not command a well recognized brand name. They also need quite some time to restructure and reposition themselves. Sadly most of them do not realize that a global educational service sector is emerging or that it is threatening their local monopoly situation.

CHAPTER 16

The Organizational Challenge for European Universities Facing Globalization

Patrick Aebischer and Jean-François Ricci

INTRODUCTION

The academic world is more global than ever: competition for talents, international mobility both of students and faculty, diversification of funding are some of the main features of this changing environment faced by universities. International rankings are blooming and contribute — despite their obvious limitations — to globalization as well as competition.

Nowadays three main markets are predominant: North America, with most of the world's leading universities, Asia, the fastest-growing and changing academic environment with a huge potential in the near future, and Europe, with a long academic tradition. Three different backgrounds, three challenging environments, and a global competition framework.

Europe is made up of nations with very heterogeneous cultures, traditions, languages and political systems. This multiculturalism has to be fully taken into account in the way academic organizations are defined and managed. But, however strong their academic roots, these academic structures and organizations need to evolve in order to accommodate this new context and challenges in education and research. This paper summarizes some of those main academic challenges and proposes some general principles in reforming the organizational structures of European universities.

CHALLENGES FOR EUROPEAN UNIVERSITIES
IN A GLOBAL WORLD

Academic institutions have defined various ways to respond to new challenges and position themselves in the changing global academic environment. Swiss universities are also affected by this evolution. In fact Switzerland is quite a special case: a population of 7.5 million inhabitants, less than 20% of whom have a university degree, but 12 universities, five of which are ranked in the top 50 according to the Newsweek Ranking 2006. In this sense Switzerland is definitely a global player and has to take these global trends into account.

This chapter gives a broad — and non-exhaustive — view of some of the main challenges facing universities and institutes of technology, as well as some specific measures and initiatives developed by academic institutions worldwide.

Recruit the best students

Recruiting first-rate students is and will remain one of the main competitive advantages of universities in the global education world. Some universities like Imperial College base admission on interviews and performance evaluations. Partially due to the current legal framework in Switzerland which allows all students with a Swiss baccalaureate degree to enter EPFL (end of high school degree), it is a deliberate option at EPFL to base the selection on a first "propédeutique" (preparatory) year to give all students a chance to meet the selection criteria. Students with a foreign high school degree are admitted on dossier, but they have to pass their first-year "propédeutique" exam to move on. But, for both approaches, the dilemma is to find the right process to attract and select the best students who will become the leaders, scientists, engineers or entrepreneurs of tomorrow.

Due to this global competition, financial aid is on the agenda of most universities. As an example Cornell, Duke or Yale claim that education programmes have to be accessible whatever the financial circumstances of students and their families. Princeton has developed a broad system of financial aid grants calculated on an individual basis. Despite low tuition (approximately $1,000 a year), recent surveys in Switzerland show that there remain social inequalities in accessing universities. There is an urgent need for a constructive debate and concrete solutions in order to give better and fair access to higher education, both in Switzerland and in Europe. Fellowships for students from low-income families need to be further developed in order to ameliorate the situation.

Europe is pursuing the reform of education according to the Bologna Declaration. However, a lot of work still needs to be done in order to effectively transform the wide range of higher education programmes into a consistent framework for Bachelor, Master and Doctoral studies. As part of this reform, European universities should consider the development of true graduate schools covering both Master and Doctoral programmes.

Along with the success of the Erasmus programme, this new educational framework will greatly contribute to promote and reinforce the international mobility of students in Europe. As a consequence of this internationalization of education, more and more programmes will be taught in English, especially at the Master and Doctoral levels. Universities will therefore have to enhance their creativity and to find niches to emphasize their "génie propre" and specificities. Again the development of fellowships at the European level will be crucial to promote the mobility of European students.

Flexibility of the curricula is another key issue in the implementation of the Bologna Declaration. One of the most distinctive characteristics of educational programmes at the University of Cambridge is their breadth in the first years. In fact, many students do not have a clear idea of the options and topics they want to follow. The "Tripos System" gives students the opportunity to explore some topics in a very wide way, to delay specialization or to select some other fields according to new areas of interests. Yale University provides some vertical flexibility within the programmes. In addition to being able to enrol in advanced-level courses, students with exceptional preparation in certain areas may be eligible to accelerate — that is, to complete their degrees and graduate early by acquiring sufficient acceleration credits.

Providing the students with an opportunity to expand their knowledge is also on the agenda of many institutions. Beyond scientific and technological competences, courses in the Humanities offer the opportunity to study subjects which can make an important contribution to science and engineering students' general education and social awareness. As an example, the Imperial College Humanities courses include topics like philosophy, ethics in science and technology, history, modern literature and drama, art and music. A very similar offer has been developed at EPFL within the SHS — Social Sciences and Humanities programme. University College London aims at promoting social responsibility, global citizenship (including sustainability) and leadership in the student body, through both the formal curriculum and extra-curricular opportunities. The strategy of Duke University aims to infuse the campus with expanded opportunities to participate in and enjoy the arts. The University of Toronto aims at developing some understanding of the histories, cultures, values and epistemologies that shape the world we have inherited, in which we live, and which we shape. It should also be noted that this open-mindedness and flexibility also include the opportunity for the students to complete part of their curriculum abroad.

Attract and retain the best faculty

Beyond statements like "our staff is our most valuable resource", universities have to innovate in order to attract and retain their best staff, especially faculty and researchers. As a consequence of globalization and international recruitment, institutions have to benchmark their start-up and hard money packages in order to be competitive worldwide. This also includes considering spouse programmes together with competitive salaries.

But European universities should also develop a clear framework for academic promotions. Together with ETHZ, EPFL has adapted the US three-level faculty system, including developing a true tenure-track approach aiming at giving young scientists the autonomy and academic freedom to develop their own research and teaching.

As part of their motivation, retaining the best faculty should also include a scheme to reward the best contributions, especially for teaching. Beyond "bean-counting" procedures, universities should define some very simple processes aimed at identifying outstanding performance. But such an approach is also crucial for detecting local problems in teaching and providing suitable corrective measures, including teaching clinics.

Promote innovation and reinforce technology transfer

Innovation is a key driver for the economy and society, and universities play a crucial role at the very origin of the economic and industrial pipeline. Many institutions have therefore developed specific initiatives to support knowledge and technology transfer projects in their very early stages. The EPFL Vice Presidency for Innovation and Technology Transfer has recently developed several tools in order to close the innovation gap: science translator officers as a bridge between business technology needs and scientific research potentials and, as an additional component to the more traditional technology transfer activities, new schemes for the management of IP, creation of Innograms as tailored supports to the best EPFL intrapreneurs, increased plasticity for the interaction with industry, increased SME access and support to universities, etc.

Interdisciplinarity is a buzzword in all institutional visions and strategies. Beyond cutting-edge research within scientific domains, more and more discoveries occur at the interface between disciplines. Many institutions like Imperial College, Yale University, KTH Stockholm, Duke University and MIT are promoting such interdisciplinarity beyond structural organizations through dedicated centres and programmes. EPFL has recently launched new initiatives in the field of design, information security, global health, cognitive neuroscience, space research and energy: these initiatives aim at bringing together scientists and researchers from various fields and domains in order to develop innovative solutions and ideas. Beyond developing new scientific topics at the interface between domains, such initiatives are also very successful in providing concrete results for the economy and industry.

Develop strategic partnerships

Strategic partnerships are increasingly becoming part of the academic environment. Academic alliances are expanding beyond countries and continents, but national collaborations both with other academic institutions as well as with industries are also relevant.

Partly due to the results of most rankings, Europe has been used to looking west. But the current global trends and developments mean that European universities also have to learn to look east in order to develop new partnerships with Asian Universities: developing joint degrees, creating joint research programmes and joint laboratories, offering courses and programmes in Asian studies as well as providing incentives for these developments.

Become less dependent on state funding

The current constraints of public financing for higher education and research put a major pressure on universities. Beyond rationalization programmes and efficiency increases — typical economic approaches — European universities have to find new ways of financing.

The Bologna reform and increased student mobility have raised the question of tuition fees, which are today quite heterogeneous around the world. Another issue is the development of fundraising and sponsoring for chairs, fellowships or even buildings. Such external funding should greatly contribute to create real endowments, which would significantly increase the flexibility and agility of European universities. Despite significant successes for some rare European institutions, a major culture change will be needed to give the universities significant financial leverage.

Improve the management of universities

Due to the complexity of both the internal academic world as well as the external political environment, managing a university requires strong commitment and leadership. But such leadership is also needed at all levels of any institution, partly due to the need for rapid changes. So promoting, developing and even training professional university administrators should, more than ever, require great attention.

As part of the necessary change management, internal communication is a key component of any corporate culture. But this notion is often quite difficult and complex to manage in an open academic environment. Some institutions like the University of Cornell or UC Berkeley have created an Employee

Assembly — a mechanism for the informal exchange of information and views between employees and university administrators. But whatever the ways for such internal communication, this should never been taken for granted. Universities should therefore consider duplicating and multiplying communication channels in order to reach a majority of the institutional community.

European universities often have deep roots in history. Over the centuries they have developed well-respected traditions which are definitely part of their corporate culture and identity. But these traditions could also strongly restrain university management from undertaking the reforms needed due to external changes. Beyond keeping their corporate identity, universities should therefore develop a more flexible organization.

Together with this evolution the university management will have to integrate more and more characteristics and tools derived from the economy and business world. Through the Workforce Planning Initiative, the University of Cornell has been developing a global strategy in order to achieve sustainable improvement in both the effectiveness and the efficiency of campus wide support functions. At Yale University the Senior Management and the Unions agreed to launch and support a strategic initiative aiming at improving the overall quality, efficiency and workplace culture. Within the UK national context VfM — Value for Money is the term used to assess whether or not an organization has obtained the maximum benefit from the goods and services it acquires and/or provides within the resources available to it. Here once again staff commitment, awareness and participation are crucial for real success and implementation.

Data management and information systems have become unavoidable components of any university management good practice: finance, human resources, student management and academic information, but also research grants and contracts, as well as governance indicators, belong to this data management portfolio. The integration and combination of these large amounts of data and their use for competitive advantage is another step and challenge for the university senior administration. But this information is also required for the purpose of public reporting. Within the framework of the four-year performance contract the ETH Domain — ETHZ, EPFL and the four Research Institutes — reports its performance to Parliament on a yearly basis.

Provide modern infrastructure

The quality of infrastructure is definitely a crucial factor for attracting excellent students as well as top faculty and scientists. EPFL has a long tradition of providing first-rate facilities to the academic community. This is the result of a long-standing investment policy over decades. But this effort needs to be constantly renewed: this is the aim of the Campus 2010 project. As a central part of this concept and the future point of entry to EPFL, the Rolex Learning Center will be a place of learning, information and living. A place where virtual and physical components combine for facilitated access to knowledge. It will offer flexibility and development potential in order to adapt itself to pedagogical, social and technical evolution.

The EPFL Campus 2010 project also includes a significant extension of student housing capacity, the creation of a hotel on campus, an extension of the Sport Center on the lake, as well as new infrastructure for industrial developments, including incubators. Additionally, a conference centre is to be planned near the EPFL campus.

Local Responsibility and Commitment

Last but not least, universities have important social responsibilities towards local and regional communities. Many North American universities have developed significant commitments for a number of years: the University of Duke through the "Duke-Durham Neighborhood Partnership", Caltech through its Office of Public Relations, and Princeton through the Office of Community and Regional Affairs (CRA) are a very few examples of this culture of openness. Despite very different backgrounds and history, European universities will increasingly have to play a significant citizen role towards local and regional communities.

ORGANIZATION, STRUCTURES AND MANAGEMENT

Many of these challenges require special efforts in shaping and re-organizing academic institutions and the way they are managed. Due to this fast-changing environment, European universities have to reflect on their mission and role in and for society, develop strategies and define goals, as well as adapt their structures and management.

University organizations are "people" structures: students, faculty and researchers, as well as technical and administrative staff, belong to the same complex and changing academic environment. Together with sometimes very deep historical backgrounds, they all contribute to creating a unique organization in size, networks, competences, leadership and culture. Despite a very broad range of organizations, one may ask which are the common organizational features of institutions like Oxford University, MIT or Nanyang University. Or, in other words, are there any organizational criteria that could contribute to success and international recognition?

In order to move towards these objectives, structure and organization need to be carefully defined. But the first question to be asked relates to the notion of structure. According to Laurie J. Mullins (2004), structure is the pattern of relationship among positions in the organization and among members of the organization. Structure makes possible the application of the process of management and creates a framework of order and command through which the activities of the organization can be planned, organized, directed and controlled. The structure defines tasks and responsibilities, work roles and relationships, and channels of communication.

Within this very general and global framework there are obviously structures and structures. A study by Burns and Stalker (1966) described two extreme and divergent systems of management practice and structure: the mechanistic system (a more rigid structure with similar features to bureaucracy) and the organic system (a more fluid structure appropriate to changing conditions). Whereas the former pattern is more appropriate to stable conditions, the latter is more suitable to tackle new problems and situations. Actually most of the organizations combine some of the characteristics of both extreme patterns of mechanistic and organic systems.

Universities are a very typical example of such a hybrid organization. The unique combination of academic and administrative staff creates a very interesting — but complex — pattern. On the one hand, academic staff often feel that organic structures are the only framework they can effectively work within. Loose coordination and as little bureaucracy as possible are the most suitable organizational features, along with the academic freedom that faculty are granted. On the other hand, technical and administrative staff have a central function in keeping the organization operational. But they often have difficulties in integrating a real customer-oriented culture towards specific academic needs. This dilemma is a potential source of tension and misunderstanding, and a perpetual challenge for universities.

Defining a structure and an organization is a first step, but it is not enough. Synergies, collaboration and interactions need to take place within a form of integrated system. Lawrence and Lorsch (1969) described the parameter of integration as the quality of the state of collaboration that exists among departments that are required to achieve unity of effort by the demands of the environment. It is the degree of co-ordination between different departments with interdependent tasks. The mechanisms used to achieve integration depend on the amount of integration required and the difficulty in achieving it.

- In mechanistic structures, integration may be attempted through the use of policies, rules and procedures.
- In organic structures, integration may be attempted through teamwork and mutual co-operation.
- As the requirements for the amount of integration increase, additional means may be adopted, such as formal lateral relations, committees and project teams.

In every system and organization, achieving the right balance and level of integration is crucial. Redundancy and unnecessary complexity as a result of too much integration may easily lead to frustration and additional costs. But too low a level of integration could on the contrary result in loose and inefficient coordination, which could finally lead to waste of resources at the global level of the organization. Every institution has to define and find the right balance which mostly depends on historical background and academic tradition, political governance and the legal framework, as well as its corporate culture and internal structure.

EUROPEAN UNIVERSITIES FACING THE FUTURE OF GOVERNANCE AND ORGANIZATIONS

The structure is never the whole story. According to Birkinshaw (2001), structure is not an end in itself, but a means of improving organizational performance. Structure is also a way of managing the economic and efficient performance of the organization and the level of resource utilization. In this context, structures need to evolve and to accommodate the various challenges universities are facing.

Global competitiveness sets the framework for alternative forms of structures and systems of governance. Ridderstrale (2001) suggests some trends and ways of improving organizations and structures:

- More decentralized and flatter structures allow quick decisions to be taken near to where the critical knowledge resides.
- The use of more than a single structure in order that knowledge may be assembled across the boundaries of a traditional organization chart.
- Converting companies into learning organizations and giving every employee the same level of familiarity with personnel and capabilities.
- The broader sharing of expertise and knowledge, which may be located in the periphery where little formal authority resides.

European universities have to (re-)create flexible structures and organization models in order to accommodate a moving and globalized academic environment. They have to find the right level and degree of integration, i.e. the right balance between internal regulations, rules and procedures. They have to find the right procedures in order to be accountable to the political governing bodies. But they also have to find the right approach to informal group and teamwork in order to achieve a real and efficient collaboration as well as dynamic synergies among all groups and components of the academic community.

As far as governance is concerned European academic institutions have to gain autonomy in relation to politicians and stakeholders. But in parallel to these increased responsibilities and competencies at all levels of the institution, senior management has to reinforce the accountability framework towards these politicians and external bodies. The current four-year performance mandate of the ETH Domain is a good example of a clear separation between politicians and academics. But there is a fine line between increased bureaucracy, internal regulations, entrepreneurship and institutional agility.

Innovation is a key mover which needs to be part of every academic organization. New opportunities resulting both from increased mobility in Europe and the globalization of higher education worldwide, new ways of teaching and access to knowledge, new scientific and human challenges calling for new solutions, new ways of collaborating with academic and industrial partners. Innovation should be present at all levels of every institution. Moving forward and pushing the limits is the best way not to lag behind the rest of the academic world.

But people are definitely the key success factor and remain at the centre of each organization. People stay beyond all structures. As the latter put organizational emphasis on some institutional missions, individuals give life and movement to this structure. Any winning organization will always depend on the effective use of talented people. The internal connections, interactions and synergies of people together with a clear definition of objectives and structure will noticeably contribute to the success or failure of the organization as well as its effectiveness. Responsibilities, sharing of expertise and knowledge, informal networks, corporate culture and communication — a real and constant challenge within the academic environment — are some key factors providing the motivation and innovation spirit which will give every European university the strength and internal dynamism to face future challenges in the global academic world.

ADDENDUM

A sample of 15 universities has been considered in this paper. Ranging from a little over 2,000 students (Caltech) to tens of thousands of students (University of Toronto), nine of these are located in North America, five in Europe and one in Asia. One of the main common features of these institutions is their excellent performance according to the Newsweek Ranking (2006).

University	Country	Ranking Newsweek '06	Nb students
CALTECH - California Institute of Technology	USA	4	2'200
Princeton University	USA	15	6'600
MIT - Massachusetts Institute of Technology	USA	7	10'200
Yale University	USA	3	11'400
Duke University	USA	14	12'200
Imperial College	UK	17	12'200
KTH Stockholm	Sweden	–	13'000
TU Delft	Netherland	–	13'400
UCL - University College London	UK	25	18'300
University of Cambridge	UK	6	19'000
Columbia University	USA	10	20'200
Cornell University	USA	19	20'400
Nanyang University	Singapore	71	24'300
UC Berkeley	USA	5	30'300
University of Toronto	Canada	18	62'800

REFERENCES

Birkinshaw, J. (2001). "The Structures behind Global Companies", in Pickford, J. (Ed.), *Financial Times Mastering Management 2.0*, Financial Times Prentice Hall, London.

Burns, T. & Stalker, G.M. (1966). *The Management of Innovation*, Tavistock Publications, London.

Lawrence, P.R. & Lorsch, J. W. (1969). *Organization and Environment*, Irwin.

Mullins, Laurie J. (2004). *Management and Organisational Behaviour*, Financial Times Prentice Hall, London, seventh edition.

Newsweek Ranking (2006). http://www.msnbc.msn.com/id/14321230/site/newsweek/

Ridderstrale, J. (2001). "Business Moves beyond Bureaucracy", in Pickford, J. (Ed), *Financial Times Mastering Management 2.0*, Financial Times Prentice Hall, London.

CHAPTER 17

Higher Education in the 21st century: Global Imperatives, Regional Challenges, National Responsibilities and Emerging Opportunities

James J. Duderstadt

INTRODUCTION

We live in a time of great change, an increasingly global society, driven by the exponential growth of new knowledge and knitted together by rapidly evolving information and communication technologies. It is a time of challenge and contradiction, as an ever-increasing human population threatens global sustainability; a global, knowledge-driven economy places a new premium on technological workforce skills through phenomena such as out-sourcing and off-shoring; governments place increasing confidence in market forces to reflect public priorities even as new paradigms such as open-source software and open-content knowledge and learning challenge conventional free-market philosophies; and shifting geopolitical tensions are driven by the great disparity in wealth and power about the globe, manifested in the current threat to homeland security by terrorism. Yet it is also a time of unusual opportunity and optimism as new technologies not only improve the human condition, but also enable the creation and flourishing of new communities and social institutions more capable of addressing the needs of our society. Such issues provide the context for higher education in the 21st century.

GLOBAL IMPERATIVES

Our world today is undergoing a very rapid and profound social transformation, driven by powerful information and communications technologies that have stimulated a radically new system for creating wealth that depends upon the creation and application of new knowledge and hence upon educated people and their ideas. As Thomas Friedman stresses in his provocative book, *The World is Flat*, information and telecommunications technologies have created a platform "where intellectual work and intellectual capital can be delivered from anywhere — disaggregated, delivered, distributed, produced, and put back together again", or in current business terms, this gives an entirely new freedom to the way we do work, especially work of an intellectual nature (Friedman, 2005).

Our economies and companies have become international, spanning the globe and interdependent with other nations and other peoples. As the recent report of the National Intelligence Council's 2020 Project has concluded, "the very magnitude and speed of change resulting from a globalizing world — apart from its precise character — will be a defining feature of the world out to 2020. Globalization — growing interconnectedness reflected in the expanded flows of information, technology, capital, goods, services, and people throughout the world will become an overarching mega-trend, a force so ubiquitous that it will substantially shape all other major trends in the world of 2020." (National Intelligence Council, 2004). It is this reality of the hyper-competitive, global, knowledge-driven economy of the 21st century that is stimulating the powerful forces that will reshape the nature of our society and our knowledge institutions.

Nations are investing heavily and restructuring their economies to create high-skill, high-paying jobs in knowledge-intensive areas such as new technologies, financial services, trade and professional and technical services. From Paris to San Diego, Bangalore to Shanghai, there is a growing recognition throughout the world that economic prosperity and social well-being in a global, knowledge-driven economy require investment in knowledge resources. That is, regions must create and sustain a highly educated and innovative workforce and the capacity to generate and apply new knowledge, supported through policies and investments in developing human capital, technological innovation, and entrepreneurial skill (Council on Competitiveness, 2004).

Markets characterized by the instantaneous flows of knowledge, capital and work and unleashed by lowering trade barriers are creating global enterprises based upon business paradigms such as out-sourcing and off-shoring, a shift from public to private equity investment, and declining identification with or loyalty to national or regional interests. Market pressures increasingly trump public policy and hence the influence of national governments. Yet the challenges facing our world such as poverty, health, conflict and sustainability not only remain unmitigated, but in many respects become even more serious through the impact of the human species — global climate change being foremost among them. The global knowledge economy requires thoughtful, interdependent and globally identified citizens. Institutional and pedagogical innovations are needed to confront these challenges and insure that the canonical activities of universities — research, teaching and engagement — remain rich, relevant and accessible.

REGIONAL CHALLENGES

Regions face numerous challenges in positioning themselves for prosperity in the global economy, among them changing demographics, limited resources, and cultural constraints. The populations of most developed nations in North America, Europe and Asia are aging rapidly where over the next decade the percentage of the population over 60 will grow to over 30% to 40%. Half of the world's population today lives in countries where fertility rates are not sufficient to replace their current populations, e.g. the average fertility rate in EU has dropped to 1.45, below the 2.1 necessary for a stable population. Aging populations, out-migration, and shrinking workforces are having an important impact, particularly in Europe, Russia, and some Asian nations such as Japan, South Korea and Singapore. The implications are particularly serious for schools, colleges and universities that now experience not only aging faculty, but excess capacity that could lead to possible closure.

In sharp contrast, developing nations in Asia, Africa, and Latin America are characterized by young and growing populations in which the average age is less than 20. Here the demand for education is staggering since in a knowledge economy, it is clear to all that this is the key to one's future security. Unless developed nations step forward and help address this crisis, billions of people in coming generations will be denied the education so necessary to compete in, and survive in, the knowledge economy. The resulting despair and hopelessness among the young will feed the terrorism that so threatens our world today.

Today we see a serious imbalance between educational need and educational capacity — in a sense, many of our universities are in the wrong place, where populations are aging and perhaps even declining rather than young and growing. This has already triggered some market response, with the entry of for-profit providers of higher education (e.g., Laureate, Apollo) into providing higher education services on a global basis through acquisitions of existing institutions or distance learning technologies. It also is driving the interest in new paradigms such as the Open Education Resources movement (Atkins, 2007). Yet, even if market forces or international development efforts are successful in addressing the urgent educational needs of the developing world, there are also concerns about whether there will be enough jobs to respond to a growing population of college graduates in many of these regions.

Growing disparities in wealth and economic opportunity, frequently intensified by regional conflict, continue to drive population migration. The flow of workers across the global economy seeking prosperity and security presents further challenges to many nations. The burden of refugees and the complexity of absorbing immigrant cultures are particularly apparent in Europe and North America. In the United States, immigration from Latin America and Asia is now the dominant factor driving population growth (53%), with the US population projected to rise from 300 million to over 450 million by 2050 (National Information Center, 2006). While such immigrants bring to America incredible energy, talents and hope, and continue to diversify the ethnic character of our nation, this increasing diversity is complicated by social, political and economic factors. The full participation of immigrants and other under-represented ethnic groups continues to be hindered by the segregation and non-assimilation of minority cultures and backlash against long-accepted programmes designed to achieve social equity (e.g., affirmative action in college admissions). Furthermore, since most current immigrants are arriving from developing regions with weak educational capacity, new pressures have been placed on US educational systems for the remedial education of large numbers of non-English speaking students.

On a broader scale, the education investments demanded by the global knowledge economy are straining the economies of both developed and developing regions (OECD, 2005). Developing nations are overwhelmed by the higher education needs of an expanding young population at a time when even secondary education is only available to a small fraction of their populations. In the developed economies of Europe and Asia, the tax revenues that once supported university education only for a small elite are now being stretched thin to fund higher education for a significant fraction of the population (i.e., massification). Even the United States faces the limits imposed on further investment in education by retiring baby boomers who demand other social priorities such as health care, financial security, low crime, national security and tax relief (Zemsky et al., 2005; Newman et al., 2004).

These economic, social and technological factors are stimulating powerful market forces that are likely to drive a massive restructuring of the higher education enterprise. Already we see many governments tending to view higher education as a private benefit (to students) of considerable value rather than a public good benefiting all of society, shifting the value proposition from that of government responsibility to support the educational needs of a society to that of university responsibility to address the economic needs of government

— an interesting reversal of responsibilities and roles. Many nations are moving toward revenue-driven, market-responsive higher education systems more highly dependent on the private sector (e.g., student fees and philanthropy) because there is no way that their current tax systems can support the massification required by knowledge-driven economies in the face of other compelling social priorities (particularly the needs of the elderly).

The changing nature of the global economy is also exerting new and powerful pressures on regional educational needs and capacity. The liberalization of trade policies coupled with the ICT revolution has allowed the emergence of global corporations characterized by weakening ties to regional or national priorities. The trend for out-sourcing of business processes and off-shoring of jobs has accelerated as many corporations are now beginning to distribute not only routine production but fundamental aspects of core business activities (e.g., design, innovation, R&D) on a global basis, leaving behind relatively little core competence in their countries of origin. While this can create new regions of high innovation, these too can out-source/off-shore activities to still less expensive, although competent, labour markets, leaving behind enterprises characterized by little value added aside from financial management and brand name — no longer a solid foundation for a prosperous regional economy. From the United States to India to Vietnam to Kenya... the out-sourcing/off-shoring practices of the global corporation continue to distribute value-adding activities ever further, wherever skilled and motivated labour is available at highest quality and lowest cost.

NATIONAL RESPONSIBILITIES

In summary then, the forces driving change in our world — changing demographics (aging populations, migration, increasing ethnic diversity), globalization (economic, geopolitical, cultural), and disruptive technologies (info-bio-nano technologies) — are likely to drive very major changes in post-secondary education as a global knowledge economy demands a new level of knowledge, skills, and abilities on the part of our citizens. The strength, prosperity and leadership of a nation in a global knowledge economy will demand highly educated citizenry and hence a strong system of post-secondary education. It will also require research universities, capable of discovering new knowledge, developing innovative applications of these discoveries, transferring them into society through entrepreneurial activities, and educating those capable of working at the frontiers of knowledge and the professions.

Yet there are broader responsibilities beyond national interests — particularly for developed nations — in an ever more interconnected and interdependent world. Global challenges such as crippling poverty, health pandemics, terrorism and global climate change require both commitment and leaderships. Whether motivated by the economic design to create new markets or the more altruistic motives of human welfare, affluent nations have a responsibility to address global issues.

The ongoing debate concerning the future of higher education in the United States provides an illustration of the tension between the traditional roles of the university and the needs of the knowledge economy.

A CASE STUDY: THE UNITED STATES

Higher education in the United States is characterized both by its great diversity and an unusual degree of institutional autonomy — understandable in view of the limited role of the federal government in post-secondary education. As *The Economist* notes, "the strength of the American higher education system is that it has no system." It benefits from a remarkable balance among funding sources, with roughly 25% from the federal government, 20% from the states and 55% from private sources (tuition, philanthropy). Again to quote *The Economist*: "It is all too easy to mock American academia. But it is easy to lose sight of the real story: that America has the best system of higher education in the world!" (*The Economist*, 2005).

Yet, while this remains true in selected areas such as research and graduate education, many other aspects of higher education in the United States raise serious concerns: an increasing socioeconomic stratification of access to (and success in) quality higher education; questionable achievement of acceptable student learning outcomes (including critical thinking ability, civic participation, communication skills and quantitative literacy); cost containment and productivity; and the ability of institutions to adapt to changes demanded by the emerging knowledge services economy, globalization, rapidly evolving technologies, an increasingly diverse and aging population, and an evolving marketplace characterized by new needs (e.g., lifelong learning), new providers (e.g., for-profit, cyber, and global universities), and new paradigms (e.g., competency-based educational paradigms, distance learning, open educational resources). Furthermore, while American research universities continue to provide the nation with global leadership in research, advanced education and knowledge-intensive services such as health care, technology transfer and innovation, this leadership is threatened today by rising competition from abroad, by stagnant support of advanced education and research in key strategic areas such as physical science and engineering, and by the complacency and resistance to change of the American research university (Augustine, 2005).

In recent years, numerous studies sponsored by government, business, foundations, the national academies and the higher education community have suggested that the past attainments of American higher education may have led our nation to unwarranted complacency about its future. Of particular importance here was the National Commission on the Future of Higher Education, launched in 2005 to examine issues such as the access, affordability, accountability and quality of our colleges and universities (Miller, 2006). This unusually broad commission — comprised of members from business, government, foundations and higher education — concluded that "American higher education has become what, in the business world would be called a mature enterprise: increasingly risk-averse, at times self-satisfied, and unduly expensive. It is an enterprise that has yet to address the fundamental issues of how academic programs and institutions must be transformed to serve the changing educational needs of a knowledge economy. It has yet to successfully confront the impact of globalization, rapidly evolving technologies, an increasingly diverse and aging population, and an evolving marketplace characterized by new needs and new paradigms."

More specifically, the Commission raised two areas of particular concern about American higher education: social justice and global competitiveness. Too few Americans prepare for, participate in and complete higher education. Notwithstanding the nation's egalitarian principles, there is ample evidence that qualified young people from families of modest means are far less likely to go to college than their affluent peers with similar qualifications. America's higher-education financing system is increasingly dysfunctional. Government subsidies are declining; tuition is rising; and cost per student is increasing faster than inflation or family income.

Furthermore, at a time when the United States needs to be increasing the quality of learning outcomes and the economic value of a college education, there are disturbing signs that suggest higher education is moving in the opposite direction. Numerous recent studies suggest that today's American college students are not really learning what they need to learn (Bok, 2006). As a result, the continued ability of American post-secondary institutions to produce informed and skilled citizens who are able to lead and compete in the 21st century global marketplace may soon be in question. Furthermore, the decline of public investment in research and graduate education threatens to erode the capacity of America's research universities to produce new the knowledge necessary for innovation.

The Commission issued a series of sweeping recommendations to better align higher education with the needs of the nation, including; 1) reaffirming America's commitment to provide all students with the opportunity to pursue post-secondary education; 2) restructuring financial student aid programmes to focus upon the needs of lower income and minority students; 3) demanding transparency, accountability and commitment to public purpose in the operation of our universities; 4) adopting a culture of continuous innovation and quality improvement in higher education; 5) greatly increasing investment in key strategic areas such as science, engineering, medicine and other knowl-edge-intensive professions essential to global competitiveness; and 6) ensur-ing that all citizens have access to high quality educational, learning, and training opportunities throughout their lives. A series of actions has been launched by government at the federal and state levels, along with colleges and universities, to implement these recommendations over the next several years.

In a global, knowledge-driven economy, technological innovation — the transformation of new knowledge into products, processes, and services of value to society — is critical to competitiveness, long-term productivity growth, an improved quality of life and national security. It is certainly true that many of the characteristics of our nation that have made the United States such a leader in innovation and economic renewal remain strong: a dynamic, free society that is continually renewed through immigration; the quality of American intellectual property protection and the most flexible labour laws in the world, the best regulated and most efficient capital markets in the world for taking new ideas and turning them into products and services, open trade and open borders (at least relative to most other nations), and uni-versities and research laboratories that are the envy of the world. Yet today, many nations are investing heavily in the foundations of modern innovation systems, while the United States has failed to give such investments the pri-ority they deserve in recent years. Well-documented and disturbing trends include: skewing of the nation's research priorities away from engineering and physical sciences and toward the life sciences; erosion of the engineering research infrastructure; a relative decline in the interest and aptitude of Amer-ican students for pursuing education and training in engineering and other technical fields; and growing uncertainty about our ability to attract and retain gifted science and engineering students from abroad at a time when for-eign nationals constitute a large and productive fraction of the US R&D workforce. (Augustine, 2005; Duderstadt, 2005)

These concerns raised both by industry and the National Academies have finally stimulated the federal government to launch a very major effort, the American Competitiveness Initiative, aimed at sustaining US capacity for innovation and entrepreneurial activities (OSTP, 2006). The elements of this initiative will span the next decade and involve doubling federal investment in basic research in physical science and engineering (from $9.75 billion/year to $19.45 B/y); major investments in science and engineering education; tax policies designed to stimulate private sector in R&D; streamlining intellectual property policies; immigration policies that attract the best and brightest sci-entific minds from around the world; and building a business environment that stimulates and encourages entrepreneurship through free and flexible labour, capital, and product markets that rapidly diffuse new productive technologies.

EMERGING OPPORTUNITIES

The information and communications technologies enabling the global knowledge economy so-called cyberinfrastructure (the current term used to describe hardware, software, people, organizations, and policies) evolve exponentially, doubling in power for a given cost every year or so, amounting to a staggering increase in capacity of 100 to 1,000-fold every decade. It is becoming increasingly clear that we are approaching an inflection point in the potential of these technologies to radically transform knowledge work. To quote Arden Bement, Director of the US National Science Foundation: "We are entering a second revolution in information technology, one that may well usher in a new technological age that will dwarf, in sheer transformational scope and power, anything we have yet experienced in the current information age." (Bement, 2007).

Many leaders, both inside and outside the academy, believe that these forces of change will so transform our educational institutions — schools, colleges, universities, learning networks — over the next generation as to be unrecognizable within our current understandings and perspectives (Duderstadt, 2005; Brown, 2006). Let me illustrate with several possibilities:

The Global University: The emergence of a global knowledge economy is driven not only by pervasive transportation, information and communications technologies, but also by a radically new system for creating wealth that depends upon the creation and application of new knowledge and hence upon advanced education, research, innovation and entrepreneurial activities. There is a strong sense that higher education is similarly in the early stages of globalization, through the efforts of an increasing number of established universities to compete in the global marketplace for students, faculty and resources; through the rapid growth in international partnerships among universities; and through for-profit organizations (e.g., Apollo, Laureate) that seek to expand through acquisition into global enterprises. New types of universities may appear that increasingly define their purpose beyond regional or national priorities to address global needs such as health, environmental sustainability and international development — what one might call "universities in the world and of the world".

Lifelong Learning: Today the shelf life of education provided early in one's life, whether K-12 or higher education, is shrinking rapidly in face of the explosion of knowledge in many fields. Furthermore, longer life expectancies and lengthening working careers create additional needs to refresh one's knowledge and skills on a continual basis. Hence, an increasing number of nations are setting the ambitious goal of providing their citizens with pervasive, lifelong learning opportunities. Of course, this will require not only a very considerable transformation and expansion of the existing post-secondary education enterprise but also entirely new paradigms for the conduct, organization, financing, leadership and governance of higher education. Yet, if successful, it could also create true societies of learning, in which the sustained development of knowledge and human capital become the key paths to economic prosperity, national security and social welfare.

The Meta University: Some of the most interesting activities in higher education today involve an extension of the philosophy of open source software development to open up opportunities for learning and scholarship to the world by putting previously restricted knowledge into the public domain and inviting others to join both in its use and development. MIT led the way with its OpenCourseWare (OCW) initiative, placing the digital assets supporting almost 1,800 courses in the public domain on the Internet for the world to use. Today over 150 universities have adopted the OCW paradigm to distribute their own learning assets to the world (Vest, 2006). Furthermore, a number of universities and corporations have joined together to develop open-source middleware to support the instructional and scholarly activities of higher education, already used by several hundred universities around the world. (Sakai Project, 2007; Moodle, 2007) Perhaps the most exciting — and controversial — effort is the Google print library project in which a number of leading universities have joined together with Google to digitize a substantial portion of their library holdings, making these available for full-text searches using Google's powerful Internet search engines (Google, 2007). For example, Michigan expects Google to complete the scanning of its entire 7.8 million volume library by 2010. While there are still many copyright issues that need to be worked through, it is our hope that we will be able to provide full access to a significant fraction of this material to scholars and students throughout the world. When combined with the holdings of the other Google book scan members — now roughly a dozen of the world's leading libraries — the potential of this project amounts to providing full-text search access (and eventually perhaps direct online text access) to over half of the estimated books in the world today — in over 400 languages.

Open source, open content, open learning and other "open" technologies become the scaffolding on which to build truly global universities — what Vest terms the "meta" university (Vest, 2006). As he observes, "the incredibly large scale of education world wide; the huge diversity of cultural, political, and economic contexts; and the distribution of public and private financial resources to devote to education are too great." Instead Vest suggests that "through the array of open paradigms, we are seeing the early emergence of a Meta University — a transcendent, accessible, empowering, dynamic, communally-constructed framework of open materials and platforms on which much of higher education world wide can be constructed or enhanced."

Universal Access to Knowledge and Learning: Imagine what might be possible if all of these pieces could be pulled together, i.e., Internet-based access to all recorded (and then digitized) human knowledge augmented by powerful search engines, open source software (SAKAI), learning resources (OCW), open learning philosophies (open universities), new collaboratively developed tools (Wikipedia II, Web 2.0); and ubiquitous information and communications technology (e.g., Negroponte's $100 laptop computer or, more likely, advanced cell phone technology). In the near future it could be possible that anyone with even a modest Internet or cellular phone connection has access to all the recorded knowledge of our civilization along with ubiquitous learning opportunities. Imagine still further the linking together of billions of people with limitless access to knowledge and learning tools enabled by a rapidly evolving scaffolding of cyberinfrastructure increasing in power one-hundred to one thousand-fold every decade. In fact, we may be on the threshold of the emergence of a new form of civilization, as billions of world citizens interact together, unconstrained by today's monopolies on knowledge or learning opportunities (Atkins *et al.*, 2007; Kelly, 2006).

Perhaps this, then, is the most exciting vision for the truly global university, no longer constrained by space, time, monopoly or archaic laws, but rather responsive to the needs of a global, knowledge society and unleashed by technology to empower and serve all of humankind.

REFERENCES

Atkins, D.E. (chair), (2003). Report of the National Science Foundation Blue-Ribbon Advisory Panel on Cyberinfrastructure, Revolutionizing Science and Engineering Through Cyberinfrastructure. National Science Foundation, Washington, D.C.

Atkins, D.E., Brown, J.S. & Hammond, A.L. (2007). External Review of the Hewlett Foundation's Open Educational Resources (OER) Program: Achievements, Challenges, and Opportunities. Hewlett Foundation, Menlo Park, CA.

Augustine, N. (chair), (2005). National Academies Committee on Prospering in the Global Economy of the 21st century, Rising Above the Gathering Storm: Energizing and Employing America for a Brighter Economic Future, National Academies Press, Washington, D.C.

Bement, A.L. (2007). "Cyberinfrastructure: The Second Revolution", *Chronicle of Higher Education*, January, http://chronicle.com/weekly/v53/i18/18b00501.htm

Brown, J.S. (2006). "New Learning Environments for the 21st century", MIT Symposium on iCampus, Cambridge, MA.

Bok, D. (2006). *Our Underachieving Colleges*. Princeton University Press, Princeton, NJ.

Council on Competitiveness. (2004). National Innovation Initiative, Council on Competitiveness, Washington, D.C., http://www.compete.org/nii/

Duderstadt, J.J. (chair), (2003). Committee on Information Technology and the Future of the Research University, Preparing for the Revolution: Information Technology and the Future of the University. National Academies Press, Washington, D.C.

Duderstadt, J.J. (chair). (2005). Committee to Assess the Capacity of the United States Research Enterprise, Engineering Research and America's Future: Meeting the Challenges of a Global Economy, National Academy of Engineering, Washington, D.C.

Duderstadt, J.J., Wulf, W.A. & Zemsky, R. (2005). "Envisioning a Transformed University", *Issues in Science and Technology*, Vol. 22, No. 1, pp. 35-41. National Academy Press, Washington, D.C.

The Economist. (2005). "The Brains Business: A Survey of Higher Education", 10 September.

Friedman, T. (2005). *The World Is Flat: A Brief History of the 21st century*. Farrar, Strauss and Giroux, New York.

Google Book Library Project. (2007). http://books.google.com/googlebooks/library.html

IBM Corporation. (2006). IBM Global Innovation Outlook, IBM Corporation, Armonk, N.Y.

Kelly, K. (2006). "Scan This Book!", *New York Times Sunday Magazine*, 14 May.

Kurzweil, R. (1999). *The Age of Spiritual Machines: When Computers Exceed Human Intelligence*. New York: Viking.

Kurzweil, R. (2005). *The Singularity Is Near: When Humans Transcend Biology*. Viking Penguin, New York.

Lynn, L. & Salzman, H. (2006). "Collaborative Advantage", *Issues in Science and Technology*, Winter, pp. 74-82. National Academy Press, Washington, D.C.

Miller, C. (chair). (2006). National Commission on the Future of Higher Education in America, A Test of Leadership: Charting the Future of U.S. Higher Education, U.S. Department of Education, Washington, D.C.

Moodle. (2007). Course Management System, http://moodle.org/

National Information Center. (2006). "Population Projects-Percent Change from 2000 to 2005", http://www.higheredinfo.org/dbrowser/index.php?level=nation&mode=data&state=0&submeasure=107.

National Intelligence Council. (2004). Mapping the Global Future, Project 2020. U.S. Government Printing Office, Washington, D.C.

Newman, F., Couturier, L. & Scurry, J. (2004). *The Future of Higher Education: Rhetoric, Reality, and the Risks of Market*. Jossey-Bass Publishers, San Francisco.

OECD. (2005). Education at a Glance: OECD Indicators 2005, OECD, Paris.

OSTP. (2006). The American Competitiveness Initiative, U.S. Office of Science and Technology Policy, Washington, D.C., http://www.ostp.gov/html/ACIBooklet.pdf

Palmisano, S.J. (2006). "The Globally Integrated Enterprise", Foreign Affairs, May/June.

Sakai Project. (2007). Collaboration and Learning Environment for Education, http://sakaiproject.org/

Vest, C. M. (2006). "Open Content and the Emerging Global Meta-University", *Educause*, May/June, pp. 18-30.

Zemsky, R., Massey, W. & Wegner, G. (2005). *Remaking the American University: Market-Smart and Mission Centered*. Johns Hopkins University Press, Baltimore, MD.

CHAPTER 18

An Open University for the 21st century

B.M. Gourley

INTRODUCTION

Many things have been forever changed by the forces of globalization that have swept the world in the last couple of decades. Higher Education is one of them. It has also been changed by the imperatives of a knowledge society, a society where knowledge increases at an exponential rate and anyone who hopes to succeed must continually update and even retrain or render him or herself unemployable. More than that, in so-called Western economies where labour costs are high, manufacturing and other lower skilled jobs have migrated to other lower cost economies and there is less and less call for lower skill employment — thus reinforcing the necessity of having a larger and larger proportion of the population with education at a tertiary level.

It is important therefore to review the trends sweeping Higher Education — and put them in the context of the social trends that technology has unleashed, social trends which are in the process of not only changing the way in which the world does business but indeed changing the way in which universities — and open and distance learning institutions in particular — will have to discharge their main functions. The conclusion describes some of the ways in which The Open University in the UK is embracing these challenges and pursuing the opportunities.

TRENDS IN HIGHER EDUCATION

It would seem to many observers that we are witnessing a seismic shift in Higher Education. The authors of a book published last year entitled *The*

American Faculty: The Restructuring of Academic Work and Careers (Schuster & Finkelstein, 2006) contend that we are seeing nothing less than a revolution — with profound consequences. "Everything is in play," they write, "as nearly every aspect of academic life is being driven by a host of inter-related developments: dazzling technological advances, globalization that permeates academic boundaries, rapid increase of tertiary students worldwide, expansion of proprietary higher education, a blurring of [the] public/private distinction, and entrepreneurial initiatives on and off campus."

To this must be added the blurring of distance and residential, of full-time and part-time study, dramatically changing government policies on the funding of higher education (with an increasing belief that it is as much a private good as a public good), increasing competition (including competition across national boundaries), and research funding becoming ever more concentrated (in itself changing the very nature of the academic contract). The amazing social changes prompted by the new technologies and media, to say nothing of fundamental shifts in the world economy, are further factors. This last is of paramount importance to Higher Education because at the heart of economic change is collection, dissemination and management of information — historically Higher Education's core social functions (ibid, p. 6).

"Taken together," the authors of the book write, "these seismic shifts are profoundly changing how knowledge is acquired and transmitted... [and] changing the face — even the very meaning — of higher education. The coming change is unprecedented, insofar as the sheer number of forces in play, and the stunning rapidity with which they are shaping academia."

In developed countries, but also increasingly in less developed countries, technology has indeed changed everything. The Internet on its own has been dramatic enough, but as other technologies have advanced we now live in a world where "merchants in Zambia use mobile phones for banking; farmers in Senegal use them to monitor prices; health workers in South Africa use them to update health records while visiting patients" and we realize that although the personal computer helped democratize computing and unleashed all sorts of innovation, it is the mobile telephone "that now seems most likely to carry the dream of the 'personal computer' to its conclusion." (*The Economist*, 29 July 2006).

With this convergence of technologies (including near universal satellite coverage), we can reach people where they are, wherever they are, making learning as accessible as possible. Content can be delivered to laptops, iPods, smartphones, and computer monitors, whatever. This clearly has revolutionary potential for the educational endeavour — and it gives the concept of mobility a whole new meaning. We now have students who are able to delegate one of their number to attend a lecture and podcast it to their classmates; students who can watch the very best academic performers on their internet sites and not suffer less than best at any particular university; students who can access more and more material on open content sites; students who can take one or more courses at universities across national (and certainly individual university) boundaries; students who indeed learn in whole new ways. These are the students who arrive in the HE environment with different benchmarks from their predecessors and indeed with more choices. These are the students who will drive change in the system — rather more change than our political masters.

The consequences for the system are colossal. They challenge the physical facilities on offer; they challenge the nature of the materials produced — especially those that do not harness the technologies available; they challenge the material produced to match up to the best on open content sites; they challenge curricula as well as learning models; they challenge the very basis on which funding models and much more besides rest. Material that is available on open content sites poses particular questions about how much content should be reinvented at individual institutions (more especially at undergraduate level). Quality benchmarks will start taking account of what is available on open content sites as well.

In a world where the mobility of students is highly prized and projects such as the Bologna Process seek to enhance mobility, in a world too where competition is intense, quality and quality assurance are high on the agenda. Indeed, quality and associated "brand" have never been more important. More and more universities for the first time are hiring marketing specialists and advertising consultants, conducting branding campaigns and generally behaving much as ordinary businesses do in a competitive environment. As students are being required to pay more for education they are increasingly alert to their job prospects and to the economic value of degree offerings. As the realities of globalisation dawn on more and more people, universities are doing more to internationalize their offerings. Employer engagement and responsiveness to employer needs are high on many governments' agendas — and as our respective governments hope to shift some costs to employers, it had better be on universities' agendas as well.

More and more corporate employers are taking matters into their own hands and establishing "corporate" universities where they tailor the material to their own preferred outcomes. Publishers (like Pearsons and Thomsons), technology providers (like Cisco and Microsoft) and a host of others are in the HE market as well.

These trends have profound consequences for the business model upon which universities run their operations — and embracing the unprecedented opportunities offered by our global technology-fuelled knowledge society and embracing collaboration represent major strategies for survival in this new world.

THE DISRUPTIVE EFFECTS OF NEW TECHNOLOGIES

Many would argue that current technological advances rank alongside the Renaissance and the Industrial Revolution in terms of the unprecedented challenge they pose to businesses in a world where history seems to be accelerating and time being compressed. Higher education is no more immune to this challenge than any other sector.

It is useful to ponder just one important trend that these technologies have triggered: amateurs are now generating their own content on Internet sites — for free — and often in collaboration with peers. This trend has prompted a number of commentators to call this the Age of Peer Production.

From Amazon.com (where much of the value comes from millions of customer reviews) to MySpace to YouTube (which Google bought for $1.65 billion), some of the most successful web companies are building business models partly or largely based on user-generated content. MySpace has 120 million users and, while it is clearly a marvellous social network, it has also taken marketing into totally new territory. Wikipedia has set in train a new way of creating information. This is presenting a major challenge to *Encyclopaedia Britannica*.

And importantly, we are also seeing in MySpace, YouTube, Linux and Wikipedia exemplars of mass collaboration, forms of peer production that entirely change our business models. Tapscott and Williams call their recent book *Wikinomics* with the subtitle, *How Mass Collaboration Changes Everything* (Tapscott & Williams, 2006). John Battelle called his recently published book *The Search* with a subtitle, *How Google and its Rivals Changed the Way the World does Business* (Battelle, 2005). Neither of these excellent books is in any way exaggerating. The technology and the social networks it has spawned have indeed changed everything.

Who would have imagined that millions and millions of people would give their time, uncompensated in monetary terms, to create this amazing library in cyberspace? But then, as John Naughton reminds us in his book *A Brief History of the Future: The Origins of the Internet* (Naughton, 2000) not a single line of the computer code which underpins the Net is proprietary; and nobody who contributed to its development has ever made a cent from the intellectual property rights in it (p. xii). This is a gift culture and its currency is something different: reputation, expression, whim, whatever it is, it is providing the energy that drives a new kind of enterprise — and it is also making the outcome better for everybody.

One of the attributes (one might even call it a trend) of this new movement is its commitment to openness. Openness was not an attribute that could be applied to organizations in the old economy. Conventional wisdom had it that coveted resources were held close, even secret. That wisdom does not hold true in the new world. The fact is that the sheer complexity of the world and the startling richness of information available make it virtually impossible for any one organization to keep track of everything they need to know. "Today, companies that make their boundaries porous to external ideas and human capital outperform companies that rely solely on their internal resources and capabilities." (Tapscott & Williams, 2006; p. 21).

If peer production is one of the most powerful industrial forces of our time then we in education will have to ask ourselves tough questions about the production of some of our teaching materials, not only because our model is an expensive one but also because it is relatively slow in a world growing so accustomed to the swift satisfaction of consumer needs. In the Higher Education community we are seeing universities subscribing to the open educational resource movement and putting teaching material on the web, free to use subject only to the protocols of the Creative Commons Licences. This is a dramatic contribution to the improvement of educational endeavours where libraries are less than good and access to modern textbooks unaffordable — and it also has the potential to dramatically reorder how universities allocate their teaching activities and hence the costing of such activities.

The mass collaboration that is taking place on the Net is also changing quite dramatically the world of research. We now have the phenomenon of "crowd-sourcing" where companies describe a research problem and put it up on the Web for anybody to solve it. In an article last year entitled "Crowd-sourcing: Milk the masses for inspiration" *BusinessWeek* reported on "Inno-Centive, a social network created by Eli Lilly, where companies like Procter & Gamble and Boeing can pay a steep fee to post the knotty problems they can't solve internally — like a process for the extraction of trace metal impurities, for example. The idea is that individual problem solvers — retired scientists, obsessive hobbyists, university students —might be able to lend a hand. If they solve the problem, they receive a hefty cash reward." (http://www.businessweek.com/magazine/content/06_39/b4002422.htm).

What has this got to do with education? Two suggestions: first — higher educational institutions are going to have to behave more like private sector companies and consider buying some of the start-up companies in educational innovation. We don't have to invent everything ourselves. Second: collaboration has to be at the heart of change, because it is only by collaborating that we can harness the richness of a very large community of scholars and students and share our common wealth.

WHAT IMPLICATIONS DOES THIS HAVE FOR THE OPEN UNIVERSITY BUSINESS MODEL?

The Open University was an early pioneer in the field of open and distance learning, and consideration of some of its history is appropriate.

There is no doubt the University holds a particular place in British history and indeed, Higher Education history, by virtue of its special mission — to be open to people, places, methods and ideas; open, in particular to people who did not have the traditional entry qualifications to university. It was born amidst much scepticism on the part of many people, not the least of whom were the academics who believed that this departure from the norm would mean a radical drop in standards.

Within a surprisingly short time it confounded all the critics — by focusing not only on the quality of its materials (of whatever media), but also the quality of its student support, with study centres and 8,000 part-time tutors distributed all over the UK. It is doing something right — it received the highest rating for student satisfaction for the second consecutive year in the 2006 UK National Student Survey. The OU also places enormous emphasis on its research in educational technology and pedagogy. Its Knowledge Media Institute and its Institute for Educational Technology are well known all over the world for the quality of their research and their participation in the teams that put together our courses — another unique feature of the operation.

Since its foundation the OU has opened the door to Higher Education for more than 2 million people, achieving over 300,000 degrees. Throughout that time it has been in the vanguard of technological advances and currently over 220,000 people are studying with the OU or with institutions validated by the OU. Of these more than 35,000 are living outside the UK — and more than 10 000 are disabled. More than that, the OU has helped establish other "open" universities all over the world, which have grown at an astonishing rate.

It has been a remarkable achievement indeed — and the OU is not complacent. It lives in a highly competitive marketplace where competition respects no national geographic borders and where technology takes it into whole new paradigms. It faces unprecedented competition.

WHERE IS IT GOING FROM HERE?

The fact is that in many, many ways the OU is much more adapted to the changes in the world than virtually any educational institution. It has a great deal of expertise in a whole range of educational technologies and open and distance pedagogies, it has strong brand backed by high quality and the last few years have seen dramatic changes in the university as it accommodates to the new realities — for example customer relationship management and virtual learning environments.

Its overarching strategy for the future is to grow and strengthen its existing business in three main areas — each with their own business models, market understanding and growth strategies. These areas have been termed OU Core, OU Plus and OU for Free.

OU Core

The OU core business model — to deliver high quality supported open learning — has been developed and refined over nearly 40 years. Delivered originally through the print and broadcast media, it has more recently utilized the huge advances in technology to deliver e-learning to people they could not previously reach. It is now able to offer UK awards cost-effectively, flexibly and directly to an increasingly diverse cohort of students throughout the world.

But it has to ask itself some hard questions as to how best to deliver "customer service" — appropriate, flexible and sustainable student support — in this new world and how it harnesses this gift culture to enhance student support with peer-to-peer mentoring and collaborative learning models; how it deals with the shifting boundaries between formal and informal learning; how it harnesses the content that is being created on the internet in this remarkable new way. It is already experimenting with incorporating user-generated content into its teaching materials in the professional areas of its curriculum to harness the expertise of students in professional practice.

What we see on the Web are people from all over the world creating communities of interest (some of them very sophisticated indeed) on a whole range of subject matter — and what we need to do is ask ourselves how we harness this energy and recognise the learning — if that is indeed useful to people as they negotiate their careers and lives. OU students have been operating a very lively on-line community for many years, including peer mentoring possibilities. Indeed it has the largest virtual student common room in the world — managing and morphing that for a broader remit is not such a huge exercise.

There are some who remain sceptical about the quality of the learning experience delivered via technology and cite the centrality of the conventional face-to-face teacher-student relationship. Throughout its history, however, the OU has explored and exploited cutting-edge technological innovations to provide a high-quality, responsive and truly interactive open and supported learning environment.

OU Plus

"Working in partnership" is one of The Open University's strategic priorities — and has been from its inception. Our oldest offspring, The Allama Iqbal Open University in Pakistan, was established barely five years after the OU was launched in 1969. It has been wildly successful, with about 1.8 million course enrolments (1 million of these being in teacher education) and 1,400 study centres around Pakistan. The youngest offspring is the Arab Open University which was only established in 2002 and already has 30,000 students throughout Kuwait, Jordan, Lebanon, Egypt, Bahrain and Saudi Arabia.

It has partnerships in both the public and private sectors, helping it produce material, adapt to local context and "internationalize" its offerings — as well as enhance its research capacity and localise student support. It encourages the mobility of teaching staff across the system, by investing more in virtual access, by offering joint degrees, by making offerings to students wherever they may be — while at the same time respecting local differences and the necessity of local support. It is by collaborating across the system that it is finding solutions to meeting the language, cultural and even disciplinary heterogeneity of a global knowledge society.

Such partnerships include educators and Higher Education institutions, donor organizations and governments from countries across the continent to improve health, services and education through targeted programmes. TESSA — the Teacher Education in Sub-Saharan Africa programme — is providing online training on a unique scale to equip educators with the resources they need to teach language, literacy, numeracy and other vital skills. DEEP — the Digital Education Enhancement Project — has so successfully piloted IT as a teaching aid to primary schools in Egypt and South Africa that the programme is about to be rolled out to many more schools in these and other African countries.

Students will increasingly obtain education from both online and campus-based providers and this means that the OU is heavily committed to accreditation and validation partnerships. It is no trivial task to set these up across multiple systems. The language issue on its own is serious enough — as can be imagined. The very ethnocentricity created by the dominance of the English language in the world of the Internet is a challenge. The OU sees it as part of their task to contribute to the creation of a global information society that genuinely values diverse cultures as well as creating a more even distribution of wealth. By setting itself up as a global distance education institution it has to pay attention to this issue.

In this globalized (and highly competitive) world, it might at first glance seem paradoxical that the OU has put partnerships and collaborations at the heart of its strategy. It is almost a cliché to claim that the world is a global village yet it is true, as Elizabeth Lank points out in her insightful book on *Collaborative Advantage: How Organizations Win by Working Together* (Lank, 2005) that our lives and organizations' lives "are set within a much greater web of connections than any previous generation would recognize", with ever-increasing competition. In the past the "unit of analysis has generally been one specific organization and the choices it makes about its own markets, competencies and processes. However, it is self-evident that no single organization can be the best, the quickest, the most cost-effective at everything. Working with others to bring the right combination of skills, experience and resources to the job at hand is becoming a necessity in a world that moves as quickly, and demands as much as ours does today. Information and communication technology has dramatically lowered the transaction costs of collaborating — and it is now much easier to find and connect with a whole range of organizational partners. It is increasingly clear that going it alone is no longer a viable option for any organisation." (p. 1). In short, partnerships and collaborations are a strategic necessity.

OU for Free

And then there is the use of open source material. The OU is already the most significant user of Moodle, the open source course management system or virtual learning environment (VLE), and the launch of the OpenLearn site last year (where a selection of OU material and learning resources is available on the Web, free to use under the Creative Commons Licence protocol) signals its determination to play a leadership role in this new world. This is a £5.65 million project, with state-of-the-art learning support and collaboration tools to connect students and educators. Already almost half-a-million learners worldwide have experienced the free learning materials made available by OpenLearn since its launch in late 2006 and the site can now boast in excess of 2500 hours of free study materials.

This initiative has all sorts of implications for the HE system and indeed the central OU business model, to say nothing of the business models of other universities. It is, however, really significant for the many people far beyond our shores who do not have access to decent libraries, textbooks and educational media. In the science and technology domains where Africa and elsewhere are so desperately short of people educated in these disciplines, it is manna from heaven. It is marvellously consonant with the OU mission and the project has lit fires of enthusiasm all over the university.

Using the "skunk works" approach to bringing innovators together the OU is also currently developing a radically new model for supported open learning — SocialLearn — which is based on the principles that animate the participatory Web, including social media's "user generated content". SocialLearn is envisioned as being an "open marketplace" for learning. By this is meant that organizations such as corporations, universities or groups of educators will be able to participate in SocialLearn to forward their particular end, including direct sponsorship of programmes and research, accredited learning activities, or the creation and licensing of courseware. Individuals will be able to participate to achieve personal, corporate, or government-sponsored learning goals, perhaps receiving government grants or stipends. And, at its most basic, the idea of a marketplace means that participants can make money through their activities, such as the creation and licensing of courseware, performing learning services for others, such as teaching or tutoring. Watch this space!

The fact that The Open University is the first British university to place material on the web should be no particular surprise. The fact that it is actively searching for new ways to create the best environment for individuals to learn, building on rich social interaction with other engaged participants, and a constantly evolving learning environment that incorporates innovative and productive technologies and techniques, whatever their source — should also come as no surprise. The philosophy of open access and technological innovation is a perfect fit with the founding principles of the OU; one could almost say it is their destiny. The marvellous resonance of the whole open source, open innovation, open educational resources movement with the very name makes it feel like destiny! What better vehicle for reaching more people, in more places, regardless of their previous qualifications?

CONCLUSION

In summary — in many ways this new world of knowledge is now a lot more democratic and open, and the OU mission to bring education to all who can benefit by it ever more possible; to say nothing of bold and exciting and important; a mission that continues to inspire all who have the privilege of working at the OU. This article has given a glimpse of the complexities of running such a large business (with such a large mission!) and there are lessons for all educators and educational institutions in what the OU is doing. It remains a benchmark in the field. Who would have thought 40 years ago when it was founded that the possibilities and potential would have been quite so limitless?

REFERENCES

Battelle, J. (2005). *The Search: How Google and Its Rivals Rewrote the Rules of Business and Transformed Our Culture Portfolio*, Nicholas Brearley Publishing, Boston, MA; London.

Lank, E. (2005). *Collaborative Advantage: How Organizations Win by Working Together*, Palgrave Macmillan, Basingstoke UK.

Naughton, J. (2000). *A Brief History of the Future: The Origins of the Internet*. Phoenix Press, London.

Schuster, J.H. & Finkelstein, M.J. (2006). *The American Faculty: The Restructuring of Academic Work and Careers*, The Johns Hopkins University Press, Baltimore.

Tapscott, D. & Williams, A.D. (2006). *Wikinomics, How Mass Collaboration Changes Everything*, Penguin USA.

CHAPTER 19

The Emerging Meta University

Charles M. Vest

INTRODUCTION

The 21st century is an age when we cannot compete nationalistically based on geography, natural resources or military might. Nations can only prosper and compete based on brainpower and innovation. Because brainpower and innovation know no political or geographic boundaries, the fact is we must all cooperate as well as compete. In my view, there is no domain of human activity in which global cooperation is more desirable than in education. It is in the interest of all people that education be available and effective worldwide. This includes the kind of "high-end" education found in research universities.

In Asia, the Middle East and elsewhere, major investments are being made to elevate the quality of existing research universities or to create new ones. Most are based on western models that have been enormously successful, especially during the last 60 years. But hopefully, new and evolving institutions will also innovate by bringing new ideas and developing modifications of this model.

As we seek to advance research universities, new and old, the role of information technology is an immediate question. The advent of the Internet and the World Wide Web, together with ever-decreasing costs of computing power and digital memory, create new opportunities and raise fundamental questions.

How will the use of so-called educational technology play out? What will be the nature of globalization of higher education? Will the Age of the Internet and what lies beyond it fundamentally reshape education and research? Are residential universities dying dinosaurs or models to be propagated further?

My personal assessment of these matters is made in the context of two admitted biases. First, I remain hopelessly in love with the residential university. Teaching is fundamentally based on personal interaction, and it is difficult for me to envision anything better than the magic that happens when a

217

group of smart, motivated, and energetic young men and women live and learn together for a period of years in a lively and intense university environment.

But I am cautioned in this assessment by my second bias, which has to do with the rate of technological development. Years ago I read a book by Princeton's Gerrard O'Neil (O'Neil, 1981) in which he looked back over the centuries at what futurists of each period had predicted, and then compared their predictions with what turned out to be the realities. The primary lesson from this study is that the rate of technological progress was almost always dramatically under-predicted, and the rate of social progress is almost always dramatically over-predicted. I share this view.

What I envision, therefore, is a way in which relatively stable and conservative institutions will develop enormous synergies through the use of ever-expanding technological tools. Indeed this is already happening in profound ways. The views I present in this chapter draw extensively on a small book I recently authored (Vest, 2007).

INFORMATION TECHNOLOGY AND HIGHER EDUCATION

Computers, of course, have had a strong influence on higher education since the 1960s, starting out as specialized tools in science, engineering and mathematics, and then propagating across the humanities, arts and social sciences, as well as to business, law and medicine. During the late 1990s, following the development of the World Wide Web, and accelerated by ever decreasing prices of storage and processing, educators everywhere began to recognize information technology as a transformative force. This coincided with the dot-com era in the world of business, so attention quickly turned to how universities could teach large numbers of students at a distance, and how they could realize financial profits by doing so. Journalists, critics and many of our own faculty concluded that classroom teaching in lecture format was doomed. Economies of scale could be garnered and many more people could afford to obtain advanced educations via digital means. For-profit distance education was assumed to be the emerging coin of our realm. University faculty and administrators across the country wrestled over the ownership of intellectual property when a professor's course was made available electronically.

The model that was proposed over and again for higher education was "find the best teacher of a given subject, record his or her lectures and sell them in digital form". There is an appealing logic to this proposition, and I very much believe that there are important roles for this kind of teaching tool, but the image of students everywhere sitting in front of a box listening to the identical lecture is one that repels me. It struck me as odd that many of the same critics who decried the lack of personal attention given to students on our campuses seemed eager to move to this model. Nonetheless, the dominant proposition was that a university should project itself beyond its campus boundaries to teach students elsewhere.

But, in the meantime, many other teaching and learning innovations were introduced on campuses. Increasingly effective computer-based tools for language learning were developed. On-line journals were published. Computer simulations were used in subjects ranging from fluid mechanics to theatre stage design. Studio style instruction with heavy use of computational tools was refined. Multiple institutions shared large scientific databases. Massive search engines made information available to anyone with a web browser, and this quietly and rapidly revolutionized the work of many students and faculty. (It also introduced new complexities and issues of ethics by blurring definitions of "original work", and plagiarism.) Informal electronic learning communities formed, both within and among universities.

In other words, information technology, usually through increasingly large accumulations of modest, local activities, was transforming much of what we do on our campuses. Information technology was bringing the world to the students on our campuses, as well as projecting campus activities outwards.

At the Andrew W. Mellon Foundation, William C. Bowen and his colleagues developed ideas about how to empower large numbers of scholars and institutions through a combination of technology and economy of scale that in 1990 coalesced in the establishment of JSTOR. JSTOR makes available digital copies of scholarly journals in the liberal arts, sciences and humanities for modest annual fees scaled to institutional size. JSTOR currently serves 3,700 institutions, almost half of which are outside the United States, and archives 730 scholarly journals from more than 440 publishers. It helps individual scholars conducting advanced study and research at major universities. It also enables small liberal arts colleges with very modest resources to collectively or individually mount courses and research programmes in areas of the arts and sciences for which they could not have afforded appropriate library collections. In 2001 the Mellon Foundation launched a second major venture, ARTstor that uses a similar approach to develop a huge, carefully developed archive of high-quality digital images of great works of art. ARTstor archives more than 500,000 images, 100,000 of which are available in 1,024 pixel resolution.

In my view, JSTOR was a particularly important development in bringing the power of the Internet, and of sharing large digital archives, to humanistic scholars and students in a wide array of colleges and universities. It pointed toward a new type of "openness" in higher education.

MIT OPEN COURSEWARE

In 1997, with generous financial support from the Mellon and Hewlett Foundations, the Institute pledged to make available on the web, free of charge to teachers and learners everywhere, the substantially complete teaching materials from virtually all of the approximately 2,000 subjects we teach on campus. For most subjects these materials include a syllabus, course calendar, well-formatted and detailed lecture notes, exams, problem sets and solutions, lab and project plans, and in a few cases, video lectures. The materials have been cleared for third-party intellectual property and are available to users under a creative commons licence so that they can be used, distributed and modified for non-commercial purposes.

OpenCourseWare is a new, open form of publication. It is not teaching, and not the offering of courses or degrees. It is an exercise in openness, a catalyst for change, and an adventure. It is an adventure because it is a free flowing, empowering and potentially democratizing force, so we do not know in advance the uses to which it will be put. Indeed, users' stories and unusual paths are almost as numerous as our users.

At this stage, we have mounted the materials for 1,800 subjects from 33 academic disciplines in all five of our schools — almost every subject taught at MIT. Visitors are located on every continent and average over one million visits per month, with the average visitor to the site using almost 10 HTML pages per visit. Although the primary content of OCW is the notes for more than 25,000 lectures, it also includes more than 40 complete texts, and over 1,000 hours of video.

The OCW site receives 43% of its traffic from North America, 20% from East Asia, 16% from Western Europe. The remaining 20% of the users are distributed across Latin America, Eastern Europe, the Middle East, the Pacific Region and Sub-Saharan Africa. International usage is growing rapidly. Roughly 15% of OCW users are educators, and almost half of their usage is directly for course and curriculum development. One third of the users are students complementing a subject they are taking at another college or university, or simply expanding their personal knowledge. Almost half of the users are self-learners.

The uses which teachers and learners worldwide have made of Open-CourseWare are astounding, and could not have been predicted.

OpenCourseWare seems counterintuitive in a market-driven world, but it represents the intellectual generosity that faculties of great American universities have demonstrated in many ways over the years. In an innovative way, it expresses a belief that education can be advanced around the world by constantly widening access to information and pedagogical organization, and by inspiring others to participate.

AN OPEN COURSEWARE MOVEMENT

As MIT's faculty had hoped, today there is an emerging open courseware movement. Indeed, there are over 60 OCW initiatives in the US, China,

Japan, France, Spain, Portugal and Brazil. Thirty more initiatives are being planned, in South Africa, the UK, Russia and elsewhere. Consistent with our open philosophy, MIT OCW has actively worked to encourage and assist this movement.

In the US, the University of Michigan, Utah State University, the Johns Hopkins University School of Public Health, and Tufts University's Health Sciences and Fletcher School of Diplomacy all have established OCW efforts. Here I use the term open courseware to denote substantial, comprehensive, carefully managed, easily accessed, searchable, web-based collections of teaching materials for entire courses presented in a common format.

In this emerging open courseware movement, it is not only the teaching materials that are shared. We have also implemented and actively encouraged the sharing with other institutions of software, "know how", and other tools developed by MIT OCW. The primary mechanism for doing this is the OCW Consortium, that includes more than 120 institutions worldwide.

The China Open Resources for Education (CORE) translates MIT OCW courses into Mandarin and is making them available across China. In return, CORE is beginning to make Chinese courses available and translate them into English. Another partner, Universia, a consortium of 840 institutions in the Spanish-speaking world, translates MIT OCW subjects into Spanish and makes them available. Finally, Utah State University's Center for Open and Sustainable Learning is a partner that does outstanding research on open learning, materials and software.

My point here is that openly accessible resources can be used in their entirety, in part, at any pace, and can be added to, deleted from, or modified to fit a teacher's or learner's purpose and context.

How will OpenCourseWare evolve in the future? Will its evolution continue to be largely by replication in other institutions? Will it grow Linux-like into a single entity with continual improvements by educators and learners around the world? Or will it be replaced by other developments? I do not know the answer to this question beyond the next few years, but I do consider the Open-CourseWare movement to be part of a broader class of open access materials.

OPEN ARCHIVING, INDEXING, AND PUBLISHING

The seminal development of JSTOR has been followed by several other open access projects for archiving, indexing and publishing scholarly work. Examples include the Google Library Book Project, Carnegie Mellon's Million Book Project and Dspace.

Google has engaged several of the world's great libraries, those of Harvard University, the University of Michigan, the New York Public Library, the University of Oxford and Stanford University. The stated goal of its Library

Book Project is to "digitally scan books from their collections so that users worldwide can search them in Google". This is a book-finding initiative, not a book-reading initiative. If a book is out of copyright, the entire book is accessible. Otherwise, one can view snippets of the book, or a few of its pages, on line and obtain information about purchasing it.

Another major digital archiving initiative is the Million Book Project, a collaboration of Carnegie Mellon University, the Online Computer Library Center (OCLC), as well as government and academic institutional partners in China and India. Its goal is to create a free-to-read, searchable digital library. This initiative is notable for its highly international collection. As of last fall, it included more than 600,000 books, of which 170,000 are from India, 420,000 are from China, and 20,000 are from Egypt; 135,000 of the books are in English.

DSpace at MIT has a different goal than the archiving projects discussed above. Its goal is to develop a digital platform to make available the scholarly output of a single university. It includes preprints, technical reports, working papers, theses, conference reports, images, etc. This is at the opposite end of the spectrum from out-of-copyright books and journals; this is the stuff of working scholarship. MIT has worked in alliance with the Hewlett-Packard Corporation to create this archive and establish a DSpace Federation to promote and enable institutions to establish such repositories using freely available open source software. Dspace has been adopted by at least 150 institutions located on every continent except Antarctica, many of which contribute to the on-going improvement of the open-source Dspace platform code.

There is an additional and potentially very important dimension to the open movement — open-access journal publication. The first major foray into this domain is the Public Library of Science (PLOS), founded in 2000. This initiative, spearheaded by Dr Harold Varmus, CEO of the Sloan-Kettering Memorial Cancer Center, and Professors Patrick Brown and Michael Eisen of Stanford and Berkeley, respectively, publishes open-access journals in biology and medicine, and promotes open access within the scientific community.

The Howard Hughes Medical Institute and the Welcome Trust encourage the open-publication movement by providing publication costs for researchers whose work they have sponsored if it is published in open-access journals.

ISSUES FACING THE OPEN ACCESS MOVEMENT

There are at least four fundamental issues to be addressed if open source materials are to reach their full potential for use by scholars, teachers, students and self-learners: Intellectual Property Rights, Quality Control, Cost and Bandwidth.

Intellectual property (IP) issues are clearly inherent in archiving projects because the publishers of books and journals mostly own the copyrights. The resolution usually is some variant of a time delay, such as open access to a book only after the copyright has expired, or open access to a journal issue only after some fixed number of years has elapsed since its publication. In the case of open courseware projects, nettlesome third party IP issues arise when a professor makes use of a graph or certain types of excerpts from books or journal articles. Crediting a figure or excerpt from a publisher's product would seem to me to be great free advertising. After all, companies pay huge amounts of money for a glimpse of their product to appear in a movie or television programme. Some publishers agree, but many do not. In any event, publishers' approaches vary, and careful screening of materials for IP is a time-consuming and expensive aspect of creating and sustaining open courseware projects.

Of course, some faculty may be reluctant to have their teaching materials freely available on-line because they plan to use them as the basis for a textbook or other commercial dissemination. It was extremely satisfying for me to observe that this was a very minor issue when the MIT faculty undertook to establish MIT OCW.

Quality control, i.e. certification of the accuracy and appropriateness of scholarly and teaching materials on the Web, is a fundamental issue. The Web is a Wild West of information that has little or no vetting or peer review. The imprimatur and standards of leading universities, professional organizations and scholarly oversight groups therefore are of great value when they establish open publication and archiving organizations.

The production, maintenance and distribution of materials on the Web have very real costs. The more sophisticated the material and distribution are, the greater the cost in general. The societal value of freely available materials and indeed the value of sharing materials among institutions, are substantial, but there still is a bottom line. I am passionate about keeping my own institution's OCW without cost to users, but that is possible only through the generosity of foundations in the first instance, and of corporate and individual partners and supporters in the longer run. MIT also has pledged to meet a fraction of the sustaining costs itself.

Most major archives have a business plan in which there are user fees, but strong efforts have been made thus far to keep these as modest as possible, and to scale them to the size of the user institution.

Bandwidth is a very serious obstacle to one of the most attractive potentials of the open and non-profit movements for scholarship and education, namely its impact in the developing world. Institution building and scholarship in these countries can be given a terrific boost from access to these materials. Yet to take the best advantage of the materials, easy access and interactive participation via broadband is very important.

Hopefully open access activities will provide further stimulus for governments and NGOs to increase the availability and lower the costs of high-bandwidth connectivity. This is key to bridging the digital divide. In the meantime, MIT OCW has deployed 76 mirror sites on local university networks throughout the developing world as a promising alternative. A single mirror site at Makerre University in Uganda generates more traffic than the total traffic from Sub-Saharan Africa to the MIT OCW site on the World Wide Web.

The ease of use and interactivity of the Internet and World Wide Web make it the most attractive option for open courseware and archive access. However, it is not necessarily the only option. Delivery of CDs could work in some instances, although the ease of updating, maintenance and interactivity would suffer. The rapidly dropping cost of computer memory suggests another option. The amount of iPOD memory per dollar is approximately doubling each year. In round numbers, in 2004 a 20 Gigabyte device cost $400. In 2005 that cost had dropped to $250, and one could purchase 60 Gigabytes for $450. Should this continue, by 2025 $400 might purchase 40 Petabytes! In any event, this suggests another mechanism for delivering courseware and archival materials. Indeed, there are a number of current initiatives using educational podcasts, and using iPods as primary delivery media.

I believe that it is likely that iLab, a project initially conceived and implemented by Professor Jesus del Alamo of MIT is a harbinger of the next stage of open content — the on-line laboratory. The principle is simple. Computers today control most experiments. Therefore they can be controlled from any distance through the Internet. This is not new in the world of research. There is a lot of experience, for example, in operating telescopes and other research instruments from great distances. The idea behind iLab is to apply this concept to experiments used in teaching.

Now iLab has expanded to partner institutions around the world, e.g. students in Britain, Greece, Sweden, Singapore and Taiwan have accessed iLab. Furthermore, the MIT group makes available iLab Shared Architecture, a toolkit of reusable modules and a set of standardized protocols for developing and managing on-line laboratories.

THE META UNIVERSITY

Day-to-day communication and data-transfer among scholars and researchers are now totally dominated by Internet communications. Large, accessible scholarly archives like JSTOR and ARTstor are growing and heavily subscribed. The use of OpenCourseWare is developing in the US, Asia, and Europe. I believe that openness and sharing of intellectual resources and teaching materials — not closely controlled point-to-point distance education — should emerge as a dominant ethos of global higher education.

In my view, a global Meta University is arising that will accurately characterize higher education a decade or two hence. Like the computer operating system Linux, knowledge creation and teaching at each university will be elevated by the efforts of a multitude of individuals and groups all over the world. It will rapidly adapt to the changing learning styles of students who have grown up in a computationally rich environment. The biggest potential winners are in developing nations.

This will happen because nation after nation is committed to enhancing and expanding their higher education, and because there are global efficiencies and economies of scale to be had by sharing high-quality materials and systems that collectively are too expensive for each institution develop independently. It will happen because this kind of sharing is not prescriptive. It is not paternalistic, and it need not be politically or culturally laden, because each individual institution, professor or learner is free to use only those parts of the material he or she chooses, and may adapt, modify or add to it in fulfillment of the local needs, pedagogy and context. Campuses will still be important, and universities will still compete for resources, faculty, students and prestige, but they will do so on a digital platform of shared information, materials and experience that will raise quality and access all around.

CONCLUSION

The Age of the Internet and inexpensive information storage presents remarkable opportunities for higher education and research in the United States and throughout the world. The rise of a Meta University of globally created and shared teaching materials, scholarly archives and even laboratories could well be a dominant, democratizing force in the next few decades. It could come to under girding and empower campuses everywhere, both rich and poor.

REFERENCES

O'Neil, Gerard K. (1981). *2081: A Hopeful View of the Future*. Simon and Schuster, New York.
Vest, Charles M. (2007). *The American Research University from World War II to World Wide Web: Governments, the Private Sector, and the Emerging Meta-University*. University of California Press, Berkeley, California.

PART V

•••••••••••••

Universities
in and of The World

CHAPTER 20

The Responsibility
of Universities to promote
a sustainable society

Luc Weber

PREAMBLE

We are living in a period of deep and rapid changes which are offering great hopes for peace and prosperity, but which are also the source of important challenges and even threats. The direction of change will depend on the capacity of governments, governmental and international non-governmental organizations, business and churches, as well as — last but not least — the contribution of education to confront these challenges.

This chapter aims at revisiting the role that universities and other higher education institutions could and should play to improve the state of the world. It is divided into two parts. In the first part, we shall briefly describe why the present time offers great hope, but also great challenges and threats. Then, we shall suggest that these challenges can be reduced to the fact that many present developments are not sustainable. The second part will be focused on the role of higher education institutions, in particular research universities. We shall recall that higher education institutions should not only be responsive to these changes, but also have a major responsibility towards society, and argue that they are often not doing all that they could and should to fulfil this responsibility. We shall try to suggest why, describe a few initiatives taken to raise their awareness about their responsibilities and propose one solution capable of improving their contribution to a better and more sustainable world.

A WORLD OF HOPES AND CHALLENGES

The new world at the beginning of the 21st century

Never has the world been changing so rapidly and deeply as today. Moreover, there are strong reasons to believe that this trend will continue to accelerate. The most significant causes are diverse and strongly interdependent:

- The scientific and technological progress which is feeding a continuous increased productivity of labour and dramatically reduces all distances.
- The fall of the Soviet Union, marking the end of the cold war. Considering that more or less at the same time, other communist regimes like those of China and Vietnam or very regulated and protected countries like India have also adopted a market type of economy and are deregulating accordingly, today's world is largely dominated by market rules. Competition is becoming the driving force in the private, but also partly in the public, sectors. These developments also mean that democracy is gaining in importance in most regions of the world.
- Another phenomenon, closely linked with the previous one, is the rapid economic take-off of China, South Korea, India, which, in a few decades, have become important economic, political and military powers. Other countries are following the same path like Malaysia, Vietnam and Brazil.
- A last interdependent factor of change is the dramatic growth of population which increased from 1.65 billion in 1900 to 6.6 billion in 2007 and is expected to reach more than 9 billion in 2050 (US Census Bureau, 2007; United Nations, 1999). At the same time, thanks to progress in medicine and improved standards of living, life expectancy is increasing continuously.

This period of economic prosperity driven by science and technology, and the search for efficiency and competition, as well as by the rapid economic emergence of densely populated countries, offers a fantastic opportunity for further developments and long-lasting prosperity at world level. However, most of these developments contain in themselves characteristics which have turned or could easily turn them into threats, which are at least equal in importance to the opportunities. These threats are global or regional, but with the potential danger to impact on the whole world; they are also interdependent:

- Today, many agree with the United Nations Intergovernmental Panel on Climate Change (2007) that the observed climate change is one of the most important threats. Even if purely natural phenomena are at work, there is widespread agreement that the present warming of the earth atmosphere is mainly due to human activities, in particular to the greenhouse gas produced by burning fossil oils and gas to heat houses and to power vehicles. The consequences of climate change are threatening in the medium term and their very long term impact is in fact unpredictable.

- A closely linked phenomenon is the threat to biodiversity, which, among others, will make nature more vulnerable.

- The rapid demographic growth is very imbalanced according to the region, which is at the origin of large migration flows, mainly from those countries which experience a fast growing population, but haven't managed to take off economically, to developed countries with aging populations.

- Another serious threat is the growing gap between the developing world and those countries which haven't be able to take off, as well as the growing tension between different cultures, those being in general more or less strongly coloured by differences in religions, even between different ethnical groups within a country. These tensions are at the origin of internal conflicts (Lebanon, Burundi), regional conflicts (Middle East) or conflicts with a world impact (Iraq war). They are also the cause of growing immigration, mainly of young people, in search of job opportunities or simply fleeing from regions of conflicts. This important consequence of globalization contributes strongly to the increased blending of population in some parts of the world, in particular in the Western world. This diversity is certainly a source of enrichment, but also of tensions.

- The impact of some of these events is reinforced by the development of global TV channels, like CNN, BBC World, Deutsche Welle, France 24 or Al Jazeera, which are quick to report any event, therefore spreading local tensions all over the world.

- Although it is difficult to measure it, the increased prosperity seems to be accompanied by an increased individualization of our societies. Individual success is increasingly well considered and rewarded. This can be observed in the increasing inequality of income distribution, in particular due to the extremely high incomes of a few. This growing cult of individual success is also accompanied by a reproving tone towards those individuals who are living on State support and/or do not manage to get out of the poverty trap. In other words, the power of money has increased compared with the power of politics and citizenship.

Today's challenge:
promoting sustainable development at world level

Obviously, recent developments bring hope, but also hold serious challenges and threats. There are many good reasons, depending on our personal mind set, to feel either optimistic or pessimistic.

One promising way to synthesize the challenge to which governments, international organizations, business and citizens, as well as educational institutions, are confronted is to state that societies should aim for sustainable development (Huber & Harkavy, 2007). Sustainability is defined here as all efforts made to secure the long-term prosperity and stability of humankind and the different societies composing it.

Well established in the framework of environmental protection, the extension of the paradigm of sustainability to other domains is, to our knowledge, new. This is relatively surprising as the problematic of short- and medium-term developments which are not sustainable in the long run and will therefore end up in costly crisis are obviously not limited to the environment, but concerns also at least the economic and political spheres. As the generalization of the concept of sustainability is still in its early development, there are different ways to name the main distinctive domains where it is applicable. We propose to distinguish between:

- environmental sustainability, in line with the well known concept of sustainable development;
- economic sustainability, where economic has to be understood exhaustively to cover all question raising economic issues;
- political and institutional sustainability, which focus on the political system.

Environmental sustainability

The tension between economic growth and environmental protection has made the notion of sustainability quite popular. The negative impact on the environment of an uncontrolled economic growth became a concern in most developed countries 40-50 years ago. The concepts of "economic development" or "sustainable development" replaced the notion of "economic growth". The reason is the necessity to take into account that what is important is not economic growth, as such, but economic development, where the positive impact of the economic growth is not more or less completely compensated by a simultaneous decrease in environmental quality.

However, even if this negative impact of economic growth was identified a long time ago (see for ex. Pigou, 1932), the willingness to avoid or reduce it was "moderate". There was a great suspicion that environmentalists are exaggerating the risk for the environment and that business is either exclusively maximizing profit or anxious that paying much attention to the environment was a threat for their survival. Moreover, the attitude in favour of the environment was quite different from one region or country to the others, Northern Europe being for example, more sensitive to the threats than Southern Europe, or North America. Moreover, being focused on their economic take-off, the new developing countries do not like to bother with environmental protection, arguing among others that they are much less responsible for the current climate change than developed countries. The situation might change today now that it appears clearly that the earth's climate — not only the pollution of rivers and air — is rapidly changing and that it is mainly due to human activity.

More than ever, today, the concept of sustainability applies perfectly to the environment. If one believes that sound economic policy promoting prosperity while safeguarding the environment and avoiding a change of climate impossible to control, economic and energy policies, to mention the two most important ones in this regard, should have as main target to be sustainable in the long run. What is the point of reaching short- or medium-term good results in terms of economic growth if this success will necessarily be followed by disruptive impacts on the environment and dramatic climate changes which will make significant parts of the world unliveable and force masses of people to flee these regions. In addition to the immediate social costs, there will inevitably be an economic cost affecting development.

Economic sustainability

The case of the environment is not the only one where incorrect economic policies are not sustainable, which means that they will sooner or later end up in crisis, source of a substantial social cost, forcing eventually the country or the firm to dramatically modify the way they are run. There are numerous examples of such failures. Let us mention for example the Weimar Republic in Germany, which failed, in the early 1930s, to control the money supply. This lead to hyperinflation and high unemployment, which created the perfect conditions for the birth and rise of Nazism. Also, after decades of relative success, the centrally planned economy of the Soviet Union began to stagnate because it was unable to cope with the increasingly diversified needs of the population and failed to plan for replacement investments. Finally, many developing countries were unable to control the expansion of the State, which was increasingly financed by issuing debt. It provoked a loss of confidence among the creditors and ended up in a (re)payment crisis and invariably in the imposition of a rigorous cure by the International Monetary Fund. These few facts prove that insane economic policies do not last for ever, even if they might have created for some time the illusion of success.

Diverging demographic trends may also be the source of economic difficulties. Rapid population growth is either supporting economic growth in those countries which are rapidly developing or imposing a high burden in those which have not taken off. In developed countries, the impact of an aging population is less visible, but nonetheless important. In particular, it might put at risk social security systems, developed during the golden period of the 1960s. Moreover, a population with a high proportion of retired people is less of a risk-taker and tends more than a young population to protect what they have acquired, rather than being entrepreneurial.

Finally, let us mention that a very unequal distribution of income and/or wealth, within a country or at world level, or a health system benefiting only part of the population, is disruptive for social cohesion. In addition to being considered unjust by part of the population, it has a negative impact on the willingness of segments of population to work and may even create costly social movements (strikes, etc.), if not the access to political power of a political majority whose politics is clearly unfavourable to economic development.

Political (institutional) sustainability

The third dimension of sustainability lies with the political and institutional organization of countries, and of the world. The political regimes and institutional organization are different, sometimes quite different, therefore not all as likely to promote long-term stability and prosperity. Dictatorial regimes, in particular, can be successful for some time. The economic performance of the Soviet Union in the 1950s and 1960s for example had not much to envy to those of the free world. However, regimes based on the tough restriction of individual liberties, on incentives based on fear of punishment and on a State which decides much for its citizens, as well as on confiscating private wealth, cannot last for ever. They all finish by collapsing like the Roman Empire, the Nazi government in Germany, the communist regime in the Soviet Union and the regimes of many African leaders.

To last, political regimes must not only respect their citizens, but also give them the possibility to participate to the running of the country. This is the essence of democracy, which has basically two types of justifications. The first one, rather pragmatic, is teaching us that it is not possible to govern for ever against the interest and wills of the population and without respecting citizens. Another one, inspired by ethical values, highlights the necessity to respect human liberty and dignity.

At the international level, even if there are already many specialized international organizations like the United Nations, the World Trade Organization, the International Monetary fund, etc., or non-governmental organizations like the World Economic Forum, all these organizations are not global and/or comprehensive enough or do not dispose of the necessary instruments to impose their decisions/resolutions. In order to cope with problems affecting the whole globe like climate change and the substitution to renewable energy, as well as man-made humanitarian disasters and/or regional conflicts, the present worlds need to be better governed by international organizations that have the tools of their missions. In other words, the challenge of the governance of the world is becoming one, if not the main, challenge for building a politically sustainable world.

THE ROLE OF UNIVERSITIES

Responsive and responsible Universities

All through their long history, the responsibilities of universities have had two faces, which are contradictory in the short term and converging in the long term (Weber, 2002). On one hand, universities should be responsive to the short-term needs of the private economy, the State and their main stakeholders, the students; in other words, universities should respond to what society demands at any one time, in particular their students, the economy and the public sector. This influence is in general positive: universities should take these needs or requests very seriously as they are legitimate public demands (Glion declaration, 1998).

On the other hand, while responding to society's needs and demands, universities have also to assume a crucial responsibility towards society (Grin et al., 2000; Weber, 2002). In addition to being one of the oldest surviving institutions, universities are best placed to secure and transmit a society's cultural heritage, to create new knowledge and to have the professional competences and the right status to analyse social problems independently, scientifically and critically. The great difference between being responsive and being responsible lies in the fact that, in the first case, universities should be receptive to what society expects from them, in the second case, they should have the ambition to guide reflection and policy-making in society. While universities excel at making new discoveries in all disciplines of science and technology, they must also scrutinize systematically the trends that might affect sooner or later the well-being of populations and, if necessary, raise criticism, issue alarm signals and make recommendations.

It is precisely this responsibility that justifies why universities have been granted "autonomy", which is unique in the whole education sector, not to speak of other sectors or the State. This responsibility used to be a strong mission of the press; however, the political and economic pressures of our time push the media to be too responsive to the tastes of their audience, their government or the business world. Therefore, the responsibility of universities is even greater (Weber, 2002).

This responsibility, as well as the principles necessary to allow universities to assume them, was confirmed with great conviction by a thousand rectors and presidents of European universities gathered in 1988 in Bologna for the ninth centenary of the oldest university in Europe. In "The Magna Charta Universitatum" signed on this occasion, it is first of all stressed that Universities "must also serve society as a whole" and "must give future generations education and training that will teach them, and, through them, others, to respect the great harmonies of their natural environment and of life itself".

The fulfilment of their responsibility towards society and in particular the contribution to improve the sustainability of societies, goes, as described above, through the three traditional channels of their basic missions: teaching and learning, research and service to collectivity. But universities should also be a site of citizenship, that is set a high standard of behaviour towards their students, within the staff (academic and non academic), in research (respect for ethical principles and honesty of approaches), and should also demand such a high standard from students, in particular the absence of cheating (Bergan, 2004; Kohler & Huber, 2006).

An example for a responsible University: the promotion of a democratic culture

Without any doubt, it is a permanent responsibility of democratic regimes and political leaders, supra-national organizations, the media and educators to act democratically, to contribute to the improvement of democratic regimes and processes and, more generally, to promote these values, fundamental for the sustainability of society, nationally and internationally.

Nationally, the basic principles are fixed in the Constitutions. Internationally, they are laid down in fundamental documents as the "Universal Declaration of Human Rights" of the United Nations adopted in 1948, the "Convention for the Protection of Human Rights and Fundamental Freedoms" of the Council of Europe adopted in 1950 or in the "Geneva conventions on humanitarian law" (first in 1864). These Constitutions or Declarations also set up the means to implement the principles, like the European Court on Human Rights, the UN Commission on Human Rights, replaced in 2006 by the Human Rights Council, or the International Committee of the Red Cross.

These principles, however noble they are, have no chance to be broadly respected if they are not taught to children from a relatively early age and repeated to a wide public on any occasion. Democracy, and its main pillars citizenship, human rights and, what has been recognized more recently, sustainability, requires — in order to last and improve — the application of the same rules as a happy and long-lasting marriage: a strong belief in its virtues, trust between partner(s) and the active and tireless commitment of all actors (Huber & Harkavy, 2007).

Primary, secondary, as well as higher education institutions share a great responsibility in heightening the awareness of school children, adolescents, as well as traditional and mature students, to democracy, human rights and sustainability, all necessary conditions for the development, or even the survival of humankind. This is not "just" a question of learning a set of theoretical principles — it is a question of learning in the true sense of the word by internalizing a set of principles and acting upon them.

The implementation of this role is not without difficulty. Regarding education, higher education institutions have to teach young and mature students how to learn and transmit to them the essence of knowledge accumulated over decades, as well as the methodologies to acquire new knowledge and finally to give them the curiosity and the drive to continuously acquire the latest knowledge. Today's requirements in any discipline mean that disciplinary programmes (courses, seminars, writing essays) are very much focused on specific academic disciplines. In other words, in Europe certainly, but less so in the US where the first year(s) of college is (are) equivalent to the last year(s) of high school in Europe, higher education institutions are no longer responsible for the general education of their students (Weber, 2007). Students who moved to higher education institutions have opted for a high level professional training or academic education in a specific topic. This means that, in general, higher education institutions, apart from those disciplines dedicated to the question, do not bother to raise the awareness of their students to the democratic culture, as they are fully focused on the core of the discipline. This does not mean however they are impermeable to values: sustainable development and ethics have gained a respectable attention in many disciplines over recent years or even decades.

The same type of limitations appears at the level of research. Although there is bias towards certain topics and methodologies at the cost of others, the research community is in principle keen on identifying new promising and relevant topics of research. Regarding the question of democratic culture, it is necessary to distinguish between democracy and human rights on one hand and sustainability on the other hand. Democracy and human rights are a standard theme of research in particular within the disciplines of law, history, political science, sociology and history. The emergence and development of democracy and the practice of democracy in specific countries, as well as the definition and practice of human rights, is the object of numerous publications and conferences. Sustainability itself must be looked at from two relatively different points of view. The imperative of economic development respectful of the environment has been a concern for many decades for economists, geographers and lawyers, as well as many scientists, in particular chemists, physicists, climatologists and applied scientists. The other aspect of sustainability, whose importance emerged more recently, that is the capacity of an economic and political system to be stable over generations, is a much more complex issue. However, we know that, for demographic, political and economic reasons, some systems are more likely to escape deep disruption than others. Europe is, for example, preoccupied by the sustainability of its social security systems in a time of rapidly aging population. Specialists of the disciplines concerned are now beginning to tackle this issue, but a much greater effort remains to be made.

Are Universities doing enough?

Are universities taking upon themselves fully the responsibility to contribute to a sustainable society? Are they doing all that they could and should do? The response to the question is obviously mixed. Researchers in universities are doing work on many aspects of the question and teachers may refer to these questions, although more in social sciences and humanities than in live and hard sciences. Assessing if they are doing enough is delicate. My point of view is, however, that it is not the case. The organization of science production, in particular the financing of research, the editorial policy of journals, the fact that renown is the main — if not the only — reward for research results and that frontier research in a specific discipline is better quoted than interdisciplinary research, as well as the tendency of most human beings to "follow the crowd", contribute to the fact that in fact relatively few researchers follow ways outside the mainstream (Weber, 2007). Moreover, pure scientific questions are, for most researchers, more attractive than complex societal ones: the former are more likely to bring renown among colleagues, whereas the latter imply a delicate civil engagement. There are encouraging exceptions to that; in particular some very renowned scientists, often physicists, are taking strong positions on societal and political issues. Finally, if a discipline like climatology benefits from large amounts of money, the financial means available to study democracy, human rights or social security systems are in general very scarce.

The comparatively low interest in questions related to society is unfortunate as good solutions to questions like intercultural and inter-religious dialogue, the acceptance of the rules of law to solve conflicts, the acceptance and good practice of democratic rules, the respect of human rights or a sustainable economic development are all win-win strategies for societies. On the other hand, the social and economic costs of dictatorship, tyrannies or wars, whatever their justification, are easy to demonstrate.

Moreover, because of the increasing specialization of disciplines and increasing standardization of their teaching, there remains in general not enough time left to cover anything else. However, there is suddenly an encouraging trend: the fact that higher education institutions are increasingly considered to have also the responsibility to contribute to the personal development of students. They should be taught to work in groups, to speak in public, to write for a different audience, to search for money, to respect ethical considerations, etc. All this is positive, but not enough. Why not include under the chapter of personal development the education for democratic culture, and more generally for sustainable development?

A few solutions

Aware of this unsatisfactory fact, a few ad hoc groupings have taken initiatives to raise awareness about the necessity for universities to promote societal values and to create a real dynamic towards this goal in the university community. In addition to the Magna Charta Universitatum mentioned above, we would like to mention three initiatives aiming at emphasizing the societal responsibilities of higher education institutions:

- the 2003 Wingspread Declaration: A national Strategy for Improving School connectedness;
- and two "Talloires declaration";
  - one initiated in 1990 by the Association of University Leaders for a Sustainable Future (ULSF) and,
  - the other one in 2005 on the Civic Roles and Social responsibilities of Higher education.

These declarations invite those universities signing them to commit to act according to the principles laid down in the declaration.

More recently, convinced by experience that democratic culture must be permanently kept in mind, examined and discussed, and convinced that higher education institutions are not doing enough in this respect, the Council of Europe and its Steering Committee for Higher Education and Research, and the US Steering Committee of the International Consortium for Higher Education, Civic Responsibility and Democracy, have decided to join forces to take a new initiative aiming at encouraging higher education institutions to assume more fully their responsibility towards democratic culture, and more generally towards sustainability, in their teaching, as well as research missions.

Even if, at first sight, this new initiative is not different, in particular from the second "Talloires declaration" on the civic roles of universities, it is to our knowledge the first time that the values to be promoted through higher education encompass both the values of democratic culture and human rights, as well as sustainability. Moreover, sustainability is given here, as mentioned since the beginning, a broader sense as traditionally, covering both environmental protection and the economic and political sustainability of societies.

Second, the initiative is convened and led by the Council of Europe, the oldest pan-European political organization, which counts 46 members, and was founded in 1949 to "defend human rights, parliamentary democracy and the rule of law". Two hundred legally binding treaties or conventions have been signed under its umbrella. Education and higher education and research have a privileged position as a means to reach the objectives of the Council.

Third, the initiative benefits from the support of the leading university organizations, both in the US and in Europe.

However, economists like to repeat: "Supply does not create demand", which means that it is not enough to have a great product or service if buyers have not realized it or do not need it. The history of industry counts numerous examples of products or services flops, despite huge marketing efforts. The situation is unfortunately similar with noble ideas beneficial for society at large. We wonder if a researcher has already measured the impact of promoting noble ideas. We hope to be wrong, but, we suspect that only a minority has been successful. This is true for international organizations passing resolutions or multilateral agreements which remained "lettres mortes", or had little impact. This is also true for many initiatives taken by associations, foundations or individuals. However, and this is encouraging, some initiatives are extremely successful. Let us mention, for example, some fund-raising campaigns launched after a natural catastrophe. The frontier between success and failure is often very thin; in other words, one falls easily on one or the other side of the ridge, without knowing why or without having made an error.

The sense of this remark about the uncertainty of success in marketing a product or service, as well as implementing a resolution, a multilateral agreement or a noble initiative, is that it is, by far, not enough to have a good idea, but that it is necessary to fight for its success, probably also that it is necessary to be accompanied by a bit of luck and, eventually, that engagement for it should be rewarded.

The challenge within universities to develop more initiatives promoting sustainable development, is basically twofold:

- to overcome a feeling or behaviour of indifference, motivated by the conviction that these values are "part of the environment", that is accepted by everyone, and therefore does not have to be repeated or promoted;
- the feeling that the "university agenda is already full" and that there is no room left to do something further, considering all that is already expected from them.

These two attitudes which contribute to neglecting the importance of doing research and promoting, through teaching and learning, a sustainable society are raising a serious question of priority setting within higher education institutions and universities. The present climate of competition pushes universities to be more responsive to the short-term needs of their stakeholders or pressures from society or politics at the cost of their long-term responsibility towards society. This means that the priority given to these domains is lower that what would be justified.

The leaders of higher education institutions should be aware of these biases and compensate for them. In other words, the recent Council of Europe — Consortium's initiative, as well as all previous initiatives, requires the full engagement of university leaders. This implies for them two challenges:

- they are convinced that not only it is a responsibility of universities, including the university he or she leads, but also that he or she is convinced enough to act;
- he or she takes the lead in an initiative. However, it might appear particularly difficult for him or her to convince faculties and researchers to do something of significance. This implies at least a strong personal involvement.

However, one knows by experience that moral suasion, whatever the origin (government, signed declaration, etc…) remains a weaker means to convince people to move into the desired direction if the existing incentives (financial or others) are going in another direction. This is true both at the level of the institution leaders and within the institutions, at the levels of deans, directors, faculty and researchers.

However, it is amazing to observe in the higher education sector the impact of financial incentives. When additional funding is potentially available, most academics are prompt in competing for those funds by way of preparing projects and being ready to implement them if their bid is successful. In other words, university leaders and academics who are slow to respond to moral suasion and tend primarily to resist change, are suddenly quite ready to "move mountains" if there is a chance of additional funding, even if this activity is not considered a priority. This is why, we argue that the best — if not the only — way to encourage higher education institutions, faculty and researchers to give more importance to their long term responsibilities towards society is to modify the set of incentives, financial or others — in particular in matter of individual visibility and power. This applies both to action to increase the relative part of funding earmarked for activities (teaching and research) focused on the promotion of a sustainable society and seriously working on the image linked to different academic activities, among others the engagement in interdisciplinary research.

BY WAY OF CONCLUSION

The world is changing at an ever-increasing speed. This strongly contributes to the prosperity of societies and bring with it great hopes for a better society. But, at the same time, the fast-changing world is bringing quite new challenges and even threats to prosperity and stability. Probably, more than ever, it appears that to be positive to society, it is not enough for development to be — for some time — positive; they have to be sustainable over time.

Basically, governments, international governmental and non-governmental organizations and big business, should contribute to sustainable development. But, education, as well as higher education and research, has a crucial role to play. Higher education institutions in particular, thanks to the autonomy they enjoy and to their mastering of scientific methods and broad scholarship, are best placed to identify unsustainable and dangerous trends, speak out about them and contribute to solve societal problems. They exercise this responsibility through their research and research-driven teaching and learning, and by showing the right example.

The question we were asking is: do they do it sufficiently? The answer is probably not. The obligation to fulfil multiple objectives in teaching and the strong competition in research mean that other considerations or objectives benefit most of the time (or in most cases) from a higher priority. This is why we argued that, even if higher education institutions are spontaneously or indirectly doing a lot in favour of a sustainable development, they could and should do more. Hence, the fundamental question of how do we make it possible. The solution to this challenge has two levels. Basically, the norms of correct behaviour should be put right. This is true for the set of regulations fixing the framework of the university autonomy and/or stating the fundamental values promoted by higher education institutions. Moreover, these norms can be declined openly and give raise to collective engagements from groups of higher education institutions committing to work for these values (Magna Charta, Talloires Declarations, etc...). But, this is not enough. It is crucial to realize that the climate of competition between institutions and faculties and researchers does not leave enough room for this type of consideration in the teaching programmes or does not put a high professional reward — in terms of scientific visibility — to those doing research in these questions. This is why we have argued that society, in particular government, should increase the financial and all other incentives to engage in this type of activities in increasing the funds available on a competitive basis for research on societal problems, as well as the rewards in terms of visibility and power.

REFERENCES

Association of University Leaders for a Sustainable Future. (1990). *The Talloire Declaration*, http://www.ulsf.org/

Bergan, Sjur (ed). (2004). *The University as res publica*, Council of Europe higher education series, No. 1, Strasbourg.

Council of Europe. (1950), *Convention for the Protection of Human Rights and Fundamental Freedoms*, http://conventions.coe.int/Treaty/Commun/QueVoulezVous.asp?NT=005&CL=ENG

Glion colloquium. (1998). *Glion declaration: the University at the Millennium*, The Glion colloquium, Geneva, 9 p. or http://www.glion.org/?a=6202&p=1512

Gore, Al. (2006). *An Inconvenient Truth; The planetary emergency of global warming and what we can do about it*, Rodale books, Emmaus, Pennsylvania.

Grin, F., Harayama, Y. & Weber, L. (2000). *Responsiveness, responsibility and accountability: an evaluation of university governance in Switzerland*, Office fédéral de l'éducation et de la science, Berne.

Huber, Josef & Harkavy, Ira (Eds). (2007) *Higher Education and Democratic Culture: Citizenship, Human Rights and Civic Responsibility*, Council of Europe higher education series No.8, forthcoming.

Kant, I. (1785/1988). *Foundations of the Metaphysics of Morals and what is Enlightenment*, Macmillan, New York and London.

Kohler. J. & Huber J. (eds). (2006). *Higher Education governance between democratic culture, academic inspirations and market forces*, Council of Europe higher education series, No. 5, Strasbourg.

International Committee of the Red Cross, http://www.icrc.org/eng

Pigou, A. C. (1932). *The Economics of Welfare*, Macmillan, New York.

The Geneva Conventions. (1864 and later). http://www.icrc.org/Web/Eng/siteeng0.nsf/html/genevaconventions

Tufts University. (2005). *The Talloires Declaration on the civic Roles and social Responsibilities of Higher Education*, http://www.ulsf.org/

The United Nations Refugee Agency. (UNHCR), http://www.unhcr.org/cgi-bin/texis/vtx/home

The United Nations Office at Geneva. (UNOG), http://www.unog.ch/

United Nations. (1948). *Universal declaration of Human rights*, http://www.unhchr.ch/udhr/

United Nations. (1999). *The World at six billion*, http://www.un.org/esa/population/publications/sixbillion/sixbilcover.pdf

United Nations Intergovernmental Panel on Climate Change. (2006). *Contribution of Working Group I to the Fourth Assessment Report of the Intergovernmental Panel on Climate Change Summary for Policymakers*, http://www.ipcc.ch/

United Nations Intergovernmental Panel on Climate Change (IPCC) Working Group I. (2007). *The Physical Science Basis*, http://www.ipcc.ch/

US Census Bureau. (2007). *World Population Information*, http://www.census.gov/ipc/www/world.html

Weber, L. (2002). "Universities' Responsiveness and Responsibilities in an Age of Heightened competition" in (chap. 6, pp. 61-72) Hirsch & Weber (eds), *As the Walls of Academia are Tumbling Down*, Economica, London, Paris, Geneva.

Wingspread Declaration. (2003). http://www.allaboutkids.umn.edu/WingfortheWeb/schooldeclaration.pdf

CHAPTER 21

Doing Good by Doing Little? University Responsibility in a Violent Setting

John Waterbury

PREAMBLE

Lebanon's very name evokes images of civil strife and destruction, of a society almost hopelessly divided and open to exploitation by state and non state actors well beyond its borders. It is estimated that as many as 100,000 (out of a population of ca. 3.5 million) Lebanese lost their lives in the years of civil war, 1976-1990, in no small measure due to sectarian animosities. Over a longer period there has been a series of political assassinations of prominent Lebanese, but also including in 1984 the then president of the American University of Beirut (AUB), Dr Malcolm Kerr. Since the fall of 2004 the assassination campaign has accelerated, punctuated by a short vicious war carried out by Israel against Lebanon but precipitated by Hizbollah, a radical Shi'ite party with a history of violence dating back to the attack on the US Marine barracks in 1983. Even old hands in the analysis of the Lebanese scene are increasingly worried that the country may drift back to the civil disturbances of 1976-90.

Yet Lebanon has one of the best-educated populations in the Middle East. It enjoyed nearly two decades of growth and prosperity after the Second World War and until the civil war left it floundering economically. It is a heavily urban society with at least half the population living in Beirut. Its educational infrastructure, especially at the university level, is the most developed in the Arab world. For many years after the Second World War, Lebanon was the darling of social scientists focusing on the "Third World". It seemed to demonstrate that a multi-sectarian society could function democratically, develop economically through reliance on private markets, and achieve very high levels of literacy and education. It seemed to confirm the assumptions of the structural-functional school of analysis that foresaw a kind of linear trajectory of economic growth, the building of educated, professional middle classes, and the spread of democracy. The main figures contributing to this view were Daniel Lerner, Walt Rostow, Gabriel Almond and Seymour Lipset, among many others. In 1975 the country and the dream came undone.

It is probably no surprise to us now that literacy and prosperity are not universal solvents of sectarian or blood identities. US society in the past few decades has demonstrated that amply. I doubt that my university, over its long history, ever bought fully into the dream or myth about Lebanon; nor did it or does it give in to the gloom that envelops the region today.

The university over which I preside, the American University of Beirut, has thrived in this prickly, dangerous environment since its founding in 1863 as a private, not-for-profit university, incorporated in the State of New York. At that time it was known as the Syrian Protestant College, reflecting its Christian evangelical origins. With the creation of the French protectorate of Lebanon after the First World War, carved out of the remnants of the Ottoman Empire, the university had to change its name to reflect the new reality. It became the American University of Beirut. It also very quickly became co-educational, several decades before many of its peer institutions in the United States.

Today, 141 years since it graduated its first students, AUB has become a fully secular, non sectarian institution made up almost equally of male and female students. Our total enrolment is at present about 7,000 with 5,900 undergraduates. The university has six Faculties: Arts and Sciences, Engineering and Architecture; Agricultural and Food Sciences; Health Sciences; Medicine (including a School of Nursing); and Business. AUB has never entered into the training of lawyers.

We are in numbers and in ethos an undergraduate institution with a growing graduate and research superstructure. We more resemble Princeton than MIT in this respect. Because of the emphasis on undergraduate education, we are very concerned about the general values of personal responsibility, civility and citizenship that we seek to instil in our young students fresh out of the lycées and high schools of Lebanon and several other countries in the region (about 20% of our students are non-Lebanese). Because Lebanon's political system is explicitly based on sectarian representation, our emphasis on non-sectarianism aims to define another reality. In describing ourselves as "secular" (a term frequently confused in Lebanon and elsewhere with atheism) we emphasize respect for all religions but honour none in particular. I shall revisit this theme in greater detail below.

A PRESIDENTIAL AND INSTITUTIONAL PUZZLE

When Luc Weber asked me to prepare a paper on the university's role in mitigating communal and sectarian strife, or, put more positively, contributing to better understanding among diverse groups, I remember feeling mildly irritated by the question, mainly because the American University of Beirut, as an institution, does nothing formal in this domain. It is not university policy nor a part of our mission statement to promote inter-communal or inter-sect understanding in Lebanon or in the broader region from which our students are drawn.

With reflection, I realized that part of my irritation stemmed from the feeling that perhaps AUB should have such a policy, and therefore, as president, I asked myself why am I not doing anything or at least not doing more? The answer to that question is the substance of my contribution. The irony for me is that because the political and social environment in which AUB operates is in such need of the values we espouse, we cannot risk espousing them too openly or too aggressively. I suspect that I am not the first president of AUB to come to confront this paradox.

The unwritten philosophy of AUB, which I inherited when I became president in 1998, is to lead by doing. In American parlance, we walk the walk but do not talk the talk, at least extra-murally. We stress to our students, staff and faculty the institutional values of tolerance, mutual respect and achieving status within the university solely on the basis of merit.

Our founder, the Reverend Daniel Bliss, in 1871, put the core message as eloquently as anyone: "This College is for all conditions and classes of men without regard to colour, nationality, race, or religion. A man, white, black or yellow, Christian, Jew, Mohammedan or heathen, may enter and enjoy all the advantages of this institution for three, four or eight years; and go out believing in one God, in many gods, or in no God. But it will be impossible for anyone to continue with us long without knowing what we believe to be the truth and our reasons for that belief."

By 1920 the mildly sexist phrasing of President Bliss's remarks was corrected when AUB became fully co-educational, admitting women to undergraduate study.

For the most part successive university administrations have tried to demonstrate our values within our walls through student-faculty relations, sect-blind admissions, internal governance procedures such as an elected faculty senate, the practice of academic freedom and critical thinking, the fostering of student activities including elected student bodies, a student-run newspaper and several dozen student clubs. This is our "walking the walk". We hope that students will absorb these values and to the extent possible practise them once they leave our campus. To some extent that has been the case, but it is only fair to say that survival, let alone prospering, in the real world of Lebanon and other countries in the region often comes at the expense of our values.

Why have we not aspired to do more? AUB is, after all, a highly respected model of best practice not only as an institution of higher learning but as a large, complex private organization that has considerable weight in the Lebanese economy. AUB is Lebanon's largest private employer with nearly 3,000 non-academic employees concentrated mainly in our 400-bed hospital. We have about $120 million in capital projects underway, and our operating budget is today is about $175 million. We employ many, buy a lot, and contract regularly for consulting services of all kinds. We are looked to for best practice standards in financial and project management, medical ethics, human resource policies, bidding procedures as well as in standard academic activities like admissions and faculty recruiting and promotion. Some years ago I delivered a speech on cheating and plagiarism at AUB, among students and among faculty. I argued that our statistics on these phenomena were worrisome, but not greatly different from what is found in the US. I stressed that this is not a cultural issue. Nonetheless, Beirut newspapers picked up on my remarks and several commentators stated that if AUB has a problem with cheating, think how much worse it is elsewhere in our society (and therefore, by implication, excusable).

I do not have a convincing answer to my own question about AUB's relatively low profile on issues of sectarianism and civility, but rather only a number of "considerations". First is the issue of when does an activist institutional role on inter-communal understanding step over the line into formal politics? Lebanon's political system is constitutionally based on religious sects. It seems to me that the line between political and social arenas is virtually non-existent, so that if we go outside our walls, we may be squarely in the political realm. I do not think any university president anywhere would want to put his or her institution in that position. To be politically neutral in Lebanon is, to some extent, to be socially neutral. Only if the political and social arenas impinge directly and detrimentally on the university's ability to function normally and honour its values would we respond institutionally. The area most likely to be breached is that of academic freedom, but mercifully I have not had to deal with any serious attempt on the part of the Lebanese government or on the part of Lebanese politicians to influence our academic practices.

Second, the stakes of any taking of public stances are higher in Lebanon and the region as a whole than they are in North America and Europe. I think often of the debates raging in the US over the teaching of evolutionary theory and the attempts of school boards and state legislatures to impose their own views of what is acceptable on schools, colleges and universities. It may seem curious to some that evolutionary theory does not produce the same heat in the Middle East as it does in the United States, but there are other issues that do — and they have to do with religion, gender and geo-politics. However, my point is that no matter how impassioned the debates in the US, violence is not a likely by-product. In parts of the Middle East, including Lebanon, it is a likely by-product. A university has to choose very carefully where and when to use the "bully pulpit".

Third, without any overt attempts at coordination, the most prestigious universities in Lebanon have tended to converge in internal practices. Whether American in inspiration, like AUB and the Lebanese American University, sectarian like Haigazian, Notre Dame, and Balamand, or of continental/French inspiration like the Université Saint Joseph, we have all adopted similar practices and values. Unfortunately the same cannot be said for Lebanese University, the public giant which absorbs about 60% of all Lebanon's university students. For many years LU has been a highly-politicized, religiously divided, and poorly administered institution. Because its parlous state has resulted from the machinations of Lebanon's political class, more successful institutions, like mine, are not inclined to reach out to LU. That is a pity because LU has many fine faculty members carrying on under profoundly discouraging conditions and many gifted students who surely deserve a great deal more than they are receiving.

Finally, I have not wanted to go outside AUB's walls purely for public relations advantage. Inter-faith dialogue, respect for the religious "other", non sectarianism are all slogans that elicit positive responses. Throwing them about in public discourse may be and frequently is no more than cheap talk. The political class mouths them constantly. It should not surprise an academic audience that there is an inverse relationship between the frequency with which they are invoked and the degree to which they are practised. It is mainly talk and very little walk.

Yet there is a foundation upon which one could build. The 1945 Lebanese constitution simultaneously enshrines sects as the basis for political representation and calls for the gradual phasing out of sectarian politics. At the end of the civil war the Ta'if agreement shifted the sectarian balance slightly and re-iterated the call for an end to sectarian politics. Poll after poll shows that Lebanese youth want to get away from sectarianism, stating (but is it true?) that they have no problem with inter-sect marriage, civil marriage and non sectarian political representation. The same polls show a simultaneous instinct to fasten more intensely onto one's sect. The danger that leads many to hope wistfully that sects will diminish in importance is the same danger that drives the same people toward greater reliance on sect and clan.

You may see where I am going. The single most important step toward the lessening of communal tensions in Lebanon would be to reform the political system, to re-write the constitutional guidelines to de-emphasize sectarianism. But that is precisely where AUB, as an institution, should not go. It is none of our institutional business. Faculty members and students are free to go there.

Indeed our former chair of the Department of Political Studies and Administration was secretary to a national commission to draft a new electoral law. Our newly founded Fares Institute for Public Policy and International Affairs is beginning to address the issue of constitutional reform.

I return to my mild irritation. It probably reflects a guilty conscience. I see for example that St Joseph University has established an Institute for Islamo-Christian Studies which will offer a masters degree in the subject matter. Perhaps AUB should be moving in the same direction. I cannot help but note, however, that St Joseph had to cancel its student elections in the fall of 2006 because of inter-Christian fighting among its students.

CONCLUSION

The past few years in Lebanon, Iraq and Palestine have shown how deep religious fissures run. There is no reason to be coy here. The main source of increased sectarian violence has stemmed from the operations of a minority of Muslims who have claimed some sort of divine sanction for what they undertake. Their movement has not only raised the deep-seated fears of non-Muslims but those of their co-religionists as well. In describing the stakes of the current struggles the word "existential" is increasingly used. In such circumstances the line between protecting the university and entering the political realm disappears. Perhaps it is time to go outside our walls and make sure our vision for an alternative to the extremists of all stripes is made clear.

There is a final consideration. Having the word "American" in the official name of AUB has been, 90% of the time, an asset, and that continues to be the case today. Nonetheless since 9/11 I have been acutely conscious of the dangers of an "American" president of an "American" university preaching, or seeming to preach about institutional values, at least outside our walls. In an altercation with a local AUB alumni group a few years back, I was referred to by some disgruntled alumni as the Paul Bremer of AUB. As an American with no family connections in the Middle East or Lebanon, I can resist being drawn into the family, sectarian and clan politics of the region. My presumed neutrality is in that respect a great asset. But my American origins, when it comes to defence of our institutional values could be used against me, but more importantly against my university.

CHAPTER 22

Has our Reach Exceeded our Grasp? Taking a Second Look at Higher Education as a Global Enterprise

Robert Zemsky

INTRODUCTION

My purpose in this essay is to draw a distinction between being "global" and being "international". I would like to begin, however, from a more personal perspective. For more than 40 years now I have spent a substantial portion of each year outside my own country. Like many academics, I have in my study a world map full of black and red pins testifying to the fact that professionally I have been busy going places I have never been before. This month I am in Switzerland; last month I was in Singapore; next month I will be in Australia — all places I have visited or worked in multiple times before.

When I first encountered Tom Friedman's *The Lexus and the Olive Tree* (1999) with his definition of globalization, it seemed as if I had spent a lifetime getting ready for the world Friedman was describing. Then, when I began using *The Lexus and the Olive Tree* in my classes, I noted universities were largely absent as principal players in the drama Friedman was describing. In his new world of global connections, universities were like warehouses, full of interesting people who were fun to drop in on and have lunch with. But universities per se were not global players, not part of the growing network of connections that defined the rampant globalism that so fascinated Friedman.

By the time Friedman came to write *The World is Flat* (2005), he had clearly changed his mind. Universities and the education and research they provided

251

were essential — both as means and as ends in themselves. But by then, however, I was not so sure. Beneath Friedman's obvious skill at story telling and his inventive cleverisms — I am particularly fond of DOS Capital 2.0 from *The Lexus and the Olive Tree* — lay a remarkably robust definition of globalization. An enterprise or industry could be said to be global if its transactions were transparent, its products widely distributed without reference to national boundaries, and its prices set in fully convertible currencies. In global enterprises both time and space come to mean less and less. Here there is no hiding, no protections, no cultural sanctuaries — only the pursuit of high value commodities (think Lexus) that eventually overwhelms yesterday's olive groves. In a global world, technology is king. Product cycles become ever shorter. Labour becomes increasingly mobile. Consumers constantly broaden their searches for better products at better prices. Individual enterprises lose their competitiveness unless they become integral parts of an expanding set of networks.

Two decades into the global revolution, it is a list of attributes that can be said to apply to few, if any, of the world's leading universities. Most observers outside the academy would argue, correctly I believe, that universities, both in their operations and their governance, remain opaque, even obtuse, rather than transparent. Few transactions can be said to be instantaneous, while the time necessary to develop new educational programmes has probably lengthened rather than shortened. True, there is an international labour market for young scholars, principally post-docs, for Asian and Latin American Ph.D.s trained in Europe and the United States returning to their own countries or continents to begin their careers, and for very senior academics with international reputations. But these transnational patterns are of long standing, suggesting in this case that globalization had little if anything to do with their emergence.

Student markets have remained decidedly local. Even less global are the mechanisms by which prices are set for a university education. In most settings and most countries, even the European Union to a still considerable extent, governmental subsidies to both students and institutions reflecting local conditions and local political considerations determine what students pay and, in some cases still, how much students are paid. While some students shop internationally for better prices as well as better products — Canadian universities continue to seek US students by offering comparable educations and degrees with lower tuitions — most international flows of students reflect the kind of local economic and political circumstances that have historically resulted in outward migrations.

The result is an academic world that has become aggressively more international without in fact becoming much more global. Students travel more; faculty wander more broadly; and leaders of these international enterprises find themselves spending more time abroad attending the interests and soliciting the support of their increasingly international alumni. They proudly proclaim

their interest in recruiting ever more international students both for the revenue they bring and the boost such students give to claims that their universities are among the world's most prestigious. Scientific research is — and for
more than three decades now has been — the principal exception. Colleagues
distributed among a half dozen or more countries now routinely comprise
major research teams that have made the Internet a major tool of global collaboration — indeed the Web owes much of its initial success to the demand
by scientists for a ready means of transmitting data and communicating results.

But, as I have tried to suggest, most of what higher education does internationally is not global in a Friedmanesque sense. To understand why, I want to
consider higher education's current fascination with things international in
terms of three broad dichotomies that lie at the heart of what it means to be
global.

CUSTOMIZED VS. STANDARDIZED

Perhaps the most visible result of economic globalism is the standardization of
products and hence production. In an era of globalization not only a rose is a
rose is a rose, but a Toyota is a Toyota is a Toyota, whether it is assembled in
the United States or South-east Asia or Europe from parts manufactured in an
even larger array of countries. Products with the same names and the same
brand identities look, feel, even smell the same worldwide. What is true of
manufacturing is equally true of banking, fast foods, consulting and retailing.
With remarkably little variation the templates are all the same.

This standardization of products is also leading to the standardization of
training among multinational companies that understand that their workers,
as well as their consumers, belong to a homogenous global community. Training yes, but not higher education. The services and products that research universities provide remain singular, unique and largely customized. Whereas global enterprises readily embrace the notion of interchange, each research
university remains steadfast in the certainty that it and it alone has both the
right and the ability to define what constitutes a successful educational outcome. In the United States a major battle is now brewing over whether governmental agencies can require either the public universities they pay for or
the private universities they charter to accept, as valid courses, credits earned
in another American college or university. In Europe, the Bologna Process is
demonstrating just how tough it is to establish a system of standardized and
hence fully convertible course credits, degrees and licences. There are also
those champions of free trade who believe that educational products can be
brought under the regulatory umbrella of the World Trade Organization,
though their cause has attracted little attention and less support among the
world's principal research universities.

Instead, what is being championed is an international competition for students and faculty in which the competing universities stress their individuality, uniqueness and nationality. Whether the student being recruited is from Thailand or China or the Czech Republic, making the sale inevitably requires the recruiting university to demonstrate why its style of university is best and why its particular national setting offers special opportunities not readily available elsewhere. It is a kind a selling in which truly global enterprises almost never engage.

HERE VS. THERE

Executives and directors of companies that have "gone global" often talk about theirs as a journey of three phases. First their companies were national or regional enterprises in which most of their customers as well as their workers were local, along with their production facilities and sales staffs. Then their companies went international which, for the most part, meant opening sales offices abroad and learning the art of exporting their domestically produced goods and services. Going global was the third stage in which the distinction between here and there was abandoned. Production began to take place everywhere as their hitherto foreign operations and branches became fully integrated subsidiaries of a multinational enterprise. While most of the company's workforce remained tied to a now global set of localities, the leaders of the enterprise began to come from and go anywhere — Chinese executives could be found running European operations, Americans running production plants in Brazil, and Europeans leading the company from its US headquarters.

For the world's research universities, however, the distinction between "here" and "there" is stronger than ever as the leaders of these institutions struggle to reconcile their interest in being global with their need to preserve the importance and vitality of their "home" campuses. Among these presidents, vice-chancellors and rectors, perhaps no one is more sensitive to this challenge than Johns Hopkins' President Bill Brody, a friend of Tom Friedman's, an articulate commentator on the what globalization is likely to mean to institutions like his and, at the same time, a stout defender and investor in Hopkins' two Baltimore campuses. When you visit Baltimore, Brody's challenge is readily understood. The medical campus is massive, dominating the skyline with a phalanx of buildings that bespeak power and money, as well as research and service. The arts and sciences, along with engineering and most of the universities undergraduate programmes, are located 10 miles across town on an expanded and newly renovated campus that is a jewel of Georgian architecture. The question Brody asks his colleagues with increasing poignancy is what has to happen on Hopkins' Baltimore campuses to make people want to "come here from around the world" — or, to put the matter more prosaically, how does Hopkins rationalize its historic investments in place and expensive physical facilities in an age of globalization?

Brody's question is probably *the* question the leaders of research universities everywhere are asking as each confronts the challenge of devising an international strategy that feeds their home campuses, providing them students, revenue and visibility. And indeed, most programmes of international education are designed to do just that. Among lesser institutions this need "to bring the cash home" is transparent. Programmes and campuses are established abroad to provide credentials that are fully recognized in the home institution's country of origin. The students pay less than students attending the home campus, costs of instruction are reduced through the use of local faculty, and the operating margins are sent back to the home institution to help defray the cost of operations there or to offset revenue losses occasioned by enrolment shortfalls or declining public appropriations or both. When students on foreign campuses later transfer to the home campus and choose to enrol for their post-graduate course work, the economic benefits to the home institution are further enhanced.

Australian higher education has probably been the most forthright in adopting this model. Shortfalls in public appropriations to universities across the system led to an expectation that upwards of 10% of their operating revenues would come from foreign students and/or foreign operations. As a result, Australian higher education has come to dominate the market for international education across much of Asia.

What is important to note about this model of international exchange is that it is more colonial than global, at least as Friedman has defined the term. The surpluses earned from foreign operations and from the recruitment of foreign students are sent home for support of and investment in the home campus. Unlike the modern multinational corporation which sees itself as a global network of sales and production facilities in which the centre is increasingly less important, the university that competes internationally is primarily a spoke and hub distribution system in which the home campus (the hub) remains at the centre of the operations connecting its international operations not to one another but to itself.

For a while, it seemed as if the world of research would be the globalized exception to this colonial model for broadly distributing educational services. CERN in Switzerland provided the model of how a well run and commonly financed research centre with facilities and services no individual campus could provide trumped the need of the home campuses to control the flow of personnel as well as capital. Perhaps the best-financed example of a nation trying to extend the lessons of CERN to gain first mover advantage was the decision by Singapore to have its universities team up with major research universities in the United States and Europe. Brody's Johns Hopkins was an early collaborator working with the National University of Singapore to develop a host of research programmes centred in the medical and health sciences. The idea was that principal researchers from Hopkins would relocate to Singapore, bringing their scientific skills, grantsmanship and research teams with them. In the end, however, the National University of Singapore severed its arrangement with Hopkins principally because the latter's research scientists, though they often visited and often for extended periods of time, were unwilling to transfer their sense of place from Baltimore to Singapore. Despite the attractions of new labs and generous support, in the final analysis, "here in Baltimore" proved more important than "there in Singapore".

REAL VS. VIRTUAL

Not by coincidence, the initial burst of enthusiasm for the globalization of higher education accompanied the dot.com revolution of the 1990s. The lure was the Web with its promise of anytime, anywhere communication and hence learning. Major universities everywhere were caught up in the contagion. In the United States, Columbia University and New York University each launched major distance learning initiatives using the Web as the delivery vehicle — initiatives in which each institution invested 40 million or more of its own capital.

At the same time, groups of universities banded together to offer cooperative educational programmes, creating in the process enterprises that on paper at least had all the characteristics of truly global enterprises: standardized products, degrees and credentials that were to be recognized worldwide, and provider networks instead of single institution-branding. All of this activity was made possible by an interconnecting technology that was becoming ubiquitous throughout the world. The best branded and financed of these networks involved some of the world's very best universities. Often the networks grew out of collaborations of business schools worldwide.

It didn't work. The products didn't catch on. There was open speculation as to the real worth of these Internet programmes despite their associations with strong brands. The technology proved both limiting and awkward, the prices out of line with the real value of the products being offered.

In the end, too few would-be students really believed a virtual experience would convey the same benefits as a real one. What students everywhere wanted was face time, contact and personal exchange. Despite their penchant for consuming standardized products in other domains, when it came to their own educations, they wanted what most students traditionally have wanted — a personal, at times even intimate, experience.

Perhaps it is too soon to declare the experiment a failure. While the first movers have largely abandoned their efforts, there remains both interest in and limited capital for a less grandiose set of educational products. Most have assumed that the earlier failures were the product of promising too much and delivering too little. My guess, however, is that something more was involved. What the first predictors of an emerging global market for higher education assumed was that education, like other service industries was about to be remade by the forces of globalization. To date, they have been proven wrong. In the meantime, however, the safer prediction is to say higher education is a different kind of product — not ready to be standardized, still associated with particular places and specific traditions, and largely immune to the pressures for consolidation and amalgamation that have transformed the global providers of other service products.

Taken together these three dichotomies — customized instead of standardized, here instead of there, and real instead of virtual — provide an interesting approximation of the preconditions that would have to be met for a truly global market for higher education to emerge.

- **Standardized educational products.** The goals, standards, and common definitions the European Union is striving mightily to achieve through the Bologna Process would necessarily become worldwide benchmarks. The three-year baccalaureate would become *the* standard degree excepted everywhere along with a full set of professional and advanced degrees. More than that, course content, and probably teaching modalities as well, would be similarly homogenized and made interchangeable much as manufacturing products today are interchangeable. Perhaps that process is already underway in preparation for the next round of WTO/GATT talks. Karen Hughes of the US State Department recently circulated to interested parties an announcement of the scope of the March 2007 Berlin meetings that discussed the definitions of educational services.
- In late 2006, the ISO Technical Management Board (TMB) established a new technical committee (ISO/TC 232 Educational Services) to work on the development of standards in the field of educational services. The proposal to ISO, submitted by Germany noted that there is a need to create a suitable framework for preparing standards in the field of educational services. It is our understanding that the technical committee will consider standards proposals relating to other areas of non-public education that share the common concern of encouraging cooperation in quality assurance, whereby particular emphasis is placed on the exchange of models and methods and the establishment of common criteria and principles. Core elements are ensuring the quality and effectiveness of the education or training and improvement of knowledge transfer whilst also enhancing the transparency and comparability of the range of educational services provided.

It is possible to read this note as pertaining only to vocational education, though the chair of the US Delegation reported that many of the participants simply assumed that the international definition of educational services would apply equally to all of post-secondary education.

- **A fundamental lessening of the importance attached to physical place and the uniqueness of campus brands across higher education worldwide.** Global enterprises are essentially multinational networks of producers and service providers. The kind of cooperative networks that have been tried in virtual education, linking otherwise competing providers in a host of countries and/or regions, would become a principal, perhaps even a dominant, mode of organizing the provision of standardized educational services. Campuses would become less important both as symbols of excellence and specific places of research and scholarship. What happened in one part of the network would become interchangeable with identically designed and delivered programmes in other parts of the network.

A successful revolution making electronically distributed and asynchronous education (e-learning) readily available worldwide. Despite the promises of the technologists, e-learning has a long way to go. For the most part it remains clunky, linear, too often little more than electronically distributed workbooks. What would be required would be a constantly growing catalogue of electronic offerings that had the same impact MRIs have had on the medical profession and that video games have had on the entertainment business. It is hard to imagine any process that achieves the first two of my necessary conditions — standardized products and truly global networks of universities — that does not depend directly on the ready availability of a growing catalogue of state of the art electronic learning products.

From where I sit, these are three conditions that are not likely to be met anytime soon. More importantly, meeting those conditions would not likely result in universities that are either more interesting or more efficient or necessarily more productive. More likely they would become increasingly dull places that were not much fun to visit let alone to work at. How much better it would be if research universities remained idiosyncratically independent and aggressively international even if much of that activity remained colonial in intent and execution. That is a future that does not exceed our grasp.

REFERENCES

Friedman, T. (1999). *The Lexus and the Olive Tree*. Farrar, Straus and Giroux, New York.
Friedman, T. (2005). *The World is Flat: A Brief History of the 21st century*. Farrar, Sraus and Giroux, New York.

CHAPTER 23

Globalization, Public Policies and Higher Education

David Ward

INTRODUCTION

G lobalization and the attendant emergence of the global knowledge economy are exerting tremendous pressures on universities around the world and reshaping some of their basic assumptions and activities. Although the size and shape of higher education systems differ considerably among nations, university-based research innovation and advanced technical and professional programmes are viewed as a key competitive resource in the rapidly emerging global knowledge economy. Universities long viewed as "ivory towers" are increasingly recognized as "oil wells" of the new economy. In some respects this recognition is more strongly held within the corridors of government and the boardrooms of our corporations than it is within our own academic community. Indeed, the impact of these external pressures to serve as an engine of innovation and economic development on the integrity of the academic enterprise remains unresolved.

The combined effects of pressures to expand research capacities and to prepare human capital suitable for the knowledge economy have had profound effects on funding sources and strategies of individual higher education institutions and on the missions of the array of institutions within a nation. For large comprehensive research universities, in particular, the support of a complex infrastructure and of specialized scientific personnel incurs enormous costs, and requires multiple sources of revenue as well as decisive budget reallocations. The extraordinary level of resources needed to sustain a comprehensive research university has necessarily restricted this mission to a limited number of institutions and others have had to focus on a narrower mission and a less expensive infrastructure.

At the same time, concerns about the quality and scale of the professional and technical skills of the labour force as a whole have affected all levels of tertiary education and have created additional pressures that have increased the differentiation of institutional missions. These pressures are keenly felt in the United States, even though many elements of mission differentiation were already well established there at the end of the 19th century. It is highly likely that a range of mission specific institutions rather than a single traditional model of a university will meet the challenges of research intensification, and that some combination of public subsidy and individual responsibility will be necessary to support broad access. How these issues will be worked out will, however, vary from country to country.

This reshaping of higher education is visible in a diverse array of institutional issues and national and international policy concerns. Many national policy issues are now preoccupied with the link between the capacity and quality of higher education and international competitiveness, and higher education has now become a component of negotiations about world trade. This essay outlines the major policy issues faced by higher education in confronting the rapidly changing global landscape and in charting a course that will enable institutions to thrive in this new environment.

GLOBALIZATION AND MISSION DEFINITION

This connection between the global knowledge economy and higher education is most emphatically demonstrated in revenues, linkages and capacities of large comprehensive research universities. One of the decisive elements of their impacts and reputations is the international visibility of their faculty, students, programmes and research. For long it was assumed that most, if not all, universities would necessarily and definitively be research institutions, but the escalating costs of facilities and talent have limited in varying degrees that aspiration. I estimate that the resources necessary to support a comprehensive research university with a medical centre are now approaching $2 billion, with perhaps less than 20% of that amount derived from state tax revenues. To be sure, in the US federal research funds often account for at least 30% to 40% of their revenues, but these funds are obtained competitively, usually by individual scholars or research teams. Research universities have not only built significant endowments capable of providing both insurance and supplementation of external research funds, but they have also built and modernized their infrastructure largely with private gifts. In 2002 about 10 US universities had annual operating revenues exceeding $2 billion, about 55 exceeded $1 billion, and about twice that number have revenues of about $0.5 billion.

While I am sceptical of the value and accuracy of many rankings of research institutions, the presence of so many US universities at the top of these rankings is in fact a result of the concentration of large scale research support on a small number of the total number of universities. Of course, there are many less visible and perhaps more creative examples of institutional adjustments to more limited resources by defining more strategic missions. Some universities have created their own specific niche with a more limited range of research capacities that focus on specific regional needs or a narrower range of expertise. Community colleges and predominantly undergraduate institutions are now attracting a growing share of foreign students primarily because they focus on adult students with specific needs for short-term professional programmes. The overall result is a higher education network with differentiated missions which are increasingly based on varying capacities to combine different sources of revenues to meet a defined mission. While this differentiation of mission provides considerable flexibility in responding to the needs of the global knowledge economy, it also creates both real and imagined concerns about the need for quality assurance and especially some capacity to demonstrate student achievements in a standardized fashion.

These changes in higher education have proceeded further in the US than elsewhere, but I do not assume that they will necessarily occur elsewhere. The continental scale and diversity of higher education in the US, combined with a specific and perhaps unique set of public policies, have intensified these developments. In other settings the belief that all universities should offer doctoral degrees and proclaim a comprehensive research mission makes it more difficult for them to focus resources on a specific set of institutions. While many other nations are also experiencing these same challenges of combining expanded access with enhanced research capacity, they are doing so with a much more limited range of institutional missions than in the US. The resources, rankings, reputations and unambiguous measures of research quality and productivity will continue to define a limited number of universities that will not only dominate higher education nationally and globally, but also will provide the underlying scientific structure of the knowledge economy. There will also be a wide range of opportunities for institutions with a national or regional reach and with a more modest resource base to engage in the internationalization of curricula and the global recruitment of students and staff. Certainly, the international reach of US higher education over the past half-century was built upon the availability of a range of institutional missions, and as we enter this new global role of higher education, this diversity may well continue to be an asset.

INTERNATIONAL STUDENTS

This international setting of higher education is clearly founded on a world economy that is based on technical innovation and accelerated communication. The international movement of students and scholars was the earliest expression of these conditions, and today it continues to be the most visible expression of the global nature of the higher education enterprise. The uneven capacities of different nations to provide access and enhance research has generated a rapid expansion of students seeking their education abroad. It has also stimulated a significant "brain drain" of not only students but also scholars and highly qualified professionals from developing nations to economies with higher capacity and more favourable remuneration. As part of a strategy to seek new revenues and enhance prestige, almost all research universities in developed countries (and some in less developed countries such as China) are engaged in efforts to promote and expand the number of international students. This desire to participate in the international market for students and scholars suggests that some aspects of a market based search for revenues have spread far beyond the US.

The recruitment of foreign students now represents an arena of international competition among nations on behalf of their universities. Originally, national support for international students and scholars was based upon cultural and political motives largely designed to extend knowledge about and the influence of specific nations. During the Cold War, these motives were clearly given high priority and received substantial state subsidies. Over the past decade or so, the revenues from foreign students and the economic advantages of highly qualified immigrant scholars have largely displaced the older cultural and geopolitical motives of the Cold War era.

By the end of the 20th century, there were approximately a half-million foreign students in the US representing about 4% of total enrolments, providing over $12 billion of foreign expenditures and representing the 5th largest service sector of the American economy. About two-thirds of these revenues were derived from payments from students and their families and about three-quarters were derived from outside the US. Clearly almost all foreign undergraduates and professional students were sources of revenue, but many postgraduates were supported by universities or foundations. As students, postdocs or researchers, they directly contributed to the talent pool that makes possible the ongoing information technology and bio-technology revolutions within the US economy.

Throughout the last decade of the last century, the number of foreign students in the US increased by 30%, but during the same decade a more competitive environment was created as the UK, Germany, France and Australia became leading destinations. Canada also became a major destination of foreign students, the numbers growing at a faster rate than the US and representing much larger proportions of their student bodies. Clearly, in a multi-lingual world, English became the "imperial" second language and gave English-speaking countries a great advantage in this expanding international market.

For several reasons, the geography of these international student movements has shifted, but changes in their long-term magnitudes are still unclear. Security precautions related to terrorism have certainly impacted the flow of foreign students to the US. In the short run, total student numbers did decline, but data since 2004 indicate that this trend has been reversed. Nevertheless, it is highly unlikely that the rate of growth of the 1990s will ever be re-established. Much of that growth is now distributed to other parts of the world and the increased availability of English-language programmes in continental Europe will no doubt increase Europe's attractiveness.

While national governments may continue to provide some incentives for foreign students, increasingly it is expected that universities themselves will create strategies to recruit students who will be expected to pay tuition and living expenses, while other students will be viewed as potential additions to the talent pool of the knowledge economy. Reflections on the shifts in the destinations of foreign students now emphasize variations in tuition levels. High tuition as well as visa problems are often cited as reasons why students do not choose to attend US universities. The growth of this international market may also be influenced by the development or expansion of indigenous university systems in several countries that are currently sending large numbers of students abroad. Some parts of this market will also be met by for-profit providers either by establishing commercial sites within other countries or perhaps by means of remote delivery.

CROSS-BORDER PROGRAMMES

While the movements of foreign students and scholars are well documented over the past half-century, the development of cross-border projects and programmes and off-shore campuses and instructional programmes are of relatively recent ancestry. Many ventures of this kind are short term and others are still in an experimental and innovative mode. Research and training programmes, including for example non-academic programmes such as training civil servants in the target country, are perhaps the most established and also the most ephemeral of cross-border programmes. Generally, states, foundations and higher education institutions have supported these cross-border activities for a specific purpose and for a specific time frame and they are frequently vulnerable to shifts in budgets and priorities. Nevertheless, longstanding collaborative relationships between institutions in different countries did result in the transplantation of programmes initially taught by visiting scholars from the host institutions, but later sustained by local scholars who were either trained in the host institution or were early products of the transplanted programme. Most of these projects were based on bilateral relationships between a host institution in a developed economy and a nascent organization in a developing country.

The development of off-shore campuses and degree programmes represents a relatively new form of international activity. Led by the UK, Ireland, the US and Australia, many universities offer a professional degree, often executive business administration programmes, in several countries. Indeed about one-third of all off-shore ventures offer a degree in only one subject. These programmes were developed by the sponsoring institution, often were staffed by their faculty and occasionally involved some small engagement at a partner or host institution. In some cases, qualified local professionals participated in the off-shore delivery, but for all intents and purposes, the off-shore facility was a branch of a well known institution with a global reputation. Some sponsoring institutions strategically decided to offer more than a single programme or course of study, to provide a wider curricular array of their offerings by establishing full "branch" campuses. Under these circumstances, the infrastructure and staff may be provided by local governments and/or local educational institutions creating complex partnerships that extend from bilateral collaborations to franchise type validation of instruction provided by a local campus.

In some settings where it would take several decades to develop a modern university system using only local providers, governments have provided incentives for a variety of off-shore developments. Singapore, Qatar and Dubai are perhaps the most highly publicized examples of combining local developments with imported enterprises. Government policies vary in their receptivity to off-shore investments and promotions, and India and South Africa in particular have been more cautious than China and South-east Asia. The majority of off-shore programmes are delivered in English and consequently English-speaking countries have provided the largest proportion of the off-shore developments. Of 80 ventures in place in 2006, about a half were connected to US institutions, 12% to Australian and 5% each to the UK and to Ireland. As noted, most European nations have begun to offer their home programmes for foreign students partly or completely in English in order to compete more effectively in a world in which English has become almost all nations' second language. Eventually these programmes may be as suitable for off-shore development as those with origins in the English-speaking world.

The full impact of instructional technology on higher education is hard to determine within nations and it is much more difficult to assess in its transnational or cross-border form. Distance delivery accounts for an extremely small proportion of current international delivery, but clearly has enormous potential. For-profit providers may have the largest ventures of this kind, along with the producers of standardized tests for university admission. These developments have aroused concerns about quality control and concerns about the impact of such programmes on national cultures. Over the past decade, the shift from international movements of students to the development and delivery of education both off-shore and across borders has now engaged international policy-makers.

INTERNATIONAL POLICY ISSUES
AND CROSS-BORDER EDUCATION

While the scale of cross-national for-profit investments and the expansion of distance delivery across borders are still small, the rapid growth in the number of international students and the increasing complexity of educational delivery have aroused the interest of national governments and several international trade organizations. Indeed, a new language of macro-economics has gradually replaced the more vernacular language of higher education in describing the new complexity in the delivery of programmes in an increasingly internationalized higher education market. Long established movements of students, faculty and staff for the purposes of visits, exchange or even migration is described in the language of trade as "consumption abroad". The term "commercial presence" describes the physical movement of the provider to the target country, as illustrated by branch campuses or franchised agreements with indigenous universities. Remote delivery is referred to as "cross-border supply". Perhaps the significance of this new language is not in its ready or immediate acceptance, but rather in the degree to which international trade organizations have attempted to reduce these connections to a model of international trade susceptible to the same kinds of negotiation as other service sectors.

The GATS and WTO negotiations with respect to higher education have attracted the interests of UNESCO, OECD and the EU. Paradoxically, at a time when market pressures on higher education have resulted in reduced government regulation, the expansion of international markets in higher education may provoke new sources of regulation. Certainly, the major concern of trade negotiations is to remove impediments to commerce, but at the same time they raise questions of quality assurance, customer rights and transferability of courses and programmes. All efforts to manage international movements of students and of programmes will have to confront long established national differences in the delivery and funding of higher education. Issues of transferability and mutual acceptance have been mediated at the institutional level, and the value of internal student exchange was derived from differences in national experiences. In short, the individuality of higher education systems gave added value to the student exchange. Transferability and recognition need not be based solely on identical standards and procedures.

These international negotiations address critical issues and may well provide an appropriate framework for some aspects of the off-shore delivery of higher education that remains in its infancy. Direct negotiations among higher education institutions or between governments and foreign providers may also be necessary. Variations in the relationships of higher education to national governments will also complicate these efforts. These relationships vary from systems that are an integral part of a national government to those which, like the US, are more directly connected to regional-state governments with varying fiscal policies. In some countries, universities retain considerable levels of autonomy and the national government provides legitimacy to regulatory policies that are administered by non-governmental entities. Consequently, specific trade issues may engage different negotiating entities in different countries. It is critical that appropriate representatives of higher education in different countries communicate directly with each other and with their governments on matters subject to international negotiation. This consultation is especially critical whenever the impacts of trade negotiations with respect to higher education are inextricably linked to other unrelated but strategic sectors of the economy that are concurrently under negotiation.

While there is a primary concern with quality assurance and related issues, negotiations will also need to consider the special concerns of small nations where the preservation of language and culture may be a critical function of higher education. In addition, negotiations will need to be sensitive to the fragile public higher education systems of less developed countries which will be especially vulnerable to any new external sources of competition. Certainly, the expansion of for-profit providers and the remote delivery of some programmes will make inevitable and desirable some kind of negotiated standards of quality and transferability. These complex international negotiations with respect to higher education represent one measure of the degree to which universities are viewed as instruments of national or regional economic interests whether they remain predominantly public in structure, more independent and market based in their revenues, or for-profit.

PUBLIC POLICY AND INTERNATIONAL 'COMPETITIVENESS'

It is more likely that agreements directly negotiated from within the international higher education community will influence the future directions of international linkages in higher education. Most institutions now function in a national policy environment that emphasizes the goals of facilitating access and enhancing quality. Higher education policies are now directly connected to concerns about scientific and technical capacity needed to compete in the global economy. In the US a growing sense of the responsiveness of the EU and of several Asian nations to these issues of capacity and quality has provoked sustained discussions about the needs and challenges of higher education under conditions of international competitiveness.

What was once regarded as a great success in opening college level education to the vast majority of high school graduates is now the subject of doubt and much critical scrutiny. For the past half-century, national policies have called for expanding access to higher education initially as part of an effort to "democratize" society and sustain social mobility. More recently, this drive has been more precisely expressed as a need to create the level and kind of human capital necessary to cope with and to compete in the global knowledge economy. It is this shift of purpose that has now raised many issues with respect to the quality of expanded access.

As noted earlier, having a differentiated system of institutions helps accomplish both goals by expanding access and promoting quality as defined by institutional mission. In the US comprehensive research universities became the dominant setting for such global activities as receiving foreign students and initiating off-shore programmes. They were also the primary source of knowledge transfer and of programmes capable of providing sophisticated professional and technical practitioners. More recently, however, the need for a broader and larger supply of technically skilled practitioners has shifted attention to concerns about the uneven quality of not only secondary schools but also undergraduate programmes as well. This anxiety has focused on the pipeline of students in the so-called STEM (science, technology, engineering and mathematics) fields.

This process of widening access began earlier and proceeded more rapidly in the United States than elsewhere. The first surge of enrolments comprised service men returning from World War II who were assisted by grants in aid for tuition and expenses authorized by the "GI Bill of Rights". This commitment to expanded access was also sustained by high levels of per-student support from state taxes in order to maintain low tuition at public institutions. The availability of grants to support the total costs of higher education at both public and private institutions made it possible for students to graduate with little or no debt. These assumptions began to collapse during the past two decades as the sheer success of the access initiative created a huge entitlement obligation that conflicted with other public needs in a political environment of tax restraint. Irrespective of any need for inflationary adjustments to individual grants, the increase in the number of eligible students placed an unsustainable revenue challenge at a time when tax levels and tax reductions became a key political issue. With respect to access, the US no longer leads the way in financial aid policies, and Australia and England are currently involved in procedures more creative than those in the US.

This debate about levels of state support has coincided with concerns about the performance of higher education as a whole. While the discussion began with criticisms of the undergraduate programmes of comprehensive research universities, it is now a more general concern with the quality of undergraduate programmes in many different kinds of institutions. Policy discussions of access and quality tend to focus on the measurement of current outcomes and only rarely explore the potentialities of innovative and experimental programmes. Indeed, public policies designed to connect investments in higher education to precise and standardized levels of accountability may inadvertently drive innovative and customized approaches to learning to the independent if not the for-profit sector. In the past, poorly designed instruments of accountability have discouraged experimentation, and much innovation in higher education is funded with private sources of revenue.

It is also clear that increased access to higher education results in higher variability in the time it may take students of different aptitudes to complete a programme. For many students completion of a programme may occur within the context of adult education. While minimum standards are critical to establish appropriate preparation for higher education, we should be seeking multiple models of delivery that meet a widening variety in the pace of and kinds of learning. Indeed, increased access of the magnitude proposed to meet the demands of the knowledge economy will depend on our ability to deliver high quality education in multiple ways.

NEW CONFIGURATIONS

Comprehensive research universities are without question the nodal points in the global network of higher education. Clearly national policies or market processes will place limits on the numbers of this kind of university. Formula-based state or national appropriations alone are insufficient to meet these new demands, and funding from research agencies and foundations, philanthropy and endowments are critical to sustain a comprehensive research mission. Indeed, many observers now recognize that the advantages in funding and governance of independent universities will make it possible for them to respond to global challenges more effectively than the very best public institutions. These resource advantages also make possible alliances of similar institutions worldwide, and these networks, partnerships if not eventually mergers may come to resemble multi-national enterprises so prevalent in other segments of the private sector. Alliances of institutions at home and abroad with diverse missions and limited resources will require greater ingenuity, but these more complex alliances and networks will be more critical to the resolution of many issues of access. Global research institutions will need to be sensitive to their role in meeting the needs of students drawn from all social strata and ensure that their research agenda also addresses long-term social and environmental problems.

In the past reputations were built upon place specific institutions that served hinterlands of varying sizes and complexity, but in the future networks of either similar or dissimilar institutions are more likely to be the unit of activity. Increasingly, the desire of foreign students to remain connected with the institution from which they received their degree has created a resource upon which international collaborations are built. Alumni networks have become a component in institutional international strategies. For long, the recruitment of foreign students was largely accomplished at the department or programme level and only rarely were there institutional or inter-institutional initiatives. In a more competitive environment, there are not only state-based initiatives, but also joint efforts of the departments of State, Commerce and Education to facilitate student recruitment. Within universities the role of Deans of International Studies has expanded to embrace a more strategic approach to academic partnerships that were for long as numerous as they were fragmented. The global extent and means of connectivity of these networks remains unclear, and it is an open question as to whether traditional university structures are flexible enough to facilitate these developments.

Perhaps the most challenging aspect of these new opportunities for global connectivity are based upon the availability of "open" software and course materials as well as the digitization and ready availability of the contents of most research source materials including entire academic libraries. Place-specific or place-bound scholarship has defined higher education since the invention of the printing press, and the recent digital communications revolution has in many respects enhanced the relative advantages of the most established and successful comprehensive research universities. The next phase in the communications revolution may redefine or undermine some of those advantages and make possible the development of rival learning delivery systems.

Under these circumstances should we assume that higher education in each country is on a convergent course towards some common outcomes of structure and delivery? Like medical care, higher education has not participated in the major productivity gains of many service industries largely made possible by the information revolution. While the globalization of higher education will without a doubt be a source of convergent developments, particularly among comprehensive research universities, in many other respects, it is possible that public policies and revenue structures will vary and result in a great deal of variability in innovation.

Clearly, the demands of research capacity and human capital development have created challenges of revenue and in turn a search for alternatives to public revenues. These developments have also focused attention on the cost effectiveness or efficiency of higher education. Future debates about the funding of higher education will continue to engage both the allocation of costs and also the legitimacy of those costs and at the same time there will continue to be pressures to find new revenues. These debates about public policies with respect to higher education do seem to transcend national boundaries. International competitiveness may be the driver of the kind of innovations necessary for the fulfilment of the vision of research intensification and mass access.

REFERENCES

Altbach, P.G. & Balan, J. (Eds.), (2007). *World class worldwide: Transforming research universities in Asia and Latin America*, Johns Hopkins University, Baltimore.

Altbach, P.G. (2004). "Globalization and the university: Myths and realities in an unequal world", *Tertiary Education and Management*, 10 (3-25).

Augustine, N. (Chair). (2006). *Rising above the gathering storm: Energizing and employing America for a brighter economic future.* National Academies Committee on Prospering in the Global Economy of the 21st century. National Academies Press, Washington, DC.

Bain, O., Luu, D. & Green, M. (2006). *Students on the move: The future of international students in the United States.* American Council on Education, Washington, DC.

Commission on the Skills of the American Workforce. (2007). *Tough choices or tough times.* National Center on Education and the Economy, Washington, DC.

Council on Competitiveness. (2004). National Innovation Initiative. Council on Competitiveness, Washington, DC.

Duderstadt, J. J. (2000). *A university for the 21st century.* University of Michigan Press, Ann Arbor, MI.

Friedman, T. (2005). *The world is flat: A brief history of the twenty-first century.* Farrar, Straus and Giroux, New York.

Knight, J. (2005). *Borderless, offshore, transnational and cross-border education: Definition and data dilemmas.* Observatory on Borderless Higher Education, London.

Miller, C. (Chair). (2006). *A test of leadership: Charting the future of US higher education.* National Commission on the Future of Higher Education in America. U.S. Department of Education, Washington, DC.

Organisation for Economic Co-operation and Development. (2004). *Internationalisation and trade in higher education: Opportunities and challenges.* Center for Educational Research and Education, Paris.

Vest, C.M. (2006). "Open content and the emerging global mata-university". *Educause*, May/June.

Vest, C.M. (2007). *The American research university, from World War II to World Wide Web.* University of California Press, Berkeley, CA.

Ward, D. (2007). "Academic values, institutional management and public policies", *Higher Education Management and Policy Journal*, 19 (2).

PART VI

•••••••••••

Summary

CHAPTER 24

The Globalization
of Higher Education

James Duderstadt, Jerry Taggart and Luc Weber

Today our world has entered a period of rapid and profound economic, social and political transformation based upon an emerging new system for creating wealth that depends upon the creation and application of new knowledge and hence upon educated people and their ideas. It has become increasingly apparent that the strength, prosperity and welfare of a nation in a global knowledge economy will demand highly educated citizenry enabled by development of a strong system of tertiary education. It will also require institutions with the ability to discover new knowledge, develop innovative applications of these discoveries and transfer them into the marketplace through entrepreneurial activities.

Yet the traditional institutions responsible for advanced education and research — colleges, universities, research institutes — are being challenged by the powerful forces characterizing the global economy: hypercompetitive markets, demographic change, increasing ethnic and cultural diversity, and disruptive technologies such as information, biological and nanotechnologies. Markets characterized by the instantaneous flows of knowledge, capital and work, and unleashed by lowering trade barriers are creating global enterprises based upon business paradigms such as out-sourcing and off-shoring, a shift from public to private equity investment, and declining identification with or loyalty to national or regional interests. The populations of most developed nations in North America, Europe and Asia are aging rapidly, while developing nations in Asia, Africa and Latin America are characterized by young and growing populations. Today we see a serious imbalance between educational need and educational capacity — in a sense, many of our universities are in the wrong place, where populations are aging and perhaps even declining rather than young and growing, driving major population migration and all too frequently the clash of cultures and ethnicity. New technologies are evolving at an exponential pace, obliterating both historical constraints such as distance and political boundaries, and enabling new paradigms for learning such as open educational resources, virtual organizations and peer-to-peer learning networks that threaten traditional approaches to learning, innovation and economic growth.

On a broader scale, the education investments demanded by the global knowledge economy are straining the economies of both developed and developing regions. Developing nations are overwhelmed by the higher education needs of expanding young populations at a time when even secondary education is only available to a small fraction of their populations. In the developed economies of Europe, America and Asia, the tax revenues that once supported university education only for a small elite are now being stretched thin as they are extended to fund higher education for a significant fraction of the population (i.e., massification). Yet their aging populations demand highest priority for public funding be given to health care, security and tax relief, forcing higher education systems to become more highly dependent on the private sector (e.g., student fees, philanthropy or intellectual property). More fundamentally, in a knowledge-driven economy, many governments are increasingly viewing higher education primarily as a private benefit to students and other patrons of the university rather than a public good benefiting all of society, shifting the value proposition from that of government responsibility for supporting the educational needs of a society to university responsibility for addressing the economic needs of government — an interesting reversal of traditional responsibilities and roles.

THE CONTEXT

The participants in the first session stressed that globalization is a far deeper and more profound phenomenon than internationalization. In higher education the latter phenomenon has traditionally referred to the mobility of staff and students and the exchange of ideas. Today students in the millions are internationally mobile in search of a university degree and a cross-cultural experience. Universities and their faculties build international linkages, attracting students from far and wide for their academic programmes, and augmenting these with exchange programmes, sabbaticals and conferences to support the free exchange of knowledge and ideas.

Yet globalization implies a far deeper interconnectedness with the world — economically, politically, and culturally. It is a process characterized by increasing economic openness, growing economic interdependence and deepening economic integration in the world economy. While internationalization presumes an international market controlled in varying degrees by nations, globalization presumes a world market, one that is beyond the reach of the nation state. Such a market economy challenges conventional social norms and institutions. The "death of distance" associated with emerging information and communications technologies contribute to the rapid spread of cultures, particularly among the young — the "digital natives". Globalization is not a value-free concept, since its logic and ideology of an unfettered world market for labour, finance, and goods fall far short of current geopolitical reality. It thrives on new forms of economic activity such as entrepreneurial capitalism while challenging older, less nimble forms such as oligarchy, state-directed or big-firm capitalism. Yet it also can be highly asymmetric, leading to interdependence of among countries in the industrialized world while creating even more dependence among developing countries.

For the past two decades both established and new "startup" companies have struggled to adapt to the demanding realities of the global, knowledge economy where radical innovation, entrepreneurial skills and global reach are essential. They have downsized, right-sized, offshored, outsourced and just about every other form of restructuring to adjust to the new rules of globalization. They have evolved from multinational to transnational, from proprietary hierarchies to open knowledge networks, assuming the new forms demanded by a continually evolving and mutating global marketplace.

Yet despite the fact that leading universities throughout history have been highly international in the nature of their students, faculty and academic programmes, they have yet to adapt to a global environment. To be sure, they are increasingly subject to influence by powerful global market forces and disruptive technologies. Markets and globalization influence universities, sometimes shaping education both in terms of what is taught and what is researched, and shifting both student interests and university offerings away from broader academic studies and towards narrower vocational programmes. There is a discernable commercialization of universities, defining their purpose increasingly in terms of their role in economic development, sometimes at the expense of more fundamental roles such as challenging the norms of society, securing and transmitting cultural heritage from one generation to the next, mentoring entrants into the professions, accrediting competency and skills, and striving to provide their students with personal understanding and the tools for societal transformation.

In the subsequent discussion, the issue of market pressures continued to be a key topic. Part of the challenge was balancing the needs of various stakeholders in higher education — predominantly the state, students, and business — and keeping all three satisfied without distorting the fundamental purpose of the university. For example, there was a growing utilitarianism associated with the role of higher education in addressing the need for human capital that could overwhelm the university's traditional social and cultural impact on society and civilization — its transformative potential through the creation, retention and dissemination of knowledge. We were witnessing across the globe a shift from general to vocationally orientated higher education aimed at supporting career development. The distinction between academic and vocational education was becoming increasingly blurred in a knowledge economy. There was a growing tendency for a range of stakeholders in higher education to use the language of "useful knowledge" in the discourse about where resources should be deployed in research, teaching and knowledge transfer that offered a very limited and partial view of the transformative potential of higher education. Should we simply assume that the state would step in to support strategic and vulnerable programmes such as the arts and humanities as greater numbers of students opted for more vocationally oriented subjects, driven in part by the financial burdens of increasing tuition levels as well as by employment opportunities? Or should this be the responsibility of university faculties and leadership?

A related market issue concerned the increasing competition not only among institutions for students, faculty and resources, but between the public and private education sectors and among nations. Private (and occasionally for-profit) institutions initially focused in most nations on the higher education needs unmet by public institutions — with the exception of the United States where much of private higher education goes after the elite marketplace. However more recently the ability of private providers to handpick programmes and faculty, without regard to broader public responsibilities and regulatory burdens, along with their increasing agility in adopting new educational paradigms such as online learning, was leading to substantial growth of this sector, albeit with some concern about educational quality. Although employment laws and regulations had restricted to some degree the development of international markets for faculty and students in some regions such as Europe, new programmes such as Erasmus, Socrates and the Bologna process were leading to more competition across borders.

Even more broadly, there was great interest among Glion participants in phenomena of ranking universities in terms of presumed measures of quality by various publications — so-called league table rankings — first appearing in the United States and Great Britain, but now propagating to global scale (e.g., London *Times*, US News & World Report, Shanghai Jiao Tong) as yet another indication of market pressures. Beyond the fact that these rankings were increasingly used to determine institutional reputation, there was growing sense that they might become as important for nation states as for individual universities. Yet there were serious concerns about whether the rankings were an appropriate proxy for institutional quality. They tended to focus to a large degree on measures of research productivity and reputation in scientific disciplines, rather than on the quality of learning and teaching. There was also a definite bias towards institutions in English-speaking nations.

Concerns were expressed that such rankings could drive homogenization in higher education by holding all institutions to the same standards; they could also create unrealistic expectations on the part of both patrons (e.g., states) and stakeholders (e.g., students). For example, what ranking would an institution have to achieve to be designated as "world-class"? Among the top 20, top 50 or top 100 in global rankings? It was suggested that since it was likely that league table rankings would continue to proliferate, perhaps higher education organizations should develop their own approach to evaluating and comparing institutional quality, much as has the US National Academy of Sciences in ranking graduate education programmes.

GLOBAL STRATEGIES FOR ESTABLISHED UNIVERSITIES

In many respects the challenges facing higher education in developed nations (e.g., OECD) are quite similar and perhaps incompatible: the need to dramatically broaden participation in higher education to build a competitive workforce (massification), to enhance the quality of both education and scholarship to compete in a knowledge-driven economy, and to reduce the relative burden on tax-payers who face other public spending priorities such as health, retirement and national security. All create strong pressures on universities to diversify their funding sources through mechanisms such as raising student fees, building relationships with industry, encouraging philanthropy and expanding the market for educational services through adult education or international students.

Within this context, the opportunities afforded by globalization look quite significant. Current estimates suggest that the number of students seeking university degrees will roughly double over the next two decades to as high as 250 million, with most of this growth in the developing world. Some nations such as Australia have already launched aggressive efforts to not only recruit fee-paying international students, but to establish overseas campuses to generate additional resources, finding that as the proportion of these students rises above 15%, their institutions begin to exhibit a more global character not only in funding, but also in governance and management.

Both national and institutional aspirations for quality also have acquired a global character with the appearance of numerous surveys (USN & WR, Shanghai Joao Tong, London *Times*) attempting to establish a world ranking of major universities. This has caused some consternation as established universities with long histories of educational excellence have fallen in the rankings. It is certainly the case that an over-emphasis on such rankings can distract both institutions and governments from more fundamental roles and objectives. But it is also clear that the concerns about the competitive quality of higher education have stimulated initiatives such as the Bologna Process in Europe aimed at overcoming fragmentation, increasing cooperation and competition, increasing investment in both universities and research systems, preparing for demographic change (particularly aging populations) and encouraging innovation and risk-taking.

Global competition among universities has also raised an awareness of the need to provide both a greater degree of institutional autonomy to enable the agility, flexibility and innovation required by today's fast-changing world, as well as a more sophisticated and strategic framework for higher education systems. Key in the latter is the acceptance of the importance of mission differentiation, since the availability of limited resources will allow a small fraction of institutions to become globally competitive as comprehensive research institutions (with annual budgets typically in the range of $1 billion or more). A differentiated system of higher education helps to accomplish both the goals of massification and promoting quality, but assigns different roles in such efforts for various institutions. Enabled both by the continental scale and its decentralized nature, the United States has achieved the most diverse system, enabling it to focus significant public and private resources to create a small set (less than 100) of world-class research universities, while distributing the broader roles of mass education and public service among a highly diverse collection of public and private institutions, albeit with an inevitable tendency toward "mission creep". Although such strategic diversification is beginning to appear in Asia, it will be particularly difficult to achieve in Europe where the Humboldt tradition of universities still resists defining the role of a college or university as primarily teaching (as opposed to scholarship).

Yet, despite the fact that one of the keys to the success of American higher education has been its great diversity and unusual degree of institutional autonomy, largely as a result of the limited role of the federal government in tertiary education, there are clouds on the horizon. A recent national commission has raised serious concerns about the increasing socioeconomic stratification of access to (and success in) American higher education; questionable achievement of acceptable student learning outcomes; cost containment and productivity; and the ability of institutions to adapt to changes demanded by the emerging knowledge services economy, globalization, rapidly evolving technologies, an increasingly diverse and aging population, and an evolving marketplace characterized by new needs, new providers and new paradigms. Furthermore, even the traditional strength of the American research enterprise, based heavily upon its world-class research universities, has begun to show some deterioration: a skewing of the nation's research priorities away from engineering and physical sciences and towards the life sciences; erosion of the engineering research infrastructure; a relative decline in the interest and aptitude of American students for pursuing education and training in engineering and other technical fields; and growing uncertainty about US immigration and foreign policy, constraining its ability to attract and retain gifted science and engineering students from abroad.

While most established universities are embracing — or at least coping with — globalization while addressing the ongoing challenges of massification, academic competition and limited public resources, local politics, culture and history shape their particular approach. Europe has chosen to utilize the Bologna Process (and related programmes such as Erasmus, Socrates, and the European Science Area) to enhance cooperation and competition among institutions, stimulate greater mobility of students and faculty, and achieve greater diversification enabling the focus of sufficient resources on a subset of institutions to achieve world-class quality. While Russia has accepted much of the Bologna philosophy, it also faces the challenge of merging its universities with the scientific institutes where most research occurs and garnering greater support from both public and private sources. Japan has focused on the incorporation of its national universities, separating them legally from the government to provide them with the autonomy and presidential authority to become more strategically aligned with the global economy.

As noted earlier, changing demographics, student demands and government policy have stimulated Australian universities to augment public support both with higher fees, enabled by a national forgivable student loan programme, and to aggressively recruit fee-paying international students both for existing campuses and new sites abroad. Although the United States already has achieved a balance between public (45%) and private (55%) support of higher education, this is shifting even further toward the private sector as an aging population shifts tax dollars away from education toward other social priorities such as health care, retirement and security. In fact, today many of the America's leading public research universities now find that less than 20% of their operating funding comes from the appropriation of tax dollars, with the remainder coming from student fees, competitive research grants, philanthropy, services such as health care, and technology licensing and spinoff companies.

The open discussion session following these presentations focused primarily on two topics: the increasing differentiation of both institutional types and missions demanded by the global marketplace and the role of the state in planning, management and regulation of higher education. It was increasingly apparent that the great diversity of higher education needs, both on the part of diverse constituencies (young students, professionals, adult learners) and society more broadly (teaching, research, economic development, cultural richness) would demand a diverse ecosystem of institutional types. Here diversity should be viewed as positive and not conflated with the concept of hierarchy. One could envision a range of models of universities ranging from the mega to the single faculty or single focus business school. Notwithstanding the differences in scale between institutions of higher education, there was still a need to ensure that each institution had the capacity to "flex its provision" to meet changing circumstances and changing demand for higher education provision, whether in the area of learning and teaching, research, knowledge transfer, and increasing and widening participation.

In regions dominated by public institutions, there was a need to think through the implications of creating new institutional forms for new private universities in Europe. These new institutions would need to be flexible and non-bureaucratic to survive in a market-led environment. There could well be a market for relatively small, flexible, world-class higher education institutions, which like some of the world-class business schools, could operate successfully on private funding from tuition fees while also competing for state funds for research and knowledge transfer. There might even be a market for the broad educational training characterizing the liberal arts colleges of the United States. Swarthmore was a model that others might follow with just over one-third of operating revenue derived from student fees and 43% derived from endowment income. Singapore is ready to experiment with the liberal arts college model on a public/partnership principle experiment requiring an initial investment of $1 billion for startup costs. However some caution was urged by observing that in the 1950s liberal arts colleges had awarded 70% of BA degrees in the United States; today that percentage has dropped to less than 3%, perhaps reflecting that students and parents were acting increasingly as consumers and opting for a more directly utilitarian higher education experience.

There was increasing government and stakeholder pressure for good governance and accountability, particularly in view of the expansion of higher education participation and the increasing important of education to prospering in the global knowledge economy. Paradoxically, in some nations even as relative government support has declined, the efforts to regulate universities and hold them accountable increased. Although some of this was stimulated by the sub-optimal activities of a relatively small number of institutions, it was perhaps also evidence of governments attempting to retain control over the sector through regulation even as their financial control waned. Yet such excessive regulation could be counter-productive in a global economy that demands agility and innovation.

The European Union is focused on creating quality standards that would operate effectively across national boundaries. In the context of research, the prospective European Research Council would drive competition among the elite European research universities. In contrast, higher education in the United States was going through yet another period of critical self-evaluation, stimulated in part by the formation of a National Commission on the Future of Higher Education (the Spellings Commission) demanding greater accountability for access, costs and learning outcomes, although there was some scepticism about whether this effort would have lasting impact. There was a paucity of debate in the US on the wider benefits of higher education at the local, regional, national and international levels.

In many higher education systems — particularly in Europe and the United States — there is increasing evidence of both under-planning and over-regulation by public bodies. The experience at both the regional and national level is that governments can regulate but they are usually unable as a corollary to develop effective plans for higher education. Yet both efforts may be for naught in an increasingly competitive global economy that will demand world-class standards for all activities, including higher education.

GLOBAL STRATEGIES FOR EMERGING UNIVERSITIES AND UNIVERSITY SYSTEMS

The challenges and opportunities presented by globalization are quite different both for and among the universities of developing economies. Nations with large populations, such as China, India and Brazil, face the dual challenge of building world-class universities even as they strive to expand the low participation in higher education (10% or less). Smaller nations such as Singapore and Korea have been able to achieve high participation rates (70% and 80%, respectively) and are now turning to forming international partnerships to enable them to build world-class universities and research activities. All recognize the importance of strong investment in both access to and excellence in tertiary education.

In order to face the challenges and demands of globalization, Chinese higher education institutions have been expanding and strengthening international academic exchange and cooperation, increasing the number of students going abroad as well as the number of foreign students studying in China, encouraging their faculty to constantly improve themselves and to develop research collaboration. A variety of mechanisms have been utilized, including inviting overseas universities to establish independent campuses in China, joint projects, programmes and institutes, and more recently overseas campuses established by Chinese universities. In an effort to boost several of its research universities to world-class status, China launched the "985" project to provide differential funding.

Although India is renowned for the quality of its engineering and management schools (IIT and IIM), it faces a serious massification challenge, with only 6% of 18- to 23-year-olds having opportunities for college education. It was noted that there are really two Indias: a global, prosperous state and an underdeveloped society with inadequate opportunities. India needs many more universities, but these need to be smaller, more nimble and responsive to change. As a result, the trend toward globalization is largely tangential to India's higher education strategy.

As a small, young nation, Singapore recognized early that its people were its greatest asset, and investment in education was key to its success in a global economy. Massification of educational opportunities of increasing sophistication has been an objective, as Singapore's economy shifted from labour-intensive to capital-driven and now knowledge-driven activities. Its three major universities have been given sufficient autonomy to chart their own directions and build on their areas of strength. In addition the government has made significant investment in research excellence, including joint programmes with leading universities in the United States and Europe. These activities exist in an ecosystem, interacting with many parties — research institutes, businesses, government agencies and the wider community — and spanning education, economic, social and cultural dimensions. Singapore's higher education policy is now focusing both on improving undergraduate education and creating lifelong learning opportunities.

Korea's strategy and experience hve evolved along a similar track. Its Confucian culture has long placed a high premium on education, and as it has made the transition from a labour-intensive to a capital-intensive economy, it has made parallel investments in higher education to achieve an unusually high level of massification (with 80% of secondary-school graduates continuing on to college). Korea believes that an important consequence of economic globalization is that only a few leading universities will dominate the world of higher education, just as a few companies are dominating different industrial sectors worldwide. To this end, it has created the Korean Advanced Institute of Science and Technology (KAIST) and provided it with the autonomy and resources to compete with leaders such as MIT.

Brazil is a large and highly diverse nation, facing the challenge of rapidly expanding participation in tertiary education (currently at 12%) and increasing investments in R&D (currently at 0.37% of GDP compared to 1.38% for OECD nations). Although Brazil has established leading industries in areas such as agriculture, biofuels and aircraft, there is a recognized need to stimulate greater industrial research, both through national policy and relationships with Brazilian universities.

In the subsequent open discussion session, the issue of massification, the extension of higher education participation to a large segment of the population, was discussed. To date this has primarily been a strategy for developed nations, but in a knowledge economy where workforce skills and human capital are paramount, it has become an equally serious concern of the developing world. The developing nations were concerned with managing growth towards a system of mass higher education in the context of high quality provision and social inclusion. Here some caution was raised about the impact of mass higher education on social inclusion. In some countries the expansion had been effectively an expansion of the middle classes and had relatively little impact on the percentage of lower working class students. Conceptually one could see examples across the globe where countries had pushed hard for mass higher education and then engaged more actively with the agendas for quality and excellence. Ideally, developing countries might fuse all three concepts into the development of their higher education systems.

The flow of students and faculty between developed and developing economies was also of particular concern. American universities actively go out in search of the brightest and the best students and young researchers. Young men and women aged 25-35 are attracted to the US for career development in respect of key research opportunities. These are the key years for young researchers. This proactive approach was not common in Europe. There is insufficient lateral movement of young researchers in Europe compared to movement from Europe to the United States.

Yet such migration of students and faculty members was a serious economic issue for some developing countries, leading to a "brain drain" of their students. It would be preferable to move towards a "brain circulation" scenario within which home countries were able to maintain a relationship with students once they had left their home country for career development overseas. It was important to maintain contact as a country and as a university with ex-students. Since the mid-1990s the Chinese government has had a policy of tracking the students taking up research opportunities overseas with the hope of attracting them back at some point in their career with the inducement of research contracts and relatively attractive salaries. This raises interesting questions about the implications for the development of scientific research and technology if Asia and Europe were able to attract back their researchers from the United States.

SHIFTING PARADIGMS

The forces driving globalization of the world's economy are both stimulating and demanding the development of new paradigms for higher education. Yet while universities continue to expand their international activities, they have yet to exhibit many of the key features of the global economy. Thomas Friedman suggests that an enterprise or industry could be said to be global if its transactions are transparent, its products widely distributed without reference to national boundaries, and its prices set in fully convertible currencies. In global enterprises both time and space come to mean less and less, and there is no hiding, no protection, no cultural sanctuaries — only the pursuit of high value commodities.

Yet the services and products research universities provide remain singular, unique and largely customized. Indeed, the unique programmes offered by leading universities are seen as key to their competitiveness. While universities encourage international student and faculty exchanges and seek both relationships and perhaps even campuses abroad, in reality they are still moored primarily to their home campus, exploiting their international activities both to attract new resources and reputation through a hub-and-spoke (or perhaps even colonial) paradigm. Finally, although information and communication technologies enable new forms of distance learning and collaboration, as yet these exist only at the margin for most institutions. Higher education continues to exhibit these three dichotomies — customized instead of standardized, here instead of there, real instead of virtual — that imply that while they are becoming more engaged with the world, they are not becoming globalized as has business and industry. It was suggested that perhaps higher education is a different kind of product — not ready to be standardized, still associated with particular places and specific traditions, and largely immune to the pressures for consolidation and amalgamation that have transformed the global providers of other service products.

Yet participants offered a number of new paradigms for higher education that were better aligned with the economic, social, political and cultural integration implied by globalization. For example, the traditional approach of university scholars stressing propositional knowledge might be wed with the prescriptive knowledge of the marketplace to create new academic value. The revolution currently underway in content development in the entertainment and communications industry, involving the merging of producers and consumers (e.g., YouTube, Wikipedia), along with new business models (e.g., Google, Amazon), suggest that universities have much to learn from these new collaborative approaches.

More generally, entirely new forms of higher education institutions might evolve. New types of universities may appear that increasingly define their purpose beyond regional or national priorities to address global needs such as health, environmental sustainability and international development — what one might call "universities in the world and of the world".

The exponential growth of new knowledge along with longer human lifespan make a sustained commitment to lifelong learning essential both for individuals and nations. An increasing number of nations are setting the ambitious goal of providing their citizens with pervasive, lifelong learning opportunities. Of course, this will require not only a very considerable transformation and expansion of the existing post-secondary education enterprise, but also entirely new paradigms for the conduct, organization, financing, leadership and governance of higher education.

One of the most exciting approaches to global connectivity is based upon an extension of the philosophy of open source software development to create new opportunities for learning and scholarship for the world by placing previously restricted knowledge into the public domain and inviting others to join both in its use and development. To the availability of open source software for educational purposes (e.g., Moodle and Sakai) and the open university movement have been added the open courseware projects led by MIT to put the digital assets undergirding thousands of courses in the public domain; the open learning initiative of Carnegie Mellon, Rice and others to provide learning materials; and most recently the massive effort by Google to digitize and provide search access to the combined collections of 25 leading academic libraries (estimated to hold over 50% of the printed material in the world). Such open educational resources provide the scaffolding on which to build truly global universities — what Charles Vest calls "meta" universities — a transcendent, accessible, empowering, dynamic, communally-constructed framework of open materials and platforms on which much of higher education worldwide can be constructed or enhanced.

Beyond this, one can only speculate about what it might mean if all of these elements could be combined: Internet-based access to all recorded (and then digitized) human knowledge augmented by powerful search engines, open source software, learning resources such as open courseware, open learning philosophies (open universities), new collaboratively developed tools (e.g., Wikipedia) and ubiquitous information and communications technology (e.g., Negroponte's $100 laptop computer or, more likely, advanced cell phone technology). In the near future it could be possible that anyone with even a modest Internet or cellular phone connection will have access to much of the recorded knowledge of our civilization along with ubiquitous learning opportunities. Imagine still further the linking together of billions of people with limitless access to knowledge and learning tools enabled by a rapidly evolving scaffolding of cyberinfrastructure increasing in power one-hundred to one thousand-fold every decade. Perhaps this, then, is the most exciting vision for the truly global university, no longer constrained by space, time, monopoly or archaic laws, but rather responsive to the needs of a global, knowledge society and unleashed by technology to empower and serve all of humankind.

While such paradigm shifts may seem radical, the Open University of the United Kingdom provides an "existence proof" that they are already being adopted and successfully implemented to a very considerable extent. The Open University portrays itself as offering higher education anywhere, anytime, on any platform and any screen, to students from 9 to 99! It has long provided leadership in the adoption of new technology and today is extending the open paradigm to new phenomena such as peer production and mass collaboration as exemplified by MySpace, YouTube and Wikipedia. It views its deep commitment to openness as a key feature of the global, knowledge economy where value is added through sharing and collaboration in developing new knowledge rather than constraining its propagation. It has gone far beyond its traditional offerings ("OU Core") and the launching of open universities else-where ("OU Plus") to launch a major effort in providing access to open edu-cational resources ("OU For Free"), accepting the mission of bring education to all who can benefit from it.

The open discussion session began with a further examination of the vari-ous forces driving the development of new paradigms for higher education. Higher education was fighting for public funding alongside many competing priorities including the needs of an aging population for healthcare and pen-sion support. In the developed nations there was some movement away from the traditional concept of higher education being a public good. Increasingly the consumers of higher education in a lifelong learning context envisioned higher education as private good. Quite different business models were emerg-ing in different countries even within the same broad policy goals. The mixed economy of private and public support for higher education will be a signifi-cant model for the future with the inevitable growth in private sector whether for academic or vocational higher education, although the debate on tuition fees remains an intensely political rather than economic one in many nations — though there are always some students who would be willing (and able) to pay a high premium for a non-standardized higher education experience of elite quality.

The college fee situation in the US was genuinely confusing in that the published fee was quite different from the discounted fee. Consumers needed to know the variations through publicly available data. The endowment situ-ation in the United States was also particularly interesting where funds were accumulating through hedge fund activity and subject to challenge on the grounds that they are being used primarily for investment rather than for the provision of scholarly activity. Here Harvard University, with an endowment of roughly $35 billion (more than the combined endowments of all public uni-versities in the US), is increasingly behaving as a bank and real estate devel-oper rather than an academic institution. For other nations to emulate this model would require major changes in tax policy, e.g., to allow the tax deduct-ibility of charitable contributions and endowment earnings.

The emerging of new needs for flexible workplace learning and vocational learning for skills development would be significant drivers of future demand in higher education and could open new markets for higher education. Yet the financial burden of continuing professional development was increasingly passing from the employer to the employee as large multinational companies were stripping out the costs and incentives for MBA and other postgraduate programmes, hence demanding new financing mechanisms such as lifelong learning accounts and educational tax credits.

The discussion then moved to a broader consideration of new paradigms in higher education. It was agreed that the globalization of higher education would lead to a range of models of provision including the bespoke customized model existing alongside the harmonized and standardized model. Diversity was the watchword for higher education development in a global marketplace. In some parts of the world the drive to mass higher education would need to be linked to distance learning and new technology as these were the most cost-effective means of communication in some countries. Mass higher education in developed and developing countries would be driven in future more significantly by eLearning and new technology. Distance learning in particular would take advantage of new technology. We could all understand the worlds of open learning and open universities alongside the more traditional worlds of the liberal arts university or multi-faculty world-class research university, but did we really understand how these various models of higher education and research could and should interact within an ecosystem of higher education? We needed a shift in the mindset of politicians to tolerate and support new models of delivery to students of all ages. We need a far greater conceptual appreciation of the needs of the learner in an age of lifelong learning.

UNIVERSITIES IN THE WORLD AND OF THE WORLD

Globalization and the attendant emergence of the global knowledge economy are exerting tremendous pressures on universities around the world and reshaping some of their basic assumptions and activities. The international movement of students and scholars was the earliest expression of these conditions, and today it continues to be the most visible expression of the global nature of the higher education enterprise. While the movements of foreign students and scholars are well documented over the past half-century, the development of cross-border projects and programmes and offshore campuses and instructional programmes are of relatively recent ancestry. Most of these projects were based on bi-lateral relationships between a host institution in a developed economy and a nascent organization in a developing country. The development of offshore campuses and degree programmes represents a relatively new form of international activity. Led by the UK, the US and Australia, many universities offer professional degrees, often executive business administration programmes, in several countries.

Paradoxically, at a time when market pressures on higher education have resulted in reduced government regulation, the expansion of international markets in higher education may provoke new sources of regulation. This level of international activities and some of the attendant concerns (e.g., the predatory role of some for-profit institutions in developing economies) have stimulated interest on the part of international organizations such as WTO and GATS. These international negotiations address critical issues and may well provide an appropriate framework for some aspects of the offshore delivery of higher education that remains in its infancy.

Part of the challenge is balancing the opportunities presented by globalization to higher education with the risks. For example, market forces driven by the threat of competition or the lure of profit can drive the transformation of some aspects of higher education into commercial businesses. Universities have traditionally been communities of individuals who come together around the joy of new knowledge discovery and the satisfaction of passing along the skills of learning to the next generation. The rewards of such academic careers have usually been intrinsic, associated with the freedom characterizing academic pursuits and the prestige accompanying faculty positions rather than monetary compensation. Yet today a knowledge-driven economy has placed high value on entrepreneurial efforts to spin off the intellectual property from research into the marketplace, leading not only to possible conflict with academic values and obligations, but also numerous battles over research sponsorship, intellectual property ownership, licensing, and commercialization.

More broadly, the globalization of higher education has significant implications for people and for nation-states. The proportion of foreign students from developing nations studying for professional degrees or doctorates in the university system of the major industrialized is large, and many stay on, contributing to brain drain. Although their home countries make the investment in their early education, the eventual returns accrue to the developed nations providing their advanced education and future employment. For the home countries of these people, there is an externalization of benefits and an internalization of costs. Since in the future, knowledge is bound to be critical in the process of economic growth and social progress, without correctives, the widening gap between the haves and the have-nots could then be transformed into a widening gap between those who know and those who know-not.

If the interest, or indeed the obligation, of mature universities in the developed world towards the developing world is to assist in development, rather than simply to exploit a market, then certain principles should be accepted: universities should accept a fundamental purpose as enlarging human freedom; universities must themselves be free institutions, free from government interference or control, places where the principles of academic freedom are understood and protected; in mature universities, the faculty should have a central role in the governance of the institution, the development of its curriculum and the selection of other faculty; mature universities should have the goal of building the capacity of universities in the developing countries; and the quality standards for education transmitted to developing countries should not be inferior to those of developed countries.

While universities must be responsive to the imperatives of a global economy and attendant to their local responsibilities, they must also become responsible members of the global community, that is, becoming not only universities in the world but also of the world. Yet the challenges facing our world such as poverty, health, conflict and sustainability not only remain unmitigated, but in many respects become even more serious through the impact of the human species — global climate change being foremost among them.

One promising approach is for universities to address their global responsibilities is to join together with government and industry in promoting sustainable development. Here sustainability is defined as the efforts made to secure the long-term prosperity and stability of humankind. In this broader sense, sustainability encompasses not only environmental issues but also political and institutional sustainability. Both the Glion Declaration of 1998 and the "Magna Carta Universitatum" signed in Bologna in 1988 by the leaders of European universities stressed this broader sense of institutional responsibility. Yet to capture both the attention and commitment of university faculty will likely require more, such as strong incentives to align their scholarship, teaching and service activities more with the needs of the world.

Deepak Nayyer reminds of us an ancient Buddhist proverb which states that "the key to the gate of heaven is also the key which could open the gate to hell". Markets and globalization provide a mix of opportunities and dangers for higher education. But the nature of higher education — and our institutions — must be shaped by higher purposes for which the university has been created, shaped and sustained throughout the last millennium.

The great difference between being responsive and being responsible lies in the fact that, in the first case, universities should be receptive to what society expects from them; in the second case, they should have the ambition to guide reflection and policy-making in society. Yet it is also the case that universities must also understand and accept that their most fundamental roles revolves about academic rather than political values. The global knowledge economy requires thoughtful, interdependent and globally identified citizens. Institutional and pedagogical innovations are needed to confront these challenges and insure that the canonical activities of universities — research, teaching and engagement — remain rich, relevant and accessible.

The last discussion session involved a wide-ranging consideration of both the opportunities and responsibilities of higher education in an increasingly interconnected and interdependent world. Is globalization igniting change or compounding change in higher education, and what particular or unique configuration will come out of the globalization of higher education? Many universities might well think and act globally, but in reality they are rooted in local and regional communities and therefore connected locally. The models of collaboration existing around the world were generally static. What would represent a step change function in these models? The biggest step change in the past two decades globally had been the growth in undergraduate student numbers absorbed in many cases within a higher education system designed initially for an elite system of higher education.

But many questions remain. Does the curriculum provided for students prepare them as "students of and for the world"? To what extent did our students receive what some would describe as the "liberal education"? Will the government policy responses be the same across the globe to the challenges of building and achieving mass higher education, world-class research excellence and the demographic challenge? What are the enlightenment values of higher education: civilizing values, rational inquiry and multiculturalism? Are we preparing our students adequately for global citizenship?

Universities are able to provide social solutions to social problems in society as well as providing science and technology solutions. A future topic for Glion might be the extent to which universities across the world could work together creatively on some of the present and future problems facing the planet. Why not use the influence and contacts of the Glion group to harness the global strengths of higher education to tackle key issues such environmental, economic and political sustainability?

Réalisé en P.A.O. par STDI - Z. A. Route de Couterne - 53110 Lᴀssᴀʏ-ʟᴇs-Cʜâᴛᴇᴀᴜx
Imprimé en France. - JOUVE, 11, bd de Sébastopol, 75001 PARIS
N° 447276X. - Dépôt légal : Janvier 2008